MORAL FOUNDATION OF THE STATE IN HEGEL'S
Philosophy of Right:
ANATOMY OF AN ARGUMENT

ELEMENTA

Schriften zur Philosophie und
ihrer Problemgeschichte

herausgegeben von

Rudolph Berlinger und
Wiebke Schrader

BAND XXXIV — 1984

1984

MORAL FOUNDATION OF THE STATE IN HEGEL'S
Philosophy of Right:
ANATOMY OF AN ARGUMENT

Michael H. Mitias

Millsaps College

CIP-GEGEVENS

Mitias, Michael H.

Moral foundation of the state in Hegel's "Philosophy of right" / Michael H. Mitias. — Amsterdam : Rodopi. — Elementa ; Bd. 34)
ISBN 90-6203-516-7
SISO 393.1 UDC 340.12
Trefw. : Hegel, Georg Wilhelm Friedrich ; staatstheorie ; rechtsfilosofie.

©Editions Rodopi B.V., Amsterdam 1984
Printed in The Netherlands

For My Children
Johnny, Peter, and Michel

ACKNOWLEDGEMENTS

Some of the essays which comprise the bulk of this volume have appeared in the following journals:
1. "Law as the Basis of the State," essay I, in *Interpretation: A Journal of Political Philosophy,* Vol. 9, 1981.
2. "The People as the Source of Political Authority," essay II, in *Interpretation: A Journal of Political Philosophy,* Vol. 10, 1983.
3. "Justice as the Basis of Punishment," Appendix I, in *Hegel-Studien,* Band 13, 1978.
4. "The Basis of Obligation in International Law," Appendix II, in *Clio,* Vol. 9, 1980.
5. "Hegel's Conception of Law," Part I of Essay III, in *Rivisita Internazionale di Filosofia del Diritto,* 1983.

These essays are reprinted with minor changes. I am grateful to the editors of these journals for permitting me to include these essays in this volume. I wish also to express the warmest of my thanks to my colleague, Dr. Robert E. Bergmark, for his encouragement and wholehearted support of my work both in my regular teaching activity and in my study of Hegel.

CONTENTS

ACKNOWLEDGEMENTS

Introductory Remark 9

Essay One, Law as the Basis of the State 15

Essay Two, The Source of Political Authority: The People 38

Essay Three, Law and Morality 58

Essay Four, Love as the Basis of the Family 114

Essay Five, Self-Realization as the End of Work 138

Essay Six, Appendix I: Justice as the Basis of Punishment 166

Essay Seven, Appendix II, Basis of Obligation in International Law 176

Notes 187

Index 196

INTRODUCTORY REMARK

In a thoughtful yet critical discussion with Reinhold Niebuhr at his home in Stockbridge, Massachusetts, in 1963 on the general importance and destiny of Idealism he told me that he was disenchanted with — indeed he abandoned — Hegel mainly because he (Hegel) did not have a place for the self, the individual, within his philosophical scheme. He just could not see how a great mind like Hegel's was willing, or perhaps inclined, to forego a worthy justification of the meaning and being of human individuality. Yet, that very year I had read the *Phenomenology of Spirit* under the recommendation and guidance of my teacher, Warren E. Steinkraus, and wrote a critical piece on this work from which I emerged enlightened, inspired, and with a rich intuition — cognitive intuition, I should add — that Hegel was passionately concerned not only with the significance of human individuality but especially with the conditions under which a person can exist as an individual. I made an effort to reason with Niebuhr on the need to revaluate his view of the self in Hegel, but instead of reasoning with me on the problem he referred me to a number of books I could read to understand why Hegel as a philosopher should be dismissed from any serious consideration in the quest for philosophical truth. I was not surprised to receive from him this advice simply because I was to him at that time a naive student who just finished his undergraduate studies and who was apparently under an unhealthy spell of Idealism.

But Niebuhr's attitude was neither singular nor uncommon in the nineteen fifties and sixties, for as I marched into my graduate studies with a Socratic zeal for the truth I discovered that most, if not all, of the professors, and scholars, I met in the meetings of learned societies assumed a negative attitude towards Hegel primarily on the ground that he was indifferent to the human individual. This sort of attitude was, and still is, accompanied by a deep seated concern for the meaning and being of freedom as a central value in human life. Although this concern has always been mine and remains on the highest point of my scale of priorities as a man and as a student of philosophy I just cannot see how this widespread attitude towards Hegel could at all be justified.

We witness at the present a growing revival of interest in Hegel on both sides of the Atlantic, even in the Far East, and philosophers like Taylor, Avineri, Pelczynski, Harris, Plant, Plamenatz (in the Anglo — American world) have made an admirable effort to re — assert the value and relevance of Hegel's philosophical intuition to our contemporary society, yet this revival is still in its infant stage. For, it is not enough for us to study Hegel's texts and discover what he meant; we should also explore the conditions under which his intuition can become relevant to our life, that is, we should articulate guidelines for translating this intuition into living reality. What counts in our effort as seekers of wisdom is not merely the construction of fancy conceptual schemes but schemes relevant to human life — our life — schemes that can transform our conduct and spiritual vision for the better.

And, in what way, I may be asked, is Hegel relevant to our life at the present? A detailed answer to this question cannot, and should not, be provided in an introduction to a small volume like this one, though scholars like Taylor, Avineri, Plamenatz, to mention just a few names, have already made headway in this direction. Some brief remarks, however, are in order. In these remarks I shall restrict myself to the field of social and political philosophy. Our socio — political consciousness is in the second half of the twentieth century in a state of crisis — paralysis. And this paralysis consists of at least four blunders. First, we have lost our sense and understanding of ourselves as a 'state'. Most people, even some educated professors, tend to identify 'state' with 'government' and to view the government as an external agency, authority, or power operating with a will of its own and with a purpose other than the purpose of 'the people'. Yet the main principle on which this nation was founded was *the* People, viz., the people are the ultimate source of political authority, while the government is the concrete realization of the authority of the people. It is unhealthy, to say the least, for the people and the government to stand opposed to each other rather than be cooperative partners in search of the same end. Second, most people live by a false sense of freedom and individuality. Broadly speaking, while freedom is nowadays understood in terms of subjective, capricious, behavior, individuality is understood in terms of psycho — physical independence. This conception and practice of freedom and individuality retards human growth and development, for how can one achieve his true happiness if he does not respond actively and constructively to the human element, or essence, of his nature as a human reality? And how can one proceed in this response apart from the cooperation of others or from society as a *cultured* community? And how can one exist as a cultured being outside the spiritual unity, or union, of society as a whole? When a society understands by 'freedom' "I do what I happen to feel like, desire, want, etc.," and by 'individuality' " Each to his own " this society is bound to be fragmented, fractured. There has been many a loud cry in recent years against this tendency in our society — what is being done about it? A people cannot live well, i.e., under the conditions of freedom and humanity, and it cannot fulfill its mission in history as a symbol of culture and as a witness to the glory of the divine spirit if it is divided unto itself. Only in unity under the auspices of rationality and morality is there strength and therefore meaningful achievement, harmony, peace, and happiness. Third, law has lost its true meaning, purpose, and dignity in our life. Most people tend to view the law as an instrument of control, on the one hand, and self — interest, on the other. Perhaps this is (mainly) why most people, especially the big corporations, try to by — pass it, bend it, or change it according to their particular interests. In some cases one feels triumphant when he 'beats' the law. Yet, suppose we ask the majority of our society: what is the law, and how does it relate to their satisfaction or freedom? What sort of answer do we receive? Unless we grasp — actually, wisely — that law embodies in principle at least our general and rational interest as a people and that it is a fertile means to freedom, our social existence will remain vitiated with fear, selfishness, and a sinister kind of anxiety. Fourth, work has become in the lives of the majority of the people a means to physical survival, killing time, acquiring a social status, or escape from internal psychological pressure rather than an activity of self — realization. If I am to heed what our psychologists and social critics say, I should say that many people do not *enjoy* their work; they look for enjoyable moments outside the sphere of their working place and time — why should this be the case? What have we done to ourselves in the area of economic, political, social, and educational organization? What can we do to structure these domains in such a way that we create a society in which citizens can live as human individuals, a society held together by a sense of community and respect for human dignity?

It is concern for these blunders which led me to investigate the fundamental principles of the *Philosophy of Right*. Taylor, Avineri, and Pelczynski have, beside other distinguished scholars, presented in the past few years a fair and constructive interpretation of Hegel's social and political philosophy, and to them we owe a great debt. But no detailed, comprehensive analysis of the main argument of the *Philosophy of Right* has yet been advanced; yet such an analysis is urgent for at least three reasons.

First, a number of Hegelian critics still persist in thinking that Hegel's view of the state is dangerously authoritarian, if not anti — democratic. This only shows a lingering skepticism about Hegel's sucess in accounting for human individuality in his socio — political scheme. Second, many of the objections which are advanced against Hegel's conception of the state are onesided; they do not take into serious consideration the depth and organic unity of Hegel's view of political reality as such. Third, Hegel's conception of man and the state are, as I indicated earlier, vitally relevant to our current social and political scene. The unusual transformation of our social institutions — business, government, technology, education, and church — has brought about an unprecedented upheaval not only in our way of life but especially in the place of the individual human being in the life of the whole, a whole that is vastly complex, powerful, and inherently threatening. As a society we are drifting away from our devotion to human community, yet this value was prized by the wise men of the past as well as by the founders of this country. But how can we restore our devotion, or respect, to our being as a human community without a genuine understanding of what *it means* for a society to exist as a human community? And how can we achieve this understanding unless we grasp the basic principles of social and political reality?

I am anxious to show that the very structure of Hegel's argument in the *Philosophy of Right* does not allow, even in principle, for a totalitarian, or as Ilting and Pelczynski have maintained, authoritarian, interpretation of the state. This is the main reason why I tried my best to let Hegel speak for himself, that is, to follow his line of reasoning in the text without much reference to commentators, critics, or other political philosophers. I have adopted this mode of analysis for two reasons: (1) to stress that if one reads the *Philosophy of Right* as a whole and as a part of Hegel's philosophy in general one should be able to see that the fundamental principles of the state are erected on *rational insight* and deep concern for the being and well — being of the human individual, for man as a free, self — determined being. (2) Most of the misunderstanding and confusion which we encounter in the extant criticism of Hegel's political philosophy stems from fragmentary, one — sided reading of the *Philosophy of Right*.

I should also add that my purpose in this book is not so much to vindicate, or defend, or protect Hegel from valid criticism or rescue him from controversial questions or charges. I was especially careful to avoid any tendency in this direction, for, as I indicated earlier, I am mainly interested in bringing into visible sight the basic structure of the *Philosophy of Right*. My hope is that once this structure is articulated we can evaluate it for what it is: only in this way can we do justice to Hegel and render some service in our efforts of understanding the amazing richness of political reality as such.

Moreover, the critical, dialectical, study which I present in this short volume is only an attempt to provide an occasion for understanding Hegel's intuition of socio — political reality. This intuition relates directly to the four blunders which I stated earlier. The basic idea which I explore is: the *possibility of human freedom*. 'Being free', for Hegel, is not a mental state, an attitude, a feeling, an act, or even a course of action: one is free when one responds to and actualizes his basic interest as a *human being*, when he achieves his rights, and duties, in the basic social institutions in and through which he attains these interests. Hence, 'freedom' is an on — going activity or quest, of self-actualization. And, the thesis which I elucidate and defend is: Hegel's conception of the state provides an adequate, i.e., rational, socio — political framework within which a member of the state can conduct his life as a human individual. A corollary to this basic claim is that the state which Hegel espouses rests on a moral foundation. This foundation consists of the following propositions: (1) law, and therefore justice, is the basis of the state. (2) This law expresses, or embodies, the highest values and moral sentiment of the people as a historical reality; accordingly the law of the land is valid, rational, inasmuch as it is grounded in the moral will of the people. (3) The end of the state is the promotion of human freedom. (4) Law and justice are the source of government in the state. (5) Although business should operate in principle on the model of free enterprise it cannot, and should not, in its accumulation of wealth ignore or endanger the economic well-being of society as a whole. (6) The principles of education, whether they apply in the family, school, or civil society, should be supervised by the state and built on a rational foundation: the end of education is the cultivation of human individuality.

I have discussed each of these propositions in depth in the five major chapters: but I have also added two more studies (as appendices) which I completed independently mainly because in writing them I was guided by the same intuition which prompted me to write this short volume. The first study, "Justice as the Basis of Punishment," is intended to show that the infliction of punishment can be justified only in so far as its reason and amount are determined on just principles. The second study, "The Basis of Obligation in International Law," is an attempt to show that Hegel is not at all indifferent to the need for an international order or that he does not provide a basis of obligation among the nations of the world in international relations.

I do not think I exaggerate if I say that Hegel's vision of the modern state which he captured in the first part of the nineteenth century remains a living reality in our times. It would accordingly help if we avail ourselves of the wisdom of a man who penetrated the essence of man and human life passionately yet objectively, rationally yet warmly, as a whole yet with an eye on the meaning and importance of the parts, empirically yet with a feeling for human dignity.

ONE
LAW AS THE BASIS OF THE STATE

Although a number of scholars have sought, in the past two decades, to vindicate Hegel from the charge that he espouses a totalitarian view of the state, this vindication is, so far as I can see, neither concrete nor complete; for there are critics who still maintain that his view is illiberal, undemocratic, conservative, and that he endows the state with a greater measure of authority than it should enjoy. Professor J. Plamenatz, e.g., writes: "Hegel was against democracy and was also in several ways illiberal." Again, "though Hegel is not a totalitarian, in the bad sense, it cannot be denied that he makes extravagant and false claims for the state."[1] But why should philosophers and political thinkers persist in characterizing Hegel's political theory as totalitarian? What are the logical or ontological stumbling blocks which stand in the way of some thinkers to see Hegel's conception of the state for what it actually is? The main reason for this difficulty is, I believe, the reluctance of most critics to elucidate clearly and in detail the *basis*, or foundation, on which the state for Hegel rests, on the one hand, and the *end* of the state, on the other. The basis of the state, I submit, is for Hegel, law and its end is human freedom. If we approach Hegel's theory with this basic intuition in mind the negative charges which have been levelled against it, esecially the charge of totalitarianism, would be undermined.

In this essay I shall, first, advance a brief analysis of Jacques Maritain's critique of Hegel's conception of the state. The purpose of this analysis is to show the logic which underlies the general charge that Hegel advocates a totalitarian view of the state. Second, I shall discuss the fundamental elements of Hegel's theory of the state. My aim in this discussion is to establish a framework within which we can critically evaluate the validity of Hegel's claim about the state. Finally, I shall argue that Hegel is not at all a supporter of totalitarianism. The propositions which I hope to establish are: (1) the basis of the state, for Hegel, is law; what rules or determines the life of the individual in the state is not an agency, or power, external to the individual but law, the law which the citizen consciously recognizes and lives as a rational and free being. Hence as a member of the state the citizen exists under the conditions of individuality and as the source of the authority, viz., the state, which determines his life and the life of society in general. (2) The end of the state is the freedom of its members. Accordingly (a) the state is the medium in which the citizen achieves his freedom as a human individual; (b) the state cannot use the citizen as a means to a selfish or particular end; on the contrary, it attains its character *qua* state only when each citizen is treated as a person, i.e. as an end in himself.

I

In his critique of Hegel's conception of the state J. Maritain focuses attention primarily on those statements and passages in the *Philosophy of Right* which relate to the ontological meaning of the state. The theme which he stresses is: (1) the state is (for Hegel) the highest objectification of universal reason, or spirit, on earth; it is the concrete realization of freedom. (2) Consequently man attains his freedom only as a citizen, i.e., *qua* member of the state, and outside the state he cannot exist as an individual. Thus a person becomes free in so far as he recognizes his organic unity with the social Whole, "and is it not in being recognized by others (a theme dear to Hegel)," Maritain asks, "that individuality is born into its true nature and its supracontigent reality?"[2] But the social Whole is not merely a means for the realization of the freedom of the individual, Maritain observes; it is what determines his essence, or being. He quotes the following statements from Hegel to substantiate his interpretation: "everything that man is, he owes to the State. He has his being only in it."..."All the worth which the human being possesses — all spiritual reality, he possesses through the State." "Since the State is mind objectified, it is only as one of its members that the individual himself has objectivity, genuine individuality and an ethical life." (*Ibid.*, pp. 163-64; see also *Philosophy of Right*, § 258). Accordingly the state is the entelechy of the individual. I may feel unique and I may discover my individuality when I am recognized by the social Whole, but on certain conditions — "on the condition that in return I recognize the Whole for what it is (that is, my entelechy), and on the condition that I am become *recognizable* to all — with no longer anything in me which is not exposed to all and to myself — each one in the uniqueness of his being — there no longer having any soul or spiritual inferiority other than the very soul of the Whole." (*Ibid.*, p. 163) This view, Maritain holds, " is the very formula, the original formula of political totalitarianism." (*Ibid.*, p. 164).

We should here remember that the essential feature of the totalitarian state is that it does not have a place for the individual. Thus if the being of the citizen — his values, habits, ideas, attitudes, world view, conscience, in short, his character — is determined by the state his experience of subjective freedom would merely be a feeling and not a genuine achievement of freedom; for the ends which he wills, and in whose realization he attains his real freedom, are dictated by the state. His subjective will and the will of the state "interpenetrate each other in a superior identity." (*Ibid.*, p. 165) The state does not anymore "impose itself from without by enslaving individuals as did the despotic empires of long ago, but subjects them to itself all the better — without submitting them to the least heteronomy — because it is the very substance and truth of their will." (*Ibid.*, pp. 164 — 65) The state is the law; it is also what defines concrete duty. Kant's "abstract categorical imperative has been replaced by the concrete *imperium* of the State. They see their duty. Its authority is over them, and it is by themselves willing this authority that they fully realize their freedom." (*Ibid.*, p. 165) Thus in Hegel, Maritain observes, the legal and the moral become identical; abstract law is replaced by the living law of the state. One is not, consequently, compelled to reflect subjectively, or to appeal to his conscience, to determine what is right or good in a concrete moral situation. All he has to do when such a situation arises is act 'from instinct' or out of habit, because this instinct, or habit, is in a sense a 'second nature' which he acquires in the process of social growth. This nature is the internalization of the moral voice which is uttered by the state. Conscience should, then, be proclaimed banished from the life of the conscientious citizen. It is a trivial, and perhaps bothersome, voice, for what counts as right or just is dictated by the state, and what is dictated by the state is instilled in the character of the citizen as a second nature. This is exactly why when one's conscience disturbs him in the face of some order or practice by the state he should not pursue the matter critically or with an appeal to a higher moral sentiment but should instead act according to the genuine moral sense which constitutes this second nature. (*Ibid.*, p. 166)

II

If the preceding interpretation of the state, and of the relationship between the state and the individual, is correct, it would certainly follow that Hegel espouses a totalitarian form of government; for, if the state, viewed as a kind of super — person, determines the essence of the citizen and provides him with the principles and means of moral and political conduct, he would not exist as a self — determined being, i.e., as an individual, but as a being determined by the state. But, as my discussion will presently show, Maritain's interpretation of the state according to Hegel is one — sided and erroneous; it also fails to do justice to his analysis of its structure and end. The true character of the state, for Hegel, can be revealed if one explores its foundation or the essential elements which give it its identity as a state. In what follows I shall explore these elements, and although I shall seek to show that Hegel does not advocate, not even by implication, a totalitarian conception of the state. I shall be more anxious to argue that constitutional law is, for him, the basis of the state. This basis is the ultimate ground on which the freedom and individuality of the citizen rest.

What is the essential nature of the state, according to Hegel? I raise this question at the outset for two reasons: (1) Unless we fully grasp what the state is, or what sustains it as a political institution, we cannot attain a clear understanding of key concepts like the source of political authority, social justice, obligations and privileges of the state, freedom and individuality, patriotism, etc.; (2) Hegel's analysis of *the state* is intricate; this intricacy is the main reason which led many critics and Hegelian scholars to varied and conflicting interpretations of what sort of theory he espouses. Accordingly a sound treatment of any basic political category should proceed from a reasonable analysis of the concept of the state.

Hegel makes a clear distinction between 'civil society' and 'state.' 'Civil society' is an association, or an organization, of men who are *pre - eminently* concerned with the attainment and protection of their personal ends. In this society, Hegel writes, "each member is his own end, everything else is nothing to him. But except in contact with others he cannot attain the whole compass of his ends, and therefore these others are means to the end of the particular member." (Addition to § 182)[3] The cooperation of others, however, is not enough; a public authority, viz., a government, is needed to balance and harmonize the interests of all the members of the society. This authority restricts, or conditions, the activities and aspirations of the various members to promote peace and order amongst them. Thus in the actual pursuit of their ends men establish "a system of complete interdependence, wherein the livelihood, happiness, and legal status of one man is interwoven with the livelihood, happiness, and rights of all." (§ 183) This system becomes the basis of the realization of individual happiness; it may be "prima facie regarded as the external state, the state based on need, the state as the Understanding (*Verstand*) envisages it." (*Ibid.*)

Civil society is, then, a kind of state — an external state; It is not yet a mature state in which the citizens are consciously and thoughtfully unified by a comon purpose and destiny, but a system of social, economic, and legal institutions erected solely to further the well — being, i.e., life, rights, property, contracts, happiness, etc., of the people. In this society a person functions primarily as a social and economic, not as a political, being; that is, he veiws the government as something external to him, not as something expressive of his will or mind. He obeys the law and cooperates with others, not out of a sense of duty, or for the sake of self — realization, but to ensure the satisfaction of his own interests. (Cf. § 157) He does not participate in the political process; indeed the business of government is indifferent to him. His end and the end of government may seem at first to go in opposite directions, for he tends to think that the law restricts his activities and the extent of his personal satisfaction; but in fact, Hegel observes, the interest of the particular person and that of the law are reciprocal and condition each other: "while each of them seems to do just the opposite to the other and supposes that it can exist only by keeping the other at arm's length, none the less still conditions the other." (Addition to § 184) A person may think, e.g., that paying taxes is harmful to his welfare. This way of thinking is erroneous, for the personal end of the people cannot be promoted without taxes: a country that does not receive taxes cannot provide services to its citizens. Hence in furthering the end of government a person furthers his own end.

Thus the members of civil society exist as a unity, and the basis of this unity is cooperation with one nother, on the one hand, and a government which dictates a general mode of behavior agreeable and applicable to all the society, on the other. This unity, however, is feeble, for, as we have seen, a basic principle of civil society is the particular person, the person whose end is his own interest: "individuals in their capacity as burghers in this state are private persons whose end is their own interest. This end is *mediated* through the universal which thus appears as a means to its realization. Consequently, individuals can attain their ends only in so far as they themselves determine their knowing, willing, and acting in a universal way and make themselves links in this chain of social connexions." (§ 187) Accordingly, the unity which characterizes civil society is a kind of partnership; it is not established consciously and on the basis of a political ideal but necessarily and on the basis of self-interest. This is the sort of unity which we encounter in the social contract theories of the state; here the basis of the contract is need, service. Advocates of these theories are able to think only on the level of Understanding, not on the level of Reason (Vernunft). They are able to see only the material, external relations which are necessary for the being of the state. This is why instead of advancing theories of *the state proper* they advanced theories of civil society. (Cf § 187, Addition to § 182)

III

Civil Society, however, is not only a kind of state; it is also an aspect, a phase in the state as such. It is a constitutive element of the state. It is, moreover, the state viewed as an empirical or external reality. It becomes a state when the following conditions are fulfilled. *First*, when it articulates, structures itself thoughtfully, consciously, and purposefully — when it becomes conscious of an end in which it expresses the will of the society as a whole. The state, Hegel asserts, "knows what it wills and knows it in its universality, i.e., as something thought. Hence it works and acts by reference to consciously adopted ends, known principles, and laws which are not merely implicit but are actually present to consciousness; and further, it acts with precise knowledge of existing conditions and circumstances, inasmuch as its actions have a bearing on these." (§ 270) The highest achievement of the modern state is the discovery of the *general will* as the foundation of the state. Hegel gives credit to Rousseau for introducing this principle; his contribution consists in the fact that, "by adducing the will as the principle of the state, he is adducing a principle which has thought both for its form and its content, a principle indeed which is thinking itself, not a principle, like the gregarious instinct, for instance, or divine authority, which has thought as its form only." (§ 258) But Rousseau does not provide an adequate account of this principle, for he views the will as something particular, determinate, and "he regards the universal will not as the absolutely rational element in the will, but only as a 'general' will which proceeds out of this individual will as out of a conscious will." (*Ibid.*) But, Hegel stresses, the basic principle of the state must be objective and independent of the desires, interests, or whims of its members: "we must remember the fundamental conception that the objective will is rationality implicit or in conception, whether it be recognized or not by individuals, whether their whims be deliberately for it or not." (*Ibid*) When we uphold the objectivity of the universal will we do not necessarily mean or imply that the thoughts, feelings, or judgments of the individuals are neglected or ignored. As we shall presently see, the subjective will of the individual must be consulted, and it asserts itself through legal channels in the modification and realization of the law. (Cf. § 298 — 319)

On more than one occasion Hegel reminds us that a philosophical treatment of 'the state' should concern itself with the *concept*, or Idea, of the state not with this or that state, nor with the conditions under which given states come into being. (Cf. § 258 and Addition to the same paragraph) The actual states of the world do not provide a model of what the true essence of the state is. On the contrary, if we cast a quick glance at the history of human society we can immediately show that any state is in some way defective or bad: "the state is no ideal work of art; it stands on earth and so in the sphere of caprice, chance, and error, and bad behavior may disfigure it in many respects." (Addition to § 258) Yet regardless of its degree of imperfection, a state is such only in so far as it realizes in its actual, historical being the Idea, or the principle of the state. This principle is rational, for it is essentially an activity of reason. But reason is a power which craves the universal whether in the realm of thought or in the realm of ethics. "The basis of the state," Hegel writes, "is the power of reason actualizing itself as will." (Addition to § 258)

Second, civil society becomes a state when it achieves internal unity, when it exists as an organism. Unlike civil society the state is an organic unity. In it the individual does not view himself as a particular being preoccupied merely with the satisfaction of his personal ends but as a member of the whole. His destiny is intertwined with the destiny of the whole: "unification pure and simple is the true content and aim of the individual, and the individual's destiny is the living of a universal life." (*Ibid.*) He is able to realize himself as an individual primarily because "the state in and by itself is the ethical whole, the actualization of freedom; and it is an absolute end of reason that freedom should be actual." (Addition to § 258) Consequently, since "the state is mind on earth and consciously realizing itself there," and since it is the highest realization of the ethical Idea on earth, it follows that whether he knows it or not the citizen cannot achieve his freedom except as a member of the state, as a member who aspires for the end which the universal will expresses.

I say "whether he knows it or not" because freedom, for Hegel, does not mean acting according to one's subjective desire, whim, inclination, opinion, or feeling but according to what is true and right or good. Concrete freedom, and we should remember that the "state is the actuality of concrete freedom," is attained when a person satisfies his subjective interests the way he would attain them in the family or civil society, on the one hand, and recognizes and wills the universal in his experience, on the other — when, in other words, he recognizes that he can achieve his true and complete end, viz., freedom, when he seeks the universal: "The essence of the modern state is that the universal be bound up with the complete freedom of its particular members and with the private well — being, that thus the interests of family and civil society must concentrate themselves on the state, although the universal end cannot be advanced without the personal knowledge and will of its particular members, whose own rights must be maintained. Thus the universal must be furthered, but subjectivity on the other hand must attain its full and living development. It is only when both these moments subsist in their strength that the state can be regarded as articulated and genuinely organized." (Addition to § 260) Thus unlike government in civil society the state does not stand as an other, or as something external, to its members, for it is the unity, or embodiment, of their rights and interests. If the end of the individual is not harmonious in some way with the end of the state, the state, Hegel insists, "is left in the air"; it assumes the status of civil society. (Cf. Addition to § 265) Thus in obeying the laws which are enacted by the state the citizen realizes his freedom, for the law which he obeys is an expression of his true end, or will — it is his own law. This is based on the assumption that the citizens "have duties to the state in proportion as they have rights against it." (§ 261)

Now we should ask: what is the objective principle, viz., the universal will, which is supposed to be the basis of the state? How does it become actual in the life of the state? Hegel repeatedly stressed that the Idea actualizes itself in the world as mind. The sphere of its actualization is the family and civil society. It cannot, however, be identified with these two spheres as empirically given orders, but with their ideality, with the principles and values whose actuality transforms them into 'the state.' More concretely, the Idea as mind becomes actual in the various institutions which make up the state as an organic unity: "the laws regulating the family and civil society are the institutions of the rational order which glimmers in them. But the ground and final truth of these institutions is mind, their universal end and known objective." (Addition to § 261) These institutions constitute the essential elements of the *constitution* of the state. Thus a society becomes a state when it articulates its will — (its desires, ideals, values, etc. — consciously in a constitution and organizes its life around this constitution. Accordingly a state is actual when it becomes conscious of its identity and when it recognizes that this identity is an expression of its will as a rational principle. The point which we should here stress is that the institutions which give content to the constitution, namely, the principle according to which the activities and privileges of society are organized, are "the firm foundation not only of the state but also the citizen's trust in it and sentiment towards it. They are the pillars of public freedom since in them particular freedom is realized and rational, and therefore there is *implicitly* present even in them the union of freedom and necessity." (§ 265) They are the medium within which the citizen realizes his actual freedom. They are also what shapes the political sentiment of patriotism; "this sentiment is, in general, trust (which may pass over into a greater or lesser degree of educated insight), or the consciousness that my interest, both substantative and particular, is contained and preserved in another's (i.e., in the state's) interest and end, i.e., in the other's relation to me as an individual." (§ 268) Thus patriotism does not mean offering oneself as an exceptional sacrifice at the altar of the state; it is rather the feeling and recognition that one's end and the end of the state are identical and that one cannot realize his destiny except in so far as he fulfills his duties in the various social institutions of which he is a member.

The patriotic sentiment is acquired only when the citizen identifies his will with the will of the state *qua* organism, i.e., with its rational principle, viz., the law. "The Idea of the state," Hegel writes in § 259, "has immediate actuality and is the individual state as a self — dependent organism — the *constitution* or *constitutional law*." Accordingly as an organism the state is essentially the constitution, and the constitution is the organization of the state; it is the method according to which the rights, duties, and activities of the citizens are distributed. Hegel distinguishes three basic powers within the state: "(a) the power to determine and establish the universal — the Legislature; (b) the power to subsume single cases and the spheres of particularity under the universal — the Executive; (c) the power of subjectivity, as the will with the power of ultimate decision — the Crown." (§ 273) These powers, he argues, must not be viewed as separate from each other, i.e., as self — subsistent; for if this happens the state would gradually meet its end. We may distinguish them, but we cannot separate them from each other. Their unity is the ultimate unity of the state.[4] What is crucial to the being and integrity of the state is the realization of rationality in its life — if, in other words, it lives according to the law which expresses its will as a state. This is exactly why Hegel argues that the question, "which form of government is better, democracy, monarchy, etc.", is not quite meaningful, for such forms are "one — sided unless they can sustain in themselves the principle of free subjectivity and know how to correspond with a matured rationality." (Addition to § 273) The test of the goodness of a state, then, is not merely the general plan it adopts in organizing its institutions but whether or not the constitution facilitates the realization of rational law in the life of its citizens, thereby enhancing the attainment of freedom. (Cf. § 272)

The constitution, however, cannot be made, nor can it be given as a gift to a nation; hence the question, who is to form the constitution? is meaningless — why? Because the question "presupposes that there is no constitution there, but only an agglomeration of atomic individuals." (§ 273) But an agglomeration of individuals, individuals who exist atomistically, discretely, as in civil society, do not have a conception of consciousness of constitution. They can speak of such a constitution only if they exist as a state and are conscious of their selfhood as a state. But if they enjoy this consciousness they would *eo ipso* possess a constitution. Thus the question, who is to frame the constitution? reduces itself to: who is to amend or alter the constitution?

Next, the constitution cannot be offered as a gift to a nation, because it is the mind of that nation: "the state, as the mind of a nation, is both the law permeating all relationships within the state and also at the same time the manners and consciousness of its citizens." (§ 274) Accordingly the constitution articulates, embodies, the spiritual reality of a society as it has objectified itself in a given historical period: "the constitution of a people is of the same substance, the same spirit as its art and philosophy, or at least its imagination, its thoughts, and its general culture — not to mention the additional, external influences of its climate, neighbors, and global position."⁴ Thus a constitution evolves with the evolution of a nation. This is why when Napoleon gave Spain a constitution, it did not work, for it was "more rational than what they had before"; it did not express their spiritual reality at that historical epoch. A society might feel a need for a better constitution, and it may enjoy the privilege of having a Socrates as one of its citizens, but unless the people as a whole rise to the value and dignity of Socrates' moral sentiment, as well as the depth of his rational character, this need for a better, more rational constitution remains on the level of wish, not genuine desire.

IV

The preceding discussion of the fundamental features of Hegel's concept of the state should provide a framework within which we can critically evaluate the charge that Hegel advocates, at least by implication, a totalitarian conception of the state. The point of this evaluation is not merely to show that such a charge reveals a gross misunderstanding of the depth of Hegel's analysis of the concept of the state but also to stress that applying labels like authoritarian, undemocratic, conservative, illiberal, etc., to Hegel's view does not serve a useful purpose, for none of these labels, at least the way they have been used by critics, can adequately describe Hegel's position.⁵ Indeed Hegel himself shies away from such labels. His main concern, as I tried to show in the foregoing pages, is simply to analyze the essential nature, or basic principle, of the state — what makes an organized society a state? Under what conditions can a member of such society achieve his human individuality, or freedom? We have seen that, to him, the form which the constitution should assume — i.e., whether it is democracy, monarchy, etc. — is not the crucial question; the important question is: in what way can a constitution, when it becomes a factor in shaping the conduct of the citizens, help the growth of the highest type of human character, the character that can determine its destiny, the character that can, in short, be good? I am here reminded by an important Pythagorean saying which Hegel quotes: "when a father inquired about the best method of educating his son in ethical conduct, a Pythagorean replied: 'Make him a citizen of a state with good laws.' (The phrase has also been attributed to others.)" (§ 152) This passage calls for the remark that the development or attainment of values takes place in a concrete medium of laws, custom, and, in general, institutions. We cannot, whether we like it or not, ignore the role of these factors in the nourishment of the human character. Accordingly, if self — determination, i.e., freedom, is an activity in which one attains and realizes these values, it should follow that an assessment of the goodness of the state cannot be divorced from a consideration of the legal structure which underlies its vital institutions, or laws.

Hegel clearly says that in analyzing the concept of the state he is not interested in examining historical or particular states, nor the conditions under which certain states conduct their activities, but the Idea of the state — more concretely, in how to understand the state as something rational. He does not do this abstractly but with a critical look at human nature, on the one hand, and the actual history of the states throughout the world, on the other; for the point in theorizing about the state is not to produce a beautiful political structure, e.g., a utopia, but to discover the fundamental principles according to the highest demands of reason and morality with an eye on practice, and with a passion to articulate those laws or values that can work effectively and which can ennoble human life. "This book, then (Hegel writes in the preface to the *Philosophy of Right*), containing as it does the science of the state, is to be nothing other than the endeavor to apprehend and portray the state as something inherently rational. As a work of philosophy, it must be poles apart from an attempt to construct a state as it ought to be. The instruction which it may contain cannot consist in teaching the state what it ought to be; it can only show how the state, the ethical universe, is to be understood." The importance of this emphasis in Hegel is that if we know what the state as such is, and if we know the conditions under which man's highest good — freedom — can be attained, then it becomes possible for a state to amend, alter, or reform its constitution.

Now let us focus our attention on this ultimate good in theorizing about the state, viz., the conditions under which freedom can be attained, and let us consider more directly the serious objection which was raised against Hegel's theory, that is, the claim that it is a totalitarian theory of the state. What do we mean when we say of a theory that it is totalitarian? Broadly speaking, we mean that according to this theory a citizen cannot exist as a self — determined being. He owes his life—his ideas, values, character traits, in short, his destiny — to a power outside himself; this power is the state. Accordingly, a citizen is absorbed in the whole — society; he is a means to the state. He exists and lives to make actual a general purpose or value for which the state as a whole stands. Such a citizen eats, plays, and goes to school; he works, gets married, and makes a family; he votes, discourses about public policies, and stands for what he takes to be his rights as a man and as a citizen; he functions as a social being, pursues ends, and performs his obligations to others and to the state. He may, in short, feel that he is the master of his life; but, in fact, he does not know that the self which he owns and enjoys is indirectly shaped, formed, by the various powers or institutions of the state. He does not, in other words, know that his character is not the result of his spontaneous and thoughtful effort; for, once more, the conditions under which he grows up were planned on his behalf for him to be a certain kind of 'individual.' This is in substance the original formula of political totalitarianism which Maritain attributes to Hegel as a political philosopher. This charge is serious, for Hegel's language and mode of analysis create an air or feeling in that direction. Some thinkers, like Plamenatz, who consciously sought to be sympathetic and do justice to Hegel could not feel comfortable with his theory. This discomfort is clearly sensed if we read this passage from his *Man and Society*: "I would not deny that there is an unpleasant tone about the writings of a man who appears to have believed that the Universal Mind had attained full self — knowledge in his philosophy. His manner is against him; it suggest a colossal arrogance. And we do well to mistrust the arrogant, especially when they speak of freedom."[6]

First, what do we mean by linguistic expressions like, "The state determines the life, or character, of the citizen," "The citizen is a means to the state, or to a goal adopted by the state," "The character of the citizen is indirectly shaped by the state," etc.? I raise this question primarily because if the state is a determing factor in the life of the citizen, and it is to a reasonable degree, we should then enquire into the principle, or value, by which this determination is effected. We should also enquire into the sort of atmosphere which the state provides for the education (Bildung) and growth of the citizen. If such principle and conditions do not allow the essential powers of human nature to grow naturally, and this under the conditions of *reason, morality,* and *spontaneous creativity,* we can certainly say that a state of this character is totalitarian. But Hegel's theory of the state does not contain such principle or conditions, for, to him, as I stressed, the fundamental principle of the state is law. Indeed we can say without hesitation that the government which Hegel advocates is government of law. This law becomes actual as the constitution, and the latter determines not only the organization of the society but also the kind of institutions within which the character of the growing citizen is nourished into maturity. Hegel condemns despotism, the view that force is, or should be, the basis of the state: "despotism means any state of affairs where law has disappeared and where the particular will as such, whether of a monarch or a mob (Ochlocracy), counts as law or rather takes the place of law; while it is precisely in legal, constitutional government that sovereignty is to be found as the moment of ideality — the ideality of the particular spheres and functions." (§ 278. Also cf. § 258)

The sovereignty of the state is, according to Hegel, the ideality of the powers which are designated by the constitution: the Legislature, the Executive, and the Crown. It means the unity, the inter — dependence, of these powers. "Sovereignty," Hegel writes, "depends on the fact that the particular functions and powers of the state are not self — subsistent or firmly grounded either on their own account or in the particular will of the individual functionaries, but have their roots ultimately in the unity of the state as their single self." (§ 278) The source and basis of this unity is the constitution. When each of the powers of the state functions independently of the others they are bound to oppose and consequently destroy each other. This would mean the end of the state. Their harmony, cooperation, and unity is, therefore, absolutely essential to the realization of the end of the state, viz., the freedom of the citizen. The monarch symbolizes the actual unity of these powers. This is why his signature is needed to implement any decision or action of the state; in his figure as the monarch he represents both the unity and sovereignty of the state, that is, its will as it is expressed in the constitution. It is perhaps hard to understand how one person can decide, act, on behalf of a nation. A remark here is in order. As a sovereign, the monarch sums in his figure the ideal unity of the state *qua* constitution. Accordingly when he acts on behalf of the nation as a whole his decision is legitimate, valid, only in so far as it is identical with the constitution, or insofar as it expresses the essential spirit of the law. Thus he cannot act capriciously, subjectively, or in the interest of any other group or power: "as a matter of fact, he is bound by the concrete decisions of his counsellors, and if the constitution is stable, he has often no more to do than sign his name." (Addition to § 279) I quote this sentence only to shed further light on my earlier claim that the government which Hegel advocates is a government of law, i.e., what determines the decisions, actions, or institutions of the state is in the final analysis the law. The 'I will', or signature, of the monarch is "the last word beyond which it is impossible to go." (*Ibid.*) And inasmuch as it is grounded in, and expressive of, the constitution it asserts the supremacy of the law in the life of the state; it also signifies a moment of self — consciousness, a moment in which the state becomes conscious of its will and its capacity to realize this will actually, concretely: "in a well — organized monarchy, the objective aspect belongs to law alone, and the monarch's part is merely to set to the law the subjective 'I will.'" (Addition to § 280)

The difficulty with Hegel's view, I may be told, is not merely his thesis that law is the basis of the state but rather his inability to show how the citizen can be a self — determined being, i.e., free. The citizen remains caught up within the web of the state; for if the government as the actual reality of the constitution determines the values and institutions of the state, and if these are formative factors of the character of the citizen, it should follow that this character is shaped by extraneous forces, by the sort of values which the state happens to promote in the life of society. A character of this sort cannot be self — determined. And in order for it to be self — determined it must create its own values, habits, or general outlook upon life; its life must be an expression of its will as a person. Accordingly, what guarantees, or safeguards, do we have that a given constitution provides the conditions *par excellence* for the realization of freedom? Or, what criterion should be met in order for a constitution to create a sociopolitical atmosphere for the highest realization of freedom? I raise these questions on behalf of the critic only to stress that, unless a citizen is somehow able to create his own individual character amidst the complex framework of social and political institutions which he encounters as he begins to become conscious of himself as person, he remains a product of society, he remains deprived of the opportunity to determine himself. Hegel is aware of this problem; for, on the one hand, he insists, as we have seen in some detail, that the fundamental principle of the state, viz. the constitution, which determines the life of the society, must be objective and independent of caprice, arbitrariness, and idiosyncratic interest, and, on the other hand, the highest form of constitution must be rational. Indeed rationality is the ultimate criterion by which we evaluate the goodness of a constitution. Thus a state is good, valid, inasmuch as it is rational; such a state is a community of self — determined beings. But, (1) what do we mean when we say a constitution is rational, or that it is good inasmuch as it is rational? (2) Under what conditions does the rationality of the constitution become actual in the life of the citizens?

"A state is absolutely rational," Hegel writes, "inasmuch as it is the actuality of the substantial will which it possesses in the particular self — consciousness once that consciousness has been raised to consciousness of the universal." (§ 258) Thus a constitution acquires the character of rationality if it meets three conditions. *First*, it should express concretely the will of the people — their values, interests, ideas, customs, etc. In this expression the will becomes both intelligible and actual. It accordingly reveals the mind, the spiritual substance, of the soceity as an organic unity. It is this translation of the general will into a concrete way of life which led Hegel to view the constitution as ethical in character: "the state is the actuality of the ethical Idea. It is ethical mind *qua* the substantial will manifest and revealed to itself, knowing and thinking itself, accomplishing what it knows and insofar as it knows it." (§ 257) As the ideal unity of the state, and as the principle of its organization, the constitution permeates all the relationships and institutions which make up the state. These institutions are rational in so far as they reflect the meaning and interest of the constitution. I should here remark that when Hegel considers the general will as the foundation of the state he in effect erects the structure of the state on reason, for, to him, reason actualizes itself in the life of a society as will. In the addition to § 258 he writes: "the basis of the state is the power of reason actualizing itself as will."

Second, a constitution is rational insofar as it expresses man's highest end — freedom: "it is an absolute end of reason that freedom should be actual." (Addition to § 258) Thus we cannot accept a constitution as rational, and consequently we cannot accept it as valid, unless it creates a satisfactory condition for the attainment of freedom. But the question to which we are seeking an urgent answer is: how is concrete freedom possible in a state with a rational constitution? Hegel is alive to the importance of this question, for at the beginning of his analysis of the *concept* of the state he writes: "Rationality, taken generally and in the abstract, consists in the thoroughgoing unity of the universal and the single. Rationality, concrete in the state, consists (a) so far as its content is concerned, in the unity of objective freedom (i.e., freedom of the universal or substantial will) and subjective freedom (i.e., freedom of everyone in his knowing and in his volition of particular ends); and consequently, (b) so far as its form is concerned, and self — determining action on laws and principles which are thoughts and so universal." (§ 258) We need to interpret this passage carefully, for it is crucial to the whole argument of this essay. A citizen in a state is an individual; he is a world of thought, feeling, and action. He is able to seek ends that are peculiar to his character. He uniquely distinguishes himself by personal interests, ideas, habits, values, and character traits. But he is also a member of the state; as such, he seeks and realizes the universal, viz., government, law, and custom in his life. This universal, whose foundation is the constitution, underlies the will of the people as a whole; it embodies their essential values and aspirations inasmuch as they have received the baptism of reason. Thus a citizen who is conscious of his membership in the state is also conscious that *qua* universal the consitution is the embodiment of his true freedom, for it is an expression of his true will. The laws which it prescribes are not any more external, indifferent commands which he has to obey if he has to achieve certain ends but his own laws, the laws which express his will as a member of the state: "they are not something alien to the subject. On the contrary, his spirit bears witness to them as to its own essence, the essence in which he has a feeling of his selfhood, and in which he lives as in his own element which is not distinguished from himself." (§ 147) This is why his freedom can be achieved only when he *wills*, in his actions, to realize the system of laws which emanate from the constitution. Put differently, the citizen determines himself, he achieves a breath of freedom, when he acts on the basis of the laws which are upheld by the constitution. Consequently, a citizen who fails to identify his personal, subjective will with the objective will which embodies the highest degree of rationality does not realize in his action his complete freedom. We cannot say that a person who ignores the objective will cannot *to some degree* be free. Hegel admits that such a person can be free, but his freedom is one — sided, abstract: "we must remember that...knowing and willing, or subjective freedom (the *only* thing contained in the principle of the individual will) comprises only one moment, and therefore a one — sided moment, of the Idea of the rational will, i.e., of the will which is rational solely because what it is implicitly, that it also is explicitly." (§ 258)

Third, a constitution is rational when the powers of the state cooperate and function as an organic unity. "The constitution," Hegel writes, "is rational in so far as the state inwardly differentiates and determines its activity in accordance with the nature of the concept. The result of this is that each of these powers is in itself the totality of the constitution, because each contains the other moments and has them effective in itself, and because the moments, being expressions of the differentiation of the concept, simply abide in their ideality and constitute nothing but a single individual whole." (§ 272) I quote this passage in its entirety only to underscore a basic condition for the rationality of the state which Hegel repeatedly emphasized. He was sharply critical of those who held that the powers of the state should be divided, i.e., separate, or self — subsistent. This view is advanced on the assumption that division promotes public freedom, but it does not, for it implies that in its very nature, each power is disharmonious and hostile to the others. But if the powers of the state function separately the end of the state is imminent. This is what happened in France during the Revolution; "the legislative power sometimes engulfed the so — called 'executive,' the executive sometimes engulfed the legislative, and in such a case it must be stupid to formulate, e.g., the moral demand for harmony." (Addition to § 272) But we must *distinguish* these powers, Hegel argues, for each performs a unique function in the life of the state; "each of them must build itself inwardly into a whole and contain in itself the other moments. When we speak of the distinct activities of these powers, we must not slip into the monstrous error of so interpreting their distinction as to suppose that each power should subsist independently in abstraction from the others. The truth is that the powers are to be distinguisehd only as moments of the concept. If instead they subsist independently in abstraction from one another, then it is as clear as day that two independent units cannot constitute a unity but must of course give rise to strife, whereby either the whole is destroyed or else unity is restored by force." (*Ibid*) This is another way of stating the doctrine that the state is an organism and that the principle of this organic character is the constitution. As in every organic structure, when all the parts function disharmoniously, separately, the whole falls apart. Thus a state exhibits the character of rationality when its powers, or institutions, function as an interdependent unity and when in this functioning they make the will of the people actual and, consequently, free.

V

A constitution, then, is rational if it (1) embodies, expresses, the will of the people, (2) promotes the freedom of the citizens, and (3) guarantees the unity and harmony of the powers and various institutions of the state. These criteria, our critic would argue, are general; they explain the sense in which a constitution is rational, or what it means for a constitution to be rational. But, how does the criterion of rationality apply actually in the life of a nation? What concrete attitude, or principle, should the state adopt towards the citizens in pursuing their ends as human individuals? We raise these questions, our critic would go on, primarily because (I) the implicit, or potential, rationality of the constitution remains abstract, theoretical, and therefore irrelevant, unless it permeates the practice, the laws, which affect the life of the citizens, and (II) the various states of the world are, as Hegel is quite aware, imperfect; they are not well — organized. This means they are not as rational as they ought to be. So, what means and principles should be adopted in order for a state, the way Hegel views it, to grow in rationality and to maximize the highest degree of freedom in the lives of its citizens?

I. A truly rational constitution should uphold the principle that a citizen ought to be accepted as a rational being, as a person; as such, he should be treated as an end in himself, never as a means. (Cf. Kant) Hegel recognizes this as a fundamental principle of the state. From the standpoint of political philosophy this means that the state must treat its members as persons. But a person is a being with rights, and he cannot attain his personality unless his rights are respected and protected. "Personality," writes Hegel, "essentially involves the capacity for rights and constitutes the concept and the basis (itself abstract) of the system of abstract and therefore formal right. Hence the imperative: 'Be a person and respect others as persons.' " (§ 36) A rational state should recognize the rights of its citizens. It cannot, e.g., condone slavery — why? Because the justification of slavery rests on the premise that man is a 'natural' being; consequently he can be owned the way we own objects. But man, Hegel argues, is not a natural object but *mind*, and as mind he is essentially free. Therefore he cannot be owned or used as a slave. (Cf § 57) Again, a man should be respected not on the basis of his race, religion, nationality, or social origin, but on the basis of his manhood, on the basis of what makes him a man, i.e., a human being: "A man counts as a man in virtue of his manhood alone, not because he is a Jew, Catholic, Protestant, German, Italian, etc." (§ 209)

One of the most important rights which is crucial to the attainment and integrity of personality is the right to property. One cannot enjoy a sense of personality unless his property is respected; hence it is the duty of the state to respect the right of the citizen to his property: "a person has as his substantive end the right of putting his will into any and every thing and thereby making it his, because it has no such end in itself and derives its destiny and soul from his will. This is the absolute right of appropriation which man has over all 'things.' " (§ 44) The point which merits special attention here is that a state is, for Hegel, under obligation to respect the property of its citizens primarily because in this way it safeguards their freedom. This respect extends to one's moral conviction, i.e., conscience. This faculty is a personal privilege; it " is the disposition to will what is absolutely good." (§ 137) In this activity a person determines what is right and obligatory in his life; none can realize this end except the citizen as a responsible individual, for he is the only one who knows himself and knows his end in life. This is why Hegel characterizes conscience as the "deepest inward solitude with oneself where everything external and every restriction has disappeared." (Addition to § 136) The will, it should be remarked, is rational inasmuch as it seeks what is *objectively right* and *good*, for in this seeking it raises itself from the level of particularity to that of universality. Accordingly, as this unity of the particular and the universal, conscience "is a sanctuary which it would be sacrilege to violate." (§ 137)

Respect for property and conscience is, for Hegel, inseparable from respect for religious belief. For if a religion, or religious conviction, is genuine, if it expresses a divine content, it does not undermine but promotes the integrity and end of the state. Thus the state should protect the church as a basic institution in the life of the nation. This means the church should have the right to property, because "the practice of its worship consists in ritual and doctrinal instruction." (§ 270) And "in addition, since religion is an integrating factor in the state, implanting a sense of unity in the depths of men's minds, the state should even require all its citizens to belong to *a* church — *a* church is all that can be said, because since the content of a man's faith depends on his private ideas, the state cannot interfere with it." (§ 270) This, it seems to me, is a clear statement of principle for the necessity of religious freedom. But Hegel goes a step further. He insists that the state should not interfere in the details of a given religion; it should, in other words, be tolerant even to a sect (e.g., the Quakers, The Anabaptists, etc.), "a sect (though, of course, all depends on its members) which on religious grounds declines to recognize even its direct duties to the state." (*Ibid.*) Hegel introduces this limitation on the ground that no institution in the state can enjoy all the rights it demands unless it performs its duties to the state, for unless it performs these duties it would obstruct the end and unity of the state. This is why if the members of a sect decline to perform a basic duty to the state, e.g., if they refuse to enlist in the army and defend the nation, they cannot have a claim to citizenship, though they may enjoy the civil rights which are guaranteed by the constitution.

One can discuss other rights in Hegel — for example, the right to education, to choose a career, to express one's ideas orally and in writing, to personal safety, to fair treatment before the law, etc. — as essential to the attainment of personality. My aim in considering, though briefly, the right to property, conscience, and religious belief is only to show that, for Hegel, a state is not truly rational unless in its laws and practice it safeguards the personality — or individuality — of its citizens. As stressed earlier, no man can be an individual unless he is a self — determined, i.e., free, being. Thus if the constitution of the state á la Hegel places the highest value on human individuality, and if the state promotes this individuality *concretely in its practice*, it should follow that such a constitution, or state, is rational.

II. Attainment of personality, however, is incomplete unless the state provides a sociopolitical atmosphere within which the citizens can prevent the state *qua* government from being or acting as a separate or independent agency. If the citizen is to actualize himself as a free being under the conditions of rationality, morality, and spontaneous creativity, the laws or institutions which regulate his activities in society should be an expression of his will. Thus unless the state, as an actual, historical event, is the *living will* of its people, the citizen of such a state cannot exist as an individual. But in order for a state to be the living will of its people the people must share in the refinement and realization of their constitution. Accordingly if what rules a state is law, and if this law embodies the will of the people *actually* we can certainly say that the state rules itself and that it is self — determined.

Now, does Hegel's theory of the state provide the means for the citizen to share in the refinement and realization of the constitution? This question assumes, with Hegel, that the states of the world are imperfect, and that their destiny consists in the constant realization of the highest possible degree of freedom. Thus, unless a citizen is actively involved in the modification, enactment, and actualization of the constitution, and unless he is responsive to the fact that the laws which determine his values and conduct emanate from his will, or that he intends them, the state becomes alienated from or external to, him. This may create the tendency or danger that those who enact and execute the laws may ignore his real will. If this happens the state ceases to be a state proper; it degenerates into a civil society.

The citizen, for Hegel, participates in the political process, that is, in the modification and realization of the law in two ways, directly and indirectly. (A) He participates *indirectly* by means of the legislature, which is an assembly of estates whose members are elected by the people. This institution performs two basic tasks: it modifies, i.e., determines, the laws of the state and structures the programs which affect the well — being of the society as a whole: "the legislature is concerned (a) with the laws as such in so far as they require fresh and extended determination; and (b) with the content of home affairs affecting the entire state." (§ 298) It is, then, the legislature which determines the extent of the rights, duties, privileges of the people as individuals and as socio — economic groups.

The legislature plays, moreover, two basic roles in the actual translation, or enactment, of the will of the people concretely. In the first place, it is a bridge; it is what mediates between the powers of the state. (Cf. § 300) It is, in other words, the institution which solidifies the unity of the state. For in determining the legal system it in effect determines the extent of action both of the monarch and the executive. As we have seen, the monarch decides, acts, on behalf of the state only in so far as the constitution allows. In a similar way the main function of the executive is to see to it that the laws which are enacted by the legislature are applied with the utmost of skill, honesty, and proficiency. (Cf. § 303) Thus the greater the efficiency in actualizing the laws which express the will of the people the greater is their freedom as citizens.

In the second place, the legislature has the sole goal and duty to modify the laws of the state according to the actual desires, interests, or aspirations of the people. I say 'actual' because the law recognized by the state at a given time must express the will of the people. This is why Hegel insisted that the constitution cannot be granted as a gift, constructed, or even copied. It simply *is*, for it is the rational articulation of the will of the people. But this does not mean it cannot be changed. On the contrary, it must grow and mature, and its growth and maturity should reflect the growth and maturity of the people as a state: "The constitution must in and by itself be the fixed and recognized ground on which the legislature stands, and for this reason it must not first be constructed. Thus the constitution *is*, but just as essentially it *becomes*, i.e., it advances and matures. This advance is an alteration which is imperceptible and which lacks the form of alteration." (Addition to § 298) This passage is extremely important, for it clarifies Hegel's position on political reform. It asserts that the law, or constitution, of the state is not final but always subject to change or reform, and this according to the criterion of rationality. In § 216 Hegel is sharply critical of the view, held mostly by German scholars during his lifetime, that a legal code should be absolutely complete or that it cannot be reformed. A legal code, like other types of code, is always the child of its age.

It would, I think, be interesting to remark here that although the Estates are entrusted with the determination of the law this task is not, and should not, be exclusive to them alone; the public servants and the ministers of the monarch may well excel in their contribution to the attainment of this end: "the Estates are a guarantee of the general welfare and public freedom. A little reflection will show that this guarantee does not lie in their particular power of insight, because the highest civil servants necessarily have a deeper and more comprehensive insight into the nature of the state's organization and requirements." (§ 301) The Estates further the freedom and welfare of the society primarily by the novel insight which they may bring to the political process and by allowing public opinion and criticism to be a constructive factor in this process. Accordingly they mediate between the government and the nation as individuals and groups. This is why they should "possess a political and administrative sense and temper, no less than a sense for the interests of individuals and particular groups. At the same time the significance of their position is that, in common with the organized executive, they are a middle term, preventing both the extreme isolation of the power of the crown, which otherwise might seem a mere arbitrary tyranny, and also the isolation of the particular interests of the persons, societies, and Corporations." (§ 302; cf. also § 314)

Hegel repeatedly emphasized that as plenipotentiaries the members of the assembly must enjoy high moral character and a sense of devotion to the well — being of the state. They must also be versatile in the business of the law. These features are the basis of the public trust in the Estates: "the important thing, then is that a member of the Estates shall have a character, insight, and will be adequate to his task of concentrating on public business. In other words there is no question of an individual's talking as an abstract single person. The point is rather that his interests are made good in an assembly whose business is with the general interest. The electors require a guarantee that their deputy will further and secure this general interest." (Addition to § 309) What counts, then, in the election of the members of the Estates is whether they are qualified, not whether they are elected directly and universally by the people. (Cf. *ibid.* and § 303, 308) Indeed Hegel shies away from universal suffrage and introduces a system whereby deputies from the major socioeconomic groups are elected; such deputies have a greater grasp of the needs, interests, or circumstances of the various sectors of the society.

(B) The citizen participates *directly* in the political process by voicing publicly his private personal opinion on matters relating to the business of the state: "the formal subjective freedom of individuals consists in their having and expressing their own private judgments, opinions, and recommendations on affairs of state. This freedom is collectively manifested as what is called 'public opinion,' in which what is absolutely universal, the substantative and the true, is linked with its opposite, the purely particular and private opinions of the Many." (§ 316) Thus, as it is expressed actually, public opinion is a mixture of the petty and the serious, the rational and the irrational, the particular and the universal. It is also expressed by individuals who differ in intelligence, temper, interest, or even motivation. This shows that public opinion is presented to the government in a disorganized way; but the state should conduct its business under the conditions of order and thoughtful planning. Accordingly it should select those ideas or views which are most expressive of the rational interest of the society as a whole. What is important in this selection is not who or how many express a given idea or view, but which idea is good or great. Great is he who can articulate the universal need of the people: "the great man of the age is the one who can put into words the will of his age, tell his age what its will is, and accomplish it. What he does is the heart and the essence of his age, he actualizes his age. The man who lacks sense enough to despise public opinion expressed in gossip will never do anything great." (Addition to § 318) We may, accordingly, despise or respect public opinion. We may despise it in so far as it contains falsehood and idiosyncratic interest; and we may respect it in so far as it contains the true interest of the nation. As such it "is a repository not only of the genuine needs and correct tendencies of common life, but also, in the form of common sense (i.e., all— pervasive fundamental ethical priniples disguised as prejudices), of the eternal, substantative principles of justice, the true content and result of legislation, the whole constitution, and the general position of the state."(§ 317)

It is, I believe, reasonable to assert that the state is not, for Hegel, an unquestioned authority; on the contrary, it derives its authority from the will of the people, not only by what the people say directly, by voicing their opinion verbally and in writing, and indirectly by means of the legislature, but also by the wisdom of those citizens who possess the richest insight into what is best for the state as a whole. I do not see at all any arrogant or pretentious claim in Hegel to an all — knowing state which assumes superior authority in knowledge and power over its citizens. What concerns Hegel pre — eminently is the need to recognize a higher standard according to which (1) reform is possible and (2) the dignity of the citizen as a person can be upheld. This standard is none other than the voice of reason. This voice does not, as I stressed, emanate from a dogmatic, absolute power; it is always checked and tested by the continued satisfaction and well — being of the human personality. Its source in the final analysis is: (1) thoughtful reflection and (2) the happiness and dignity of the citizen as a human individual.

In view of the preceding discussion in its entirety I can say, contrary to the critics referred to in the first part of this essay, that in Hegel's view the citizen *qua* individual is the corner stone of the state. The constitution which emanates from the will of the people is the ultimate principle according to which the activities and the institutions of the state are organized. Within this organization no activity, whether it is legal, economic, religious, social, educational, etc., is valid or justified if it does not uphold the personality or individuality of the citizen. The latter cannot in any way be viewed as shaped or 'formed' by the state, for the structure within which the citizen grows is essentially rational. It does not limit the development of the natural powers or forces which constitute his nature as a human being. He exists as a free person. This freedom is not a privilege identified with capricious, fitful, or aimless behavior, but with that sort of behavior which is conducive to the realization of the *human* element in his being. The criterion by which this realization can be effected is the law of reason. What is valid in the *state* which Hegel supports "derives its authority, not at all from force, only to some extent from habit and custom, really from insight and argument." (Addition to § 316)

Two

THE SOURCE OF POLITICAL AUTHORITY:THE PEOPLE

Having reflected with some patience on the last part of the preceding essay, my critic would advance the following objection. It is not clear to me, he would say, that Hegel's account of how the will of the people becomes actual, or embodied in the law of the state, is adequate. The democratic form of government seems to be a more viable means of organizing the various institutions and activities of the state. Unless the people individually or as a majority participate in the political process their wills would, at least in principle, be ignored, and if their wills are ignored they would not exist as self — determined beings, i.e., as free. On Hegel's view, the ordinary people do not have to be consulted when the law is enacted, modified, or reformed; for the legislative power is not restricted to the Legislature but also extends to the monarch and his ministers. The monarch is in effect the final authority on what laws should be adopted or rejected. Thus the question arises: if we hold, as Hegel does, that the basis of the constitution is the will of the people, how can this will become concrete? How can we be certain that the final legal authority always acts in the interest of the people?

As an immediate response to this objection on behalf of Hegel let me ask: has there ever been a political system in the history of human civilization in which all the people participated, or could participate, in the process of government?[1] Again, how can a people of the *modern* state share individually or directly in the political process? I raise these questions not because I am here interested in discussing the arguments which validate or invalidate democracy as a political system but because I am anxious to focus attention on the central question of this essay: viz., given a society in a certain place and historical period, how can the people of that society express and assert their will effectively? What sort of governmental structure should a state establish to ensure the continued growth of freedom in the lives of its citizens? Or, under what conditions can a citizen participate in the political process in some fashion and feel in his heart that he counts and that the policies adopted by the state reflect his genuine interests as an individual? We may construct and defend a democratic, aristocratic, monarchical, or perhaps another form of constitution, and we may pride ourselves, at least in theory, that we espouse the most logical and humanistic form. The history of political theory from the days of Plato until the present is replete with such forms. But for Hegel the question which we should consider most of all when we analyze political reality is not whether this or that form of government is 'idealistic' or logically neat but whether it provides a social structure, a political atmosphere, within which a citizen can exist under the conditions of rationality, morality and creativity, whether he can function as an individual. Hegel's criticism of Rousseau and Fichte, and the thinkers in their tradition, is based mainly on this premise. In each case he analyzed the basic principle advocated by the philosopher only to see whether that principle is (1) philosophically sound and (2) provides an opportunity for the citizen to realize himself as an individual.

In this essay I shall first discuss the major arguments which Hegel advances against some aspects of the democratic form of government and then, on the basis of this discussion, proceed to a critical treatment of why he adopts the constitutional form of government which I defended in the first essay. Here I shall argue that (1) the fabric and the end of the legislative proeess is the general interest of the people; (2) within the political framework which Hegel recommends the people can, and should, express their wants, needs, or desires to the Legislature directly and indirectly; and (3) the final authority which enacts the laws of the land is the state as a sovereign power.

I

In discussing Hegel's critique of democracy we should first of all focus attention on three basic ideas in Rousseau's theory of the state. I do this simply because Hegel has mainly Rousseau in mind in this critique.[2]

First, the state is a union of men in which every member has voluntarily agreed to alienate his rights to the community as a whole for the sake of preservation and prosperity. The unity of these rights produces what Rousseau calls the *general will*. This will is the fundamental principle of the state. In a society governed by the general will people are free because: (1) since every person has alienated all his rights to the whole none would be left with extra rights or power to dominate or control the others. (2) Since each person gives himself to the community as a whole he gives himself to none; consequently he gives himself only to the general will which is his own will. Thus in obeying this will he in effect obeys himself. (3) There is in principle no reason for any person to usurp the rights of others, for since "each one gives his entire self, the condition is equal for everyone, and since the condition is equal for everyone, no one has an interest in making it burdensome for the others."[3]

Second, the state is sovereign; it is, in other words, the ultimate source of political authority.[4] Sovereignty, however, derives its being from the sanctity of the contract according to which private individuals form a state, or a republic.[5] Rousseau makes a clear distinction between 'general will' and 'will of all'. The former consists of the general interests which are common to the people as a whole, as a community. The latter consists of the private, particular interests. These interests are subjective and not necessarily shared by every citizen. Thus since the general will aims exclusively at the well — being of the whole state it "alone can guide the forces of the State according to the end for which it is instituted, which is the common good."[6] This is based on the assumption that "it is uniquely on the basis of this common good that society ought to be governed."[7] Therefore, "sovereignty, being only the exercise of the general will, can never be alienated, and that the sovereign, which is only a collective being, can only be represented by itself. Power can perfectly well be transferred, but not will."[8] But the question which we should ask is: how does the general will become concrete, living, in the life of society? It becomes concrete in and through the corpus of laws, i.e., constitution, which regulates the public activities of society. In the enactment of these laws the lawgiver should not have before his eyes the universal as such, or the good in itself, but only the true interest of the society as it exists in a certain place and time.

Third, the government is a public force; it is "an intermediate body established between the subjects and the sovereign for their mutual communication, and charged with the execution of the laws and the maintenance of civil as well as political freedom."[9] We can immediately see from this definition that the existence of government is not justified on the basis of a contract between it and the people; on the contrary, it is a commission, "a function in which, as simple officers of the sovereign, they exercise in its name the power that has been entrusted to them by the sovereign, and that the sovereign can limit, modify, and take back whenever it pleases, since the alienation of such a right is incompatible with the nature of the social body and contrary to the goal of the association."[10] Accordingly, the legislative power is a function of the people. But on what principle does a people promulgate new laws? The main task of the popular assemblies is, for Rousseau, to enact laws that are expressive of the general will. The deputies of the people must not be viewed as 'representatives', for the general will cannot be represented; they are its agents. Thus when there is a need for a new law or the modification of an older one the duty of the people's assembly is to discover the new law or to change the old one so as to be expressive of the general will. In such an assembly it is not usual for the deputies to agree unanimously on what law should be adopted or rejected. Whenever this happens a majority vote is appealed to. But one may ask: can we determine the validity of a law by a majority vote? For if a minority is of a different opinion, if this minority does not consent to the adoption of the law, it would not feel free when compelled to act according to it later on. Rousseau is aware of this difficulty. He thinks the whole question is badly put, for "when a law is proposed in the assembly of the people, what they are being asked is not precisely whether they approve or reject the proposal, but whether it does or does not conform to the general will that is theirs. Each one expresses his opinion on this by voting, and the declaration of the general will is drawn from the counting of the votes. Therefore when the opinion contrary to mine prevails, that proves nothing except that I was mistaken, and what I thought to be the general will was not."[11] This of course presupposes that "all the characteristics of the general will are still in the majority. When they cease to be, there is no longer any freedom regardless of the side one takes."[12]

II

Hegel agrees with Rousseau that the fundamental principle of the state is not gregarious instinct or divine authority but rather the general will of the people. This will is viewed as a universal and rational principle "which has thought both for its form and content." (§ 258) Its end is, as we have seen, the common interest, not the interest of this or that particular person or group of persons. But unfortunately, Rousseau, Hegel complains, abandoned this notion of will and replaced it by what he called the 'will of all': "he (Rousseau) takes the will only in a determinate form as the individual will, and he regards the universal will not as the absolutely rational element in the will, but only as a 'general' will which proceeds out of this individual will as out of a conscious will. The result is that he reduces the union of individuals in the state to a contract and therefore to something based on their arbitrary wills, their opinion, and their capriciously given express consent." (*Ibid.*) Now, if the fundamental principle of the state is not the general will as something universal and rational, or, put differently, if the law which I must obey does not express my rational will but the capricious will of the majority of the society to which I belong, then I cannot be free. Early in the *Social Contract* (Book I, chap. 6,7 and Book II, chap. 1,2,3) Rousseau advanced a concept of will that is both general and rational, a will that cannot be alienated, divided, and mistaken, a will that is above the desires, values, and interests of the people as particular individuals. This will aims at the *general* interest of all, and this interest could not be articulated by any specific member of the community. Again, in his discussion of Law and the Legislator, Rousseau repeatedly stressed that the people are not the best judges of what is truly good for them: "how will a blind multitude, which often does not know what it wants because it rarely knows what is good for it, carry out by itself an undertaking as vast and as difficult as a system of legislation?"[13] This is why they need a person of superior wisdom to draft their laws, or constitution: "the discovery of the best rules of society suited to nations would require a superior intelligence, who saw all of the men's passions yet experienced none of them; who had no relationship at all to our nature yet knew it thoroughly; whose happiness was independent of us, yet who was nevertheless willing to attend to ours; finally one who, preparing for himself a future glory with the passage of time, could work in one century and enjoy the reward in another. Gods would be needed to give laws to men."[14] But when he came to discuss the legislative power, the assembly which has the task of articulating the laws of social behavior, Rousseau maintained, as we saw above, that a law is adopted or rejected by a majority vote. He did insist that the assembly should enact the general will, yet what the assembly articulates as law is nevertheless decided by the will of the majority, that is, "their arbitrary wills, their opinions, and their capriciously given express consent." We should therefore disagree with S. Avineri when he states that "Hegel misses the significance of Rousseau's distinction between *la volonté generale* and *la volonté des tous*. Hegel apparently sees Rousseau's 'general will' as a pure aggregate of individual wills and overlooks the fact that it represents a higher, community — oriented level of consciousness, transcending the 'lower' will which is oriented towards merely individual goals."[15] Hegel is fully aware of Rousseau's distinction between the general will and the will of all, but he is also aware that Rousseau himself reduced the notion of the general will to that of the will of all.[16]

Thus although Rousseau formulated a rational principle of the state this principle remained abstract and ineffective in the management of the affairs of the people. The real social contract, the contract that is actually operative, does not seem to be expressed in the general will but in the contract established by the will of all. Rousseau failed to bridge or to provide a principle according to which the two wills can be unified. "For this reason, when these abstract conclusions came into power, they afforded for the first time in human history the prodigious spectacle of the overthrow of the constitution of a great actual state (France during the French Revolution) and its complete reconstruction *ab initio* on the basis of pure thought alone, after the destruction of all existing and given material. The will of its refounders was to give it what they alleged was a purely rational basis, but it was only abstractions that were being used; the Idea was lacking; and the experiment ended in the maximum of frightfulness and terror." (§ 358)[17]

The crux of this criticism is that an abstract idea of the general will is not fruitful in reforming or re—structuring an already existing state. The main task of an adequate political theory is to help in building on what already exists; the attainment of rationality is a gradual process of achievement. It is a mistake to think that a state can be built on the basis of pure thought alone. The defects, injustices, or blunders of a state may be exposed or condemned but the reality of the state cannot be denied or obliterated. Moreover, basing a state merely on the idea of a contract *ab initio* does not in fact lead to a well — organized or smoothly functioning state; on the contrary, it only produces a loosely organized political body, for the customs, values, or interests of a society which constitute the heart of its constitution evolve gradually. They arise out of the existential conditions of the people through a historical period. I should here immediately add that Hegel does not mean to say that there cannot, or should not, be an ideal which stands above the actual; but, as I shall argue in some detail later on, there must be within the state a viable mechanism, or principle, which facilitates the realization of the ideal in the life of the people. This principle is absent from Rousseau's political theory. Rousseau held that the state is composed of two basic powers, the executive power and the legislative power. As an executive power, the government is an intermediary between the sovereign and the people. But the sovereign becomes concrete in the general will, i.e., in the constitution. The people alone are entrusted with the legislation of all laws. Rousseau's reluctance to allow any other power or agency to assist in the enactment of laws led him necessarily to invest the popular assembly with the full power to enact all the laws. This is the main reason why he was forced in the final analysis to reduce the general will to the will of all.

Upholding an abstract idea of the general will leads to another undesirable consequence: the freedom of the individual would be disregarded. For if the general will is sovereign, and as such inalienable, indivisible, and cannot err, then it should follow that every member of the state should submit his will completely to it. This premise is made explicit by Rousseau: "in perfect legislation, the private or individual will should be null; the corporate will of the government very subordinate; and consequently the general or sovereign will always dominant and the unique rule of all the others."[18] But if the end of the state is the freedom of the individual, and if this individual does not, at least in principle, participate in the legislative process, if in other words, his actual will is ignored, then any claim to his freedom would be a fiction and not a reality. Hegel is, it seems to me, quite aware of this weakness in Rousseau's concept of the general will; for in the same section where he discusses the concept he insists that rationality exists concretely in the state when objective freedom, the freedom implicit in the universal, in the general will, is unified with subjective freedom, with the freedom of the particular, private will. (§ 258)

But the general will becomes concrete in the popular assembly, that is, in the legislative process. This process is the heart of what is usually called the democratic process, for in it the people are expected to declare their will, to articulate this will as a law, and to adopt the law as a rule of social behavior. But we should here ask: under what conditions is the popular assembly to arrive at the true content of the general will? Are the people qualified, or in a position, to discover the common good? I raise these questions for two reasons: (1) they place the problem of freedom into sharp focus; (2) the method of articulating and realizing the general will is, for Hegel, a central question of political theory; for if the end of the state is freedom we should explain not only the meaning of freedom but also the conditions under which it is possible. Now let us ask again: is the conceptual framework within which Rousseau analyzes the concept of the general will and the way this will is actualized concretely adequate? The answer to this question is, for Hegel, in the negative. In what follows I shall explain why.

We have seen that, for Rousseau, the people are sovereign: their will is the source of political authority. This premise underlies Rousseau's insistence that the legislative power must be restricted to the people in events of popular assemblies. In these assemblies they vote on those laws which they take to be expressive of the general will, of the will of the people as whole. This task cannot be relegated to 'representatives' for two reasons: (1) the people are most qualified to judge what is in their best interests; and (2) the will of the individual cannot be represented. Hence in articulating a needed law the people must be present and each person must deliberate and decide on the appropriateness or inappropriateness of a proposed law. This line of reasoning seems at first look attractive and convincing, for it asserts the sovereignty of the people in a genuine fashion. It also seems to account for the possibility of freedom effectively. Hegel, however, rejects it for the following reasons.

First, "to hold that every single person should share in deliberating and deciding on political matters of general concern on the ground that all individuals are members of the state, that its concerns are their concerns, and that it is their right that what is done should be done with their knowledge and volition, is tantamount to a proposal to put the democratic element without any rational form into the organism of the state, although it is only in virtue of the possession of such a form that the state is an organism at all." (§ 308) What Hegel means when he says that the idea of popular government lacks rational form is that it ignores the aspect that a state is an organic whole and that the individuals who compose it are concrete, unique wills: "the rational consideration of a topic, the consciousness of the Idea, is concrete, and to that extent coincides with a genuine practical sense." (*Ibid.*) A citizen in the state is not merely a number or an abstraction. And the people are not, to borrow a term from Herbert Marcuse, 'one-dimensional' in every possible respect. Their wills are not, in other words, homogeneous.[19] The state is a concrete whole; as such, it is composed of groups, classes, associations, or corporations. In whatever an individual feels, thinks, or does he reflects the interests of the group to which he belongs. Thus a citizen is not merely a universal interest or consciousness which he shares with the rest of society; "this consciousness and will, however, lose their emptiness and acquire a content and a living actuality only when they are filled with particularity, and particularity means determinacy as particular and a particular class — status," (§ 308) What Hegel is here stressing is that it is a grave mistake to think that in any society it would be possible for all the members of that society to agree unanimously, equally, on a certain matter or proposal primarily because people exist as individuals and as groups who share certain ideas and interests.[20] A person realizes himself as an individual only in so far as he belongs to such a group: "the single person attains his actual and living destiny for universality only when he becomes a member of a Corporation, a society, &." (§ 308) Accordingly if individuals participate in the legislative process, "whether individuals are to choose representatives for this purpose, or whether every single individual is to have a vote in the legislature himself," the state would be reduced to an atomistic and abstract level. (§ 303 The 'people' become the 'many', and as such they exist "as an aggregate, a formless mass whose commotion and activity could therefore only be elementary, irrational, barbarous, and frightful." (*Ibid.*) If this happens the state would cease to be a will or a unity of purpose; it would instead exist under the sway of particular wills or interests. Hegel makes this point forcefully when he discusses the possibility of electing the monarch directly by the people: "in an elective monarchy, I mean, the nature of the relation between king and people implies that the ultimate decision is left with the particular will, and hence the constitution becomes a Compact of Election, i.e., a surrender of the power of the state at the discretion of the particular will. The result of this is that the particular offices of state turn into private property, the sovereignty of the state enfeebled and lost, and finally the state disintegrates within and is overthrown from without." (§ 281)

Second, the claim that each person should participate in the legislative business of the state presupposes that "everyone is at home in this business — a ridiculous notion, however commonly we may hear it sponsored. Still, in public opinion a field is open to everyone where he can express his purely personal political opinions and make them count." (§ 308) In *Reason in History* Hegel characterized this presupposition as false and dangerous, for then "each popular faction can set itself up as the People.

What constitutes the state is a matter of trained intelligence, not a matter of 'the people'."[21] Hegel insists that we must clearly distinguish between what the 'people' will actually and its ability to will the universal. In a popular assembly a people may agree on a certain law, but in this agreement there is no guarantee that what they have willed is the universal. If they fail to will the universal they achieve only one kind of freedom — subjective freedom. But the determination of the universal, of the general interest of the people, requires "a comprehensive insight into the nature of the state's organization and requirements." (§ 301) This insight is not, under normal conditions, generously present in the minds of ordinary men. Its attainment requires skill, dedication, wisdom.[22]

Third, if we hold that the laws of the state should be decided by the people directly we undermine the very idea of the constitution: the need for a constitution becomes superfluous: "the only institution necessary would be a neutral, centrally located observer who would announce what in his opinion were the needs of the state, a mechanism of assembling the individuals, casting their vote, and the arithmatical counting and comparison of the votes on the various propositions — and this would already be the decision."[23] This is a serious consequence of the idea of popular sovereignty; for, as we argued earlier, the 'state' is an abstract entity; its foundation is the general will.[24] Accordingly it needs to be translated concretely. This translation is what gives rise to the whole machinery of governmental and social institutions without which social life and culture are impossible. But the detailed determination of the general will is the very structure of the constitution: "only in the constitution does the abstract entity of the state assume life and reality."[25] Moreover, if we do away with the constitution we in effect ignore the validity of the universal, the ideal, in the life of the people. If this happens any attempt at rational progress or reform would necessarily come to a halt.

Fourth, in order for popular government to be effective, in order for it to work, the people must enjoy a high degree of political consciousness; but in fact, at least in Hegel's time, this requirement does not seem to be fulfilled. An expression of this difficulty is electoral apathy. Hegel thinks that popular suffrage especially in large states "leads inevitably to electoral indifference, since the casting of a single vote is of no significance where there is a multitude of electors. Even if a voting qualification is highly valued and esteemed by those who are entitled to it, they still do not enter the polling booth. Thus the result of an institution of this kind is more likely to be the opposite of what was intended; election actually falls into the power of a few, of a caucus, and so of the particular and contingent interest which is precisely what was to have been neutralized." (§ 311) We may here ask: why does popular suffrage lead to electoral apathy? I raise this question, for it would seem that casting one's vote on a matter of social significance is a political obligation. Hegel is certainly alive to this point. He holds that the main reason for electoral apathy is, as I have just indicated, lack of political consciousness; this lack is itself a consequence of a more rooted problem, namely: most people do not have a substantial conception and sense of freedom. They conceive of freedom abstractly, i.e., as an activity of personal satisfaction. But in order for one to be fully free he should acquire both understanding and skill in realizing the universal in his personal experience. This happens only when a person views his destiny as an integral achievement of the life of the state as a rational whole.

III

Hegel, then, agrees with Rousseau that in order for a state to be free it must express and realize the common interest, or the general will of the people. He, however, disagrees with him on how this will becomes actual, on how its content can be articulated as a valid law. While Rousseau insists that the people as a whole should directly participate in the legislative process because they, as a people, are sovereign, Hegel thinks that his procedure is impractical and does not ensure the gradual realization of the general will as a rational principle in the life of the whole.

The central problem for political theory, for Hegel, is not whether we should adopt a democratic, aristocratic, or monarchical form of constitution, but whether we can determine "the *best constitution*, namely, that institution, organization, or mechanism of government which most securely guarantees the purpose of the state."[26] Thus we should ask: since the end of the state is freedom, what sort of political organization is most conducive to the realization of this end? "A free constitution," Hegel writes, "is for us dependent upon the idea of representative government, and this has become a firm prejudice."[27] We should immediately add that when Hegel speaks of representation he means *indirect* representation: "our states are so big and their people so many, that they cannot directly, but only indirectly through representatives, contribute their will to political decisions."[28]

My critic may here object: how can a person be represented indirectly? I shall discuss this question in detail later on; but for now let me make the following remark. Suppose the will of a person can be reresented directly or indirectly, what is the purpose of this representation? Now suppose it cannot be represented at all, does it not have the right to seek and attain its true interest? Again, does it not become free in realizing these interests? Thus the question for Hegel is not whether the will can, or cannot, be represented by another person or an assembly of persons but whether the real interests of the people can be discovered, systematized, and enacted into law. Here my critic may ask once more: who, on Hegel's view, is qualified to enact the laws of the state? Hegel holds that the enactment of the laws is the task of the legislative power. This power is a function of the state *qua* sovereign. But sovereignty is an abstract entity; it is the ideality of the state. It exists concretely in the three powers of the state: the Crown, the Executive, and the Legislature: "the organic unity of the powers of the state itself implies that it is one single mind which both firmly establishes the universal and also brings it into its determinate actuality and carries it out." (§ 299) Thus unlike Rousseau, Hegel maintains that the enactment of the law is not restricted to the Legislature, viz., the Assembly of Estates, but to all the powers of the state. This point is clearly stated in the following passage: "in the legislature as a whole the other powers are the first two moments which are effective, (i) the monarchy as that to which ultimate decision belongs; (ii) the executive as the advisory body since it is the moment possessed of (a) a concrete knowledge and oversight of the whole state in its numerous facets and the actual principles firmly established within it, and (b) a knowledge in particular of what the state's power needs. The last moment in the legislature is the Estates." (§ 300) My critic would once more interject: this view undermines the people's authority in determining the laws of the state, for the legislative task is, for Hegel, the monopoly of the monarch and his advisory council. But unless the people speak for themselves, or declare their own will directly, there would not be any guarantee that the enacted laws will express their true interests. This argument is mistaken for at least two reasons.

First, Hegel avers that the legislative power is a function of the state, i.e., *the people*, but as sovereign. However, as I just indicated, sovereignty is an abstract ideal; its concrete determinations are the three basic powers. If we restrict the legislative business to the Legislature alone we face two difficulties: (1) we violate the integrity of the sovereignty of the state; for if the sovereignty of the state becomes concrete in its three governing powers it would necessarily follow that the exclusion of any of these powers would limit the authority of the people in the formulation of its laws; (2) we further the separation, or independence, of the powers of the state. Hegel, as we saw in the preceding essay, repeatedly stressed that if the powers of the state remain separated its unity would be destroyed; the state would consequently meet its end: "the idea of the so — called 'independence of powers' contains the fundamental error of supposing that the powers, though independent, are to check one another. This independence, however, destroys the unity of the state, and unity is the chief of all desiderata." (Add. to § 300)

Second, the claim that 'the people' should declare and enact their will into law is vague and misleading; for, what do we mean by 'the people'? Do we mean, for example, 'all' or 'many' of the people? "The phrase 'the Many'" Hegel writes, "denotes empirical universality more strictly than 'All', which is in current use. If it is said to be obvious that this 'all' prima facie excludes at least children, women, &., then it is surely still more obvious that the quite definite word 'all' should not be used when something quite indefinite is meant. " (§ 301) So when political thinkers and critics speak of "the people with reference to legislative business they usually mean 'summoning' the Estates;" they assume that "(i) the deputies of the people, or even the people themselves, must know best what is in their best interest, and (ii) their will for its promotion is undoubtedly the most disinterested." (§ 301) But this assumption is mistaken — why?

Hegel holds that we should make a distinction between what one wills, on the one hand, and willing the universal, on the other. Willing the universal, which is the proper business of the legislative powers, requires "profound apprehension and insight." It is a mistake to think that the Assembly of Estates is in a position to determine the universal. I discussed this point in the first part of this essay. I should, however, add here that in universal legislation our end is to promulgate a law, a statement which is both general and determinate: "the distinction, however, is not a hard and fast one, because a law, by being a law, is *ab initio* something more than a mere command in general terms (such as 'Thou shalt not kill'). A law must in itself be something determinate, but the more determinate it is, the more readily are its terms capable of being carried out as they stand." (§ 299) Thus although law is a general proposition it has an empirical character; for without this character it cannot be relevant or applicable to the life of the people. But in order for one to enact such law he should have a synoptic knowledge of the affairs of the state. He should have a profound grasp of its external and internal problems; he should also know these problems as inter — related. A popular assembly is not in a position to possess this sort of knowledge; it is only qualified to articulate what the people actually will under given circumstances. Hence it should function as a link, i.e., intermediary, between the government and the nation: "the Estates have the function of bringing public affairs into existence not only implicitly, but also actually, i.e. of bringing into existence the moment of subjective formal freedom, the public consciousness as an empirical universal, of which the thoughts and opinions of the Many are particulars." (§ 301) In this way it becomes a major factor in guaranteeing the well — being and freedom of the people.

But its ability to render this service to the nation does not lie merely in its status of being the representative of the people, but especially in its political insight, "(a) in the *additional* insight of the deputies, insight in the first place into activity of such officials as are not immediately under the eye of the higher functionaries of the state, and in particular into the more pressing and more specialized needs and deficiencies which are directly in their view; (b) in the fact that the anticipation of criticism from the Many, particularly of public criticism, has the effect of inducing officials to devote their best attention beforehand to their duties and the schemes under consideration, and to deal with these only in accordance with the purest motives." (§ 301) I quote this passage at length only to stress that, for Hegel, the determination of the universal requires political skill, experience, and wisdom. This is a main reason why he held that the executive power is in a better position than the Estates to contribute to the legislation of the law; they have a deeper and more comprehensive insight; "they are also more habituated to the business of government and have a greater skill in it, so that even without the Estates they are *able* to do what is best, just as they also continually *have* to do while the Estates are in session." (*Ibid.*) Hegel is here aware of the possible charge that if the monarch, or the executive power, becomes the ultimate factor in the legislative business there will be a tendency, at least in principle, towards despotism. But this charge assumes that the will of the executive is bad or less good than the will of the Estates. This assumption, Hegel argues, is "characteristic of the rabble or of the negative outlook generally." (*Ibid.*) We cannot conduct the affairs of the state on the assumption that its various powers are antagonistic to one another, otherwise the state would be doomed to failure sooner or later: "the attitude of the executive to the Estates should not be essentially hostile, and a belief in the necessity of such hostility is a sad mistake. The executive is not a party standing over against another party in such a way that each has continually to steal a march on the other and wrest something from the other. If such a situation arises in the state, that is a misfortune, but it cannot be called health." (Add. to § 301) Moreover, we should remark that by its very nature the executive has the universal as its end while the Estates proceed in their business as private individuals; they start, Hegel writes, "from isolated individuals, from a private point of view, from particular interests, and so are inclined to devote their activities to these at the expense of the general interests, while *per contra* the other moments in the power of the state explicitly take up the standpoint of the state from the start and devote themselves to the universal end." (§ 301)

Hegel thinks that "it is one of the most important discoveries of logic that a specific moment which, by standing in an opposition, has the position of an extreme, ceases to be such and is a moment in an organic whole by being at the same time a mean." (§ 302) This moment is the

Estates; it is a mediating organ between the government and the nation. While the first intends the universal, the second, viz., the Estates, intends the particular interests of the people. From the standpoint of civil society, the nation exists as a conglomeration of individuals who give pre — eminence to their particular interests without due consciousness or concern for the well — being of society as an organic whole. But in the Estates the people *qua* members of civil society acquires its "political significance and efficacy;" it here appears "neither as a mere indiscriminate multitude nor as an aggregate dispersed into its atoms, but as what it already is, namely, a class subdivided into two, one sub — class (the agricultural class) being based on a tie of substance between its members, and the other (the business class) on particular needs and the work whereby these are met. It is only in this way that there is a genuine link between the particular which is effective in the state and the universal." (§ 303)

Although this point has been made before I reiterate it only to focus attention on the need to view the state as a harmonious unity, not only (as I shall argue in the next essay) because outside it ethical life is impossible but also to establish on a firm foundation the claim that the people are the ultimate source of political authority. For the people cannot be the source of such authority unless they exist as a unified will and unless there is a framework within which the rational and general aspect of this will can be enacted into law.

IV

A brief consideration of this framework, viz., the Assembly of Estates, should throw more light on the role of the people in the legislative process. The principle around which this framework is organized is this: society elects its representatives *as a society*, on the one hand, and the legislative power enacts the laws of the nation as an organic unity, as unity of will, on the other. Let me discuss the dynamics of this principle.[29]

The Assembly of Estates is composed of two houses: the first represents the agricultural class and the second represents the business class. The first class is "one whose ethical life is natural, whose basis is family life, and, so far as its livelihood is concerned, the possession of land." (§ 305) This class is composed of farmers and an educated elite. Like the monarch, its members acquire their land and socio-political position by birth. Hence they do not depend for their living either on the state or on the other classes; they have a will of their own. Their socio-economic status allows them to be in a position to contribute constructively to the well — being of the state. "This class", Hegel states, "is more particularly fitted for political position and significance in that its capital is independent alike of the state's capital, the uncertainty of business, the quest for profit, and any sort of fluctuation in possessions. It is likewise independent of favour, whether from the executive or the mob. It is even fortified against its own wilfulness, because those members of this class who are called to political life are not entitled, as other citizens are, either to dispose of their entire property at will, or to the assurance that it will pass to their children, whom they love equally, in similarly equal divisions." (§ 306) But although the right of this class is based on the natural principle of the family, and although it has the universal immediately realized in its life, it cannot sever its political outlook or interest from that of the nation as a whole, i.e., from the general interest of society. (Cf. Add. to § 306) It thus has the unique role of being an intermediary between the monarch and the executive, on the one hand, and civil society, on the other. With the monarch it shares the aspect of economic and political independence and with civil society it shares similar rights and needs. Its virtue consists (1) in bringing about a more reasonable and prudent judgment in legal matters and (2) in enhancing the unity between the Estates and the Executive.

The second house of the Assembly of Estates represents the interests of the business class. This class does not participate in politics directly but *indirectly* by means of deputies or representatives, because (1) it is the largest segment of society and (2) because it is composed of various associations. Each of these associations is grouped together on the basis of mutual economic or professional interests. It is extremely difficult, if not impossible, to harmonize and articulate these diverse interests by means of direct participation in the legislative process. Thus since the deputies of this class "are the deputies of civil society, it follows as a direct consequence that their appointment is made by the society as a society. That is to say, in making the appointment, society is not dispersed into atomic units, collected to perform only a single and temporary act, and kept together for a moment and no longer. On the contrary, it makes the appointment as a society, articulated into associations, communities, and Corporations, which although constituted already for other purposes, acquire in this way a connexion with politics." (§ 308) But my critic would at this point insist: how can the deputies of these diverse associations discover the unity of the will of the people? Put differently, how can the diverse interests of these associations be harmonized and articulated as a law. Again, can the deputies *represent* the will of the people? These questions call for a two — fold clarification. First, what does it mean for a society to appoint its deputies *as a society*? Second, what does it mean for the deputies to *represent* the people?

First, when Hegel asserts that society, *qua* society, should appoint its deputies he means that the people are the electorate, and that the concrete interests of the people as a whole must be expressed and must play a role in the legislative process. But 'the people' is not an abstract or a homogeneous mass of human beings. The term 'people' refers to human beings who exist in society as individuals with personal interests, values, intellectual capacities, emotional inclinations, desires, and world outlooks. A quick look at how the people actually conduct their activities in social life shows that they exist as groups, or associations, or as Hegel would call them, Corporations. What makes a corporation possible is unity of socio — economic and professional interests. In civil society a corporation is usually pre — occupied with its particular interests: the attainment of these interests is the basis of its satisfaction. Accordingly if the interests of the people are to be represented in the Legislature comprehensively and concretely each corporation should elect its deputies. But the activity of representing would not be useful or effective unless the deputies are competent or qualified for the task. Hegel is sensitive to this condition: "the guarantee that the deputies will have the qualification and disposition that accord with this end, he writes, "is to be ... above all in the knowledge (of the organization and interests of the state and civil society), the temperament, and the skill which a deputy acquires as a result of the actual transaction of business in managerial or official positions and then evinces in his actions." (§ 310) Thus a deputy of the people should enjoy a political and administrative sense; he should be devoted and responsive to the needs of his community; and, above all, he should be capable of making a wise judgment. (Cf. § 311)

I am aware of the possible objection that the differentiation of society into associations or corporations is *démodé* or perhaps does not apply to our own society at the present.[30] But the crucial point which we should recognize, however, and which is the crux of Hegel's argument, is not whether society exhibits a certain mode of economic or professional organizations but that if a system of representation is to be successful it should take into serious consideration the interests of *all* the people. This 'all' exists as a diversity, or multiplicity, of interests. Accordingly the deputies should be the deputies of the various interests of the people. Only in this way does a society act as an electorate concretely and not abstractly as a conglomeration of atoms. (§ 311)

Second, when Hegel characterizes the deputies as representatives of the people or of their will he does not mean "simply the substitution of one man for another; the point is rather that the interest itself is actually present in its representative, while he himself is there to represent the objective element of his own being." (§ 311) It is a notorious presumption to claim that an elected official can, regardless of his intellectual achievements or political position, know the actual content of the people. Hegel is aware of this difficulty. He clearly states that the deputies are not "agents with a commission and specific instructions." (§ 309) Two arguments are advanced in support of the claim. (1) "since deputies are elected to deliberate and decide on public affairs, the point about their election is that it is a choice of individuals on the strength of confidence felt in them, i.e. a choice of such individuals as have a better understanding of these affairs than their electors have and such also as essentially vindicate the universal interest of a society or a Corporation in preference to that interest." (*Ibid.*) (2) The Assembly of Estates "is meant to be a living body in which all members deliberate in common and reciprocally instruct and convince each other." (*Ibid.*) The point which merits special emphasis here is that the substance of the legislative activity is what is right, or good, not merely for this or that individual or group of individuals but the whole of society given as a diversity, indeed complexity, of interests. This activity is deliberative; its content, viz., the common good, is not given as a ready made or clearly formulated principle. On the contrary, it is conceived, articulated, on the basis of understanding the actual social condition and rational aspirations of the state as an organic whole. This is why Hegel reminds us that "representation is grounded on trust, but trusting another is something different from giving my vote myself in my own personal capacity. Hence majority voting runs counter to the principle that I should be personally present in anything which is to be obligatory on me. We have confidence in a man when we take him to be a man of discretion who will manage our affairs conscientiously and to the best of his knowledge, just as if they were his own." (Add. to § 309) Accordingly when I vote for a person I declare confidence in this person's qualification to discover and promote the common good. In this act I function as a citizen; I do not think merely of my subjective interest but also of the well — being of the state as a sovereign power.

But the Assembly of Estates, or peoples' assemblies in general, may not be honest, skilled, or wise; they may not, in other words, be qualified to participate effectively in the legislative process. Indeed if we look at the history of political institutions we find that in most cases the peoples' assemblies of the various states did not exercise the highest degree of wisdom or competency. Hegel knew this fact very well. This is one main reason why he refused to restrict the power to enact laws only to the Legislature, viz., the Estates; he insisted, as we saw, that the people themselves, including the monarch and his advisory council, should also contribute to this task.

Hegel strongly believes that the people should voice their opinions and make recommendations on the political business of the state. This is a basic way in which they can exercise their political freedom: "the formal subjective freedom of individuals consists in their having and expressing their own private judgments, opinions, and recommendations on affairs of state. This freedom is collectively manifested as what is called 'public opinion,' in which what is absolutely universal, the substantative and true, is linked with its opposite, the purely particular and private opinions of the Many." (§ 316) I discussed the importance and political implications of public opinion in the preceding essay. Here I would like to emphasize two points. (1) For Hegel, the Assembly of Estates is a public forum in which the problems, needs, aspirations, and interests of the state are evaluated, debated, and settled. In this forum the Executive as well as the citizens can, directly or by means of the press, contribute their objections, views, or wisdom. They can, moreover, cooperate in determining what is best for the nation. The relation between the people and the government is not contractual. The latter is not, moreover, instituted on the basis of trust. It should, instead, be viewed as an instrument of the general will, for its main task is to apply the law, to bring the particular under the universal. It is the power which realizes or makes the will of the people actual. Moreover, while the main interest of the Assembly of estates is to discover and exchange what the people actually want, the main interest of the government is to discover the objective rational aspect of these interests and enact them into law. But it cannot do this unless it knows the mind of the people as members of corporations, i.e., concretely, and unless it shows respect for their rights and interests. The proper strength of the government lies in its associations: "in them the executive meets with the legitimate interests which it must respect, and since the administration cannot be other than helpful to such interests, though it must also supervise them, the individual finds protection in the exercise of his rights and so links his private interest with the maintenance of the whole." (Add. to § 290) Again, "just as civil society is the battlefield where everyone's individual private interest meets everyone else's, so here we have the struggle (a) of private interests against particular matters of common concern and (b) of both of these together against the organization of the state and its higher outlook. At the same time the corporation mind, engendered when the particular sphere gain their title of rights, is now inwardly converted into the mind of the state since it finds in the state the means of maintaining its particular ends." (§ 389) This is enough to show that for Hegel the work of the government and the Assembly of Estates should not, as we argued earlier, be viewed as antagonistic but as complementary to each other.

(2) In being an open forum, the Assembly of Estates provides a realistic education for the people in the affairs of the state; in its meetings they learn best how to recognize the true character of their interests. "The idea usually dominant is that everyone knows from the start what is best for the state and that the Assembly debate is a mere discussion of this

knowledge. In fact, however, the precise contrary is the truth. It is here that first begin to develop the virtues, abilities, dexterities, which have to serve as examples to the public. Of course such debates are irksome to ministers, who have to equip themselves with wit and eloquence to meet the criticism there directed against them. None the less, publicity here is the chief means of educating the public in national affairs. A nation which has such public sittings is far more vitally related to the state than one which has no Estates Assembly or one which meets in private." (Add. to § 315) The Assembly of Estates, then, performs two important functions: (1) it informs the government about the people's needs or problems; (2) it brings to focus, to the attention of the people, the problems of the state as a whole internally and externally. It is in this dual function that the Assembly of Estates acts as an intermediary, i.e., as a unifying bond between the government and the nation.

But the power responsible for the enactment of the laws is the monarch and his advisory council: "the second moment in the power of the crown is the moment of particularity, or the moment of a determinate content and its subsumption under the universal. When this acquires a special objective existence, it becomes the supreme council and the individuals who compose it. They bring before the monarch for his decision the content of current affairs of state or the legal provisions required to meet existing needs, together with their objective aspects, i.e. the grounds on which decision is to be based, the relative laws, circumstances, etc. (§ 283) It should be clear from this passage that though the monarch has the final authority on what laws should be adopted his decision in such matters is not strictly personal or subjective but assisted, indeed determined, by the wisdom of the executive council, on the one hand, and the articulated needs or demands of the Legislature, on the other. The monarch, *qua* ruler, enjoys the privilege of being a final authority because he sums up in his person the sovereignty of the state: "the power of the crown contains in itself the three moments of the whole, viz., (a) the *universality* of the constitution and the laws; (b) counsel, which refers the particular to the universal; and (c) the moment of ultimate decision, as the *self - determination* to which everything else reverts and from which everything else derives the beginning of its actuality." (§ 275) Thus when Hegel states that the final legal authority is the monarch he does not in any way mean to advocate a despotic or 'authoritarian' type of government. The only authority, for him, which should rule the state is, as we saw in the last essay, the authority of the law. His only concern is to establish a political framework within which the state can function and express itself as a unified whole. This framework is based, as I have so far argued, on three basic principles: (1) the substance of the legislative process is the actual and general interest of the people; (2) the people participate in the legislative process indirectly by electing deputies who represent their interests concretely and directly by voicing their opinions in the press and the recognized means of public communication; (3) the monarch as the concrete element of the sovereignty of the state decides what laws should be accepted or rejected. This decision is based on the recommendations of the Legislature and the advisory council of the state as such.

THREE
LAW AND MORALITY

What you have tried to show in the preceding essay, my critic would argue, is that in a constitutional state the people *qua* sovereign is the ultimate source of political authority. It follows from this premise that when a citizen acts according to the established legal system consciously, thoughtfully, and willingly he is free; for the law which he obeys expresses his interests — it is the law of his will. But, of his *political will*, not *moral* will, my critic would quickly add. You have discussed a political framework within which the actual will of the citizen may, under historical conditions, be expressed and articulated as law. Yet the ultimate authority which determines the form and content of the law is the state *qua* sovereign. But beyond this law no higher authority, or voice, exists. Although the individual may be free to express his opinion publicly, and although his will may be represented indirectly in the legislature by honorable deputies, still there is no room for conscientious objection, for objection based on a higher moral claim, mainly because Hegel has destroyed the gap between the moral and the legal; he has replaced the Categorical Imperative by the *Emperium* of the state: "departing ... from the Lutheran separation between the juridical and the moral, Hegel has now succeeded in tracing his curve and closing the circle; it is the law — not certainly the purely formal law of abstract Law, but the living and concrete law of the divinely real State — that defines duty. The legal — the concrete legal — has become the moral."[1] In reducing the moral to the legal, Hegel has in effect revaluated the whole meaning and status of moral conduct. Morality cannot anymore be viewed as a reflective, deliberative activity performed by a *human individual*, i.e., by a responsible, self — determined being, primarily because what is right, or good, is dictated by a state law which should be recognized and adopted by every member of the society. Accordingly, conscience is not the source of moral judgment; for duty is in a strict sense prescribed by the state. This means that morality in the Kantian sense is replaced by what Hegel calls 'ethical life' or 'social morality', *Sittlichkeit*, "or *Ethicity* which constitutes the moral life in its pure and authentic, stable and consistent, or completely rational form, and which, developing from its origin in the familial community, has for its keystone the state. Then I am no longer obliged to 'reflect on the object of my activity ' in order to form my 'own conviction'; I do my duty 'as it were from instinct', because it is my 'second nature'. The rule of conscience is finally transcended."[2] Thus although a citizen may feel he is free, for in his 'moral' conduct he deliberately acts according to what he takes to be the supreme moral law, he is not actually free, because the very recognition and adoption of this law as the highest moral authority is already instilled in him as such. His moral nature, or substance, is acquired during his social development. His moral sense is the internalization of the external moral voice which the state has legislated as public law. This is a main reason why he does not have to reflect on or choose the right or moral course of action: his subjective will is identical with the objective will, with the will of the Whole. Thus a citizen may receive an order from the state and he may happen to find the order wrong, immoral, or contrary to his conscience, and he may feel guilty or agonize about the supposed morality of his prospective act — so what! His anxiety has a subjective value only. He should, accordingly, arm himself with civil courage and adopt the objective point of view; he should, in other words, adopt the following attitude: "I know that I am fulfilling the absolute requirement of a truly ethical mode of conduct, *absolute duty – that which* is — by doing that which the State, that is Spirit, prescribes for me, and I know that the State itself, including within itself the sphere of abstract law and that of morality but superior to both, is subject neither to the rules of law nor to those of good and evil as the conscience understands them. In willing what the State wills as if it were my own being, I possess the *real freedom*, and I am covered, not only by my hierarchical superior but by the unshakeable certitude of the objective and universal order in which God manifests Himself."[3]

If valid, this whole line of reasoning which I developed in the foregoing paragraph would constitute a devastating blow to Hegel's analysis of human freedom and morality. But it is not valid, not only because Hegel does not naively identify *law*, or Right, with the positive law of the state but especially because in his treatment of law, will, and moral experience his main concern is to provide a social basis for human freedom and individuality. We should, for example, ask: what does Hegel mean by law, Recht? What is the relationship between law and morality? What makes an act moral? What does Hegel mean by *Sittlichkeit*? Is this concept based on the premise that moral law is identical with the positive law of the state? Again, what does Hegel mean by 'individual'? It is contrary to the philosophical spirit, to the Socratic spirit indeed, to take a few quotations from a rich and complex work like Hegel's and draw hasty conclusions from them. Before we draw such conclusions we should first understand the *assumptions* and the basic elements, i.e., content, of Hegel's view. This is what I intend to do in the following discussion. I shall study: (1) the fundamental principles of Hegel's view of moral experience, viz., law and will; (2) the relationship between law and morality; and (3) the conditions under which individuality can be realized in the state. It is, I think, extremely difficult to have an adequate and fair assessment of Hegel's conception of 'morality' and 'Sittlichkeit' unless we first understand his notion of Right, for the idea of Right is, for him, the basis, the source, of law in general and, consequently, of moral experience in particular: "right exists only as a branch of a whole or like the ivy which twines itself round a tree firmly rooted on its own account." (Add. to § 141) Thus if we begin our discussion with an account of Hegel's notion of Law and then proceed to a treatment of the relationship between law and morality we shall certainly discover that his conception of the state does not undermine the possibility of freedom and morality; on the contrary, he was anxious to construct a political system on a firm moral foundation. For him, the moral remains the highest authority in formulating the laws of the state and the laws of social behavior.

I. *Essential Nature of Law*

"The principle of rightness," Hegel writes, "becomes the law (Gesetz) when, in its objective existence, it is posited (gesetzt), i.e., when thinking makes it determinate for consciousness and makes it known as what is right and valid; and in acquiring this determinate character, the right becomes positive law in general. (§ 211) Thus in order for a statement to be law two conditions must be fulfilled; the statement should be a universal; it should, in other words, prescribe a general rule of conduct which applies without exception to all the members of society; (2) the statement should express, or embody, a degree of rightness. Accordingly law-making is an activity in which the legislator posits, lays down, concretely an element of rightness in a universal form. But what counts in this activity is not merely the form or the formulation of the rule which may be enforced in some way or another but the intuition, the articulation, of what is right regarding a certain relation or feature of human behavior in a given historical setting: "making a law is not to be represented as merely the expression of a rule of behavior valid for everyone, though that is one moment in legislation; the more important moment, the inner essence of the matter, is knowledge of the content of the law in its determinate universality." (*Ibid.*)

Hegel stressed more than once that although the content of the law is, or should be, rightness, it does not follow from this premise that if a given law is bad it ceases, *ipso facto*, to be law. In other words, he rejects the view that a bad or unjust law is not a law or that a citizen should not obey a bad law. He holds that laws are made by man during the historical development of human culture. Once a law is adopted in a society it assumes the status of a 'positive law' regardless of the degree of its goodness or the conditions under which it is enacted. "A particular law," Hegel writes in the Introduction to the *Philosophy of Right*, "may be shown to be wholly grounded in and consistent with the circumstances and with existing legally established institutions, and yet it may be wrong and irrational in its essential character, like a number of provisions in Roman private law which followed quite logically from such institutions as Roman matrimony and Roman *patri potestas*. But even if particular laws are both right and reasonable, still it is one thing to *prove* that they have that character — which cannot be truly done except by means of the concept — and quite another to describe their appearance in history or the circumstances, contingencies, needs, and events, which brought about their enactment." (§ 3) It should be clear from this passage that Hegel would agree with legal positivists like Bentham, Austin, Hobbes, Hart, or Kelsen that it is one thing to acknowledge the existence of the law and another to ask whether or not the law is valid.

But the central question, for Hegel, in the philosophical study of law is not that laws exist, but, how do we establish the validity of an existing law or a code of law? This question is urgent for at least two reasons. First, men may discover that a positive law is contrary to the dictates of their conscience or sense of right; they may discover, in other words, that the law does not embody what *ought to be*. This conflict, or antagonism, between what is absolutely right and "the arbitrary determination of what is recognized as right" creates unhappiness in their hearts and prompts them to see and study the means by which they can rationally justify a given law. (Add. to Preface, p.4) Second, the existing laws of most societies today are being challenged on the ground that they are not valid. Although Hegel had in mind what the French revolutionaries did as an example we see this happening throughout the world on a much larger scale in the twentieth century. Most of the developing countries in Asia, Africa, Latin America, and the Middle East have questioned the validity of the laws which they have inherited from a distant past, and they have in some cases thrown away a constitution and replaced it by a completely new 'modern' one. In situations like this one cannot but ask: how should a nation fashion and adopt a valid *law*? We cannot explain or justify a law, Hegel argues, by expounding its "proximate or historical causes;" this sort of study may show how a law may have come into being but not whether it is valid or derived from the *concept* of law: "by dint of obscuring the difference between the historical and the Philosophical study of law, it becomes possible to shift the point of view and slip over from the problem of the true justification of a thing to a justification by appeal to circumstances, to deductions from presupposed conditions which in themselves may have no higher validity, and so forth." (§ 3) As legal scientists, we may classify the statutes of a law, determine their meaning and application, and we may study their implications with the utmost of care — still, having done all this, we may ask: is the law rational or valid?

A law, for Hegel, is rational and valid in as much as it is right: "it is only because of this identity between its implicit and its posited character that positive law has obligatory force in virtue of its rightness." (§ 212) But how does the idea of right become determinate and applicable to a certain state? The laws of the various states differ, yet in spite of this difference every state may proclaim its law as valid. This only shows that we may have different valid conceptions of what is right. Hegel is aware of this problem. He holds that outside the sphere of law Right is abstract, indeterminate. Essential to its rational determination into law, i.e., legislation, are four basic conditions.

First, in order for a law to be valid it should, as we have just seen, express a determinate content of right (gesetzt) and declare this content as a law (Gesetz). Though determinate, the right which the law expresses is general; it applies without distinction or exception to all the members of the state. As such it is indifferent to their idiosyncracies or individual interest: "when right is posited as law and is known, every accident of feeling vanishes together with the form of revenge, sympathy, and selfishness, and in this way the right attains for the first time its true determinacy and is given its due honor." (Add. to § 211) Peculiar to this concept of law is that it embodies the highest yet most general moral and social values of a people; it is accordingly the supreme principle of justice according to which all clashes among the people should in the final analysis be settled.

Second, in order for a law to be valid it "must be universally known." For if a law is to be considered obligatory, binding, on every citizen, then every citizen should know its content, otherwise, it is extremely difficult to hold them responsible before its pronouncements: "law is concerned with freedom, the worthiest and holiest thing in man, the thing man must know if it is to have obligatory force for him." (Add. to § 215)

Third, a law is not valid unless it is supported or enforced by a public authority. The task of this authority is to see to it that in cases of conflict over right between the citizens or in cases of violating the law, justice is done. The point which we should here stress is that, for Hegel, although the existence of public authority is a necessary condition for the being of the law this authority is not what grants the law its status as law. Put differently, a judicial decision or pronouncement is not law because it can be enforced by the public authority; on the contrary, it is enforceable by the public authority because it is right, i.e., law: "that force and tyranny may be an element in law is accidental to law and has nothing to do with its nature." (§ 3) A consideration of the historical origin of the law, the conditions under which it was adopted by a people, or the manner of its application in society are irrelevant to an understanding of the rational or essential nature of the law. Hegel makes this point clear in his criticism of Herr von Haller's view on the matter: "the point is that legal and political institutions are rational in principle and therefore absolutely necessary, and the question of the form in which they arose or were introduced is entirely irrelevant to a consideration of their rational basis." (Add. to § 219)

Fourth, a law is not valid unless it assimilates and expresses the spirit of the people as a historical reality, namely, its values, aspirations, customs, outlook upon life, and the impact of its geographical setting upon its cultural temper. Hegel gives credit to Montesqieu for pointing out this important aspect in the concrete determination of the idea of right: "legislation both in general and in its particular provisions is to be treated not as something isolated and abstract but rather as a subordinate moment in a whole, interconnected with all the other features which make up the character of a nation and an epoch." (§ 3) Again, "right in this positive form acquires a positive element in its content (a) through the particular national character of a people, its stage of historical development, and the whole complex of relations connected with the necessities of nature." (*Ibid.*) Hegel is aware that this activity is never perfect or complete, for it may be vitiated with ignorance, prejudice, and all sorts of clashes between the prevelant socio-economic powers. (Cf. § 212) Yet, in spite of such imperfections the legislator should fashion a law that fits the needs and aspirations of the people to whom it should apply, otherwise it would be irrelevant to them, though it might be relevant to the ruler or to some powerfully interested groups.

But, my critic may ask: exactly what kind of features or relationships can, or should, a legislator consider in the enactment of the law? Can he, for example, legislate morality? Hegel is alive to this question. He categorically states that we cannot legislate morality: "morality and moral commands concern the will on its most private, subjective, and particular side, and so cannot be a matter of positive legislation." (§ 213) Put differently, matters relating to the subjective, personal domain of the individual should remain outside the sphere positive law. Even in matters like marriage, "love, religion and the state, the only aspects which can become the subject of legislation are those of such a nature as to permit of their being in principle external." (Add. to § 213) Hegel is, for example, critical of a Chinese law according to which a husband should love his first wife more than his other wives. (*Ibid.*)

It would, I think, be interesting to observe at this point of our discussion that the concrete determination of rightness, or put differently, legislative activity, does not, for Hegel, stop with the legislator's proclamation of a positive law. For, after all, the law must apply to a single, isolated case of theft, of murder, of divorce, etc.; but as universal, it does not contain any reference or judgments to such single cases. For example, what sort of punishment should be imposed on a man who steals three loaves of bread in a specific situation to feed his hungry children? A complex description of all the elements or factors which attend a legal case are usually unpredictable; therefore, the sort of judgment which should be pronounced on them is the task of the judge. This task is basically a legal. i.e., legislative, one, for it is essentially an activity of determining positively what is right. But in this activity the judge works within the general bounds of positive law. An unusual case may appear; accordingly, he may have to exercise a spontaneous initiative in deciding what is right in this case; but regardless of its extra — ordinary nature the judge cannot, under normal conditions, violate the general requirements of what is acknowledged as right in the society: "it is true that the law does not settle these ultimate decisions required by actual life; it leaves them instead to the judge's discretion, merely limiting him by a maximum and minimum. But this does not affect the point at issue, because the maximum and minimum are themselves in every instance only round numbers once more. To fix them, therefore, does not exempt the judge from making a finite, purely positive, decision, since on the contrary such a decision is still left to him by the necessities of the case." (§ 214) Thus Hegel would be sympathetic with legal realists like Lon Fuller and Holmes who hold that law is the activity of decision — making in the court room, for it is in such a room that the final determination of right, or justice, takes place; but it would be a mistake to think that what takes place in the court room is, or should be, divorced from or unrelated to the web of statues, customs, and moral values which are upheld in society and which reflect that sense of right which is the ultimate foundation of positive law.

II. *Freedom of the Will*

Now Right is not only the content, essence, of valid positive law; it is also the basis of freedom. The attainment of right is what makes man free. But in what sense is man free? In answering this question, I shall first discuss Hegel's view of 'free will' and then proceed to consider the relationship between the idea of freedom and the idea of *person*, or personality.

"The basis of right", Hegel writes, "is, in general, mind; its precise place and point of origin is the will. The will is free, so that freedom is both the substance of right and its goal, while the system of right is the realm of freedom made actual, the world of mind brought forth out of itself like a second nature." (§ 4) What does Hegel mean when he says that the basis of right is mind and that its point of origin is the will? Again, what is the relationship between mind and will?

Hegel holds that freedom is an activity of will; it is the essence of the will. Accordingly in thinking of will we cannot but think of freedom. The relation between the two concepts is similar to the relation between weight and matter. Weight is not an accidental attribute of matter; for we cannot think of the idea of matter without thinking of the idea of weight: "matter is rather weight itself. Heaviness constitutes the body and is the body. The same is the case with freedom and the will, since the free entity is the will. Will without freedom is an empty word, while freedom is actual only as will, as subject." (Add. to § 4) But will cannot, moreover, be viewed as something separate from or opposed to mind; like thought, or intelligence, will is an activity of mind. I purposely say 'activity' simply to stress that we cannot imagine "that man is half thought and half will, and that he keeps thought in one pocket and will in another, for this would be a foolish idea." (*Ibid.*) The distinction between the two, Hegel contends, is a distinction between two types of attitude, theoretical and practical.

The theoretical attitude is assumed in the act of thinking. When I think an object I have an idea of it; the idea is mine and belongs to my consciousness — it exists in my mind. Thus when I penetrate the object in an act of thinking, when I think it in the fulness of its essence, the object ceases to be another; it becomes mine: "just as Adam said to Eve: 'Thou art flesh of my flesh and bone of my bone', so mind says: 'This is mind of my mind and its foreign character has disappeared.'" (*Ibid.*) But an idea is a general concept, and to form such a concept is to think. Accordingly, in so far as I am in this state of mind, that is, in so far as the content of my ego is thought, my ego is universal, abstract, and as such empty. Thus in the theoretical attitude I think the world around me, I reflect on it in my consciousness, and make its content my own. The practical attitude, on the other hand, begins with thinking, but it translates a thought into action; it is the urge to actualize an idea in experience. Thus the practical attitude is characteristic of the sphere of action in which I determine myself concretely according to a given aim, purpose, or desire. Now, what I realize in my action *did* already exist in my mind; the act is the concretization, or realization, of the purpose I reflected on, approved, and proceeded to seek. This, I think, shows that the will cannot exist without thought, i.e., mind; for it determines itself first inwardly, subjectively. What I will exists first in my mind as an idea, as an object of thought. Later on, when I act, the idea becomes the essence of my action:

"an animal acts on instinct, is driven by an inner impulse and it too is practical, but it has no will, since it does not bring before its mind the object of its desire. A man, however, can just as little be theoretical or think without a will, because in thinking he is of necessity being active. The content of something thought has the form of being; but this being is something mediated, something established through our activity. Thus these distinct attitudes cannot be divorced; they are one and the same; and in any activity, whether of thinking or willing, both moments are present." (*Ibid.*)

It is worth remarking here that in stressing the unity of will and thought Hegel ingenuously surpasses yet assimilates and reconciles two important legal traditions — the one holds that the source of law is reason, or intellect, and the other holds that it is will, viz., the will of the sovereign. But, as we have just seen, this way of stating the issue is misleading, for it erroneously assumes that will and intellect are two separate faculties charged with separate functions. It is more correct to say that the source of law is the *rational will*. We can thus argue, as I did in the preceding essay, that although the sovereign is the source of positive law the will of this sovereign is not arbitrary but acts, and should act, according to the requirements and demands of reason.

Now corresponding to the theoretical and practical attitude of the mind *qua* unity of will and intellect are two basic moments. The first is the will's capacity to be free and withdraw itself from "every restriction and every content either immediately presented by nature, by needs, desires, and impulses, or given and determined by any means whatever." (§ 5) In this act the ego refrains from committing itself to any thing, purpose, or desire; it can, moreover, sacrifice everything, life included: it "can commit suicide." (Add. to § 5) An animal cannot do this; "it always remains merely negative, in an alien destiny to which it merely accustoms itself. Man is the pure thought of himself, and only in thinking is he this power to give himself universality, i.e., to extinguish all particularity, all determinacy." (*Ibid.*) However, this ability to fly away from every restriction or determination produces what Hegel calls 'negative freedom' "or freedom as the Understanding conceives it." (§ 5) It is 'negative' simply because it does not achieve anything concrete or meaningful; in exercising it a person turns himself away from the world, he ignores what is significant or important in human life. He becomes a fanatic. Hegel reminds us that this sort of freedom is a frequent occurence in the history of human society. For example, in religion the ideal of the Hindu is to free himself from the given human interests, desires, or endeavors and to focus his attention in a steady fixation exclusively upon himself with the hope of discovering identity and remaining in oneness with this identity forever. "In this way man becomes Brahma; there is no longer any distinction between the finite man and Brahma. In fact in the universality every difference has disappeared." (*Ibid.*) In politics, the fanatics of negative freedom can be seen in the behavior of the French Revolutionaries (during the Terror Period) who gave themselves almost totally to abstract ideals and goals. They could not tolerate any distinction of difference of opinion; put differently, they could not tolerate anything particular or specific. This is why they destroyed once more the institutions which they had made themselves, since any institution whatever is antagonistic to the abstract self — consciousness of equality." (*Ibid.*)

The second moment of the will is the ego's ability to posit or to seek a determinate content or object as its goal, i.e., purpose. In this activity it negates its earlier state of abstract indeterminacy and identifies itself with something concrete. Now, "my willing is not pure willing but the willing of something; and what I will may be given by nature or it may be the result of a spontaneous, creative act of my mind. But in willing something particular I restrict myself, for I cancel the state of indeterminacy to which I gave myself earlier. And, in cancelling this state I abandon the point of view of abstract universality; I become finite. Thus to be finite means to be particular; it means to deny the possibility of indeterminate alternatives and to give oneself to a specific mode, or course, of action.

But both these moments, the capacity to will the abstract and also the particular, are one — sided. First, to will the abstract universal is one — sided, for to will such a universal is to will 'nothing'. Moreover, a will that identifies itself with something abstract and indeterminate is itself determinate, for "being abstraction from all determinacy" is itself a kind of determinacy — hence, restriction, or finitude. Second, to will something particular is *ipso facto* a restriction; "thus particularization is what as a rule is called finitude." (Add to § 6) But the will, as an activity of freedom, is the unity of these two moments. In this unity it determines itself, it realizes something concrete in its experience, yet remains itself, "i.e., in its self — identity and universality." (§ 7) The will, or ego, Hegel contends, "as such is in the first place pure activity, the universal which is by itself." (Add. to § 7) Thus when it exercises its freedom in a specific act this universal becomes the particular object of interest of the will. In this activity, the will relates itself to itself; that is, it relates the universal which is the content of its reflection to its concrete, immediate experience. The universal becomes determinate. When this happens the will, or ego, is said to be self — determined. A self — determined will is an *individual*. Yet, we should stress, in determining or restricting itself in realizing its individuality, the will "remains by itself and does not cease to keep hold of the universal." (Add to § 7) An act of self — determination, then, is an event in which the will realizes the universal concretely in its experience; in this experience it becomes determinate, particular, but it also claims and keeps hold of itself as something universal. We possess this sense of freedom, e.g., in the form of feeling in friendship and love: "here we are not inherently one — sided; we restrict ourselves gladly as ourselves. In this determinacy a man should not feel himself determined; on the contrary, since he treats the other as other, it is there that he first arrives at the feeling of his own self — hood. Thus freedom lies neither in indeterminacy nor determinacy; it is both of these at once." (*Ibid.*)

Accordingly an act of self — determination in which the will exercises its essential nature, viz., freedom, consists of two basic types of activity. In the first the will determines its purpose, namely, the sort of goal or aim which it approves for realization and with which it agrees to identify itself. In the second, the will actualizes this purpose concretely. At first, the purpose exists inwardly, subjectively; it exists as an idea, as an idea worthy of attainment. But this is not enough; the idea should become objective. The activity of objectifying it is the process in which the purpose is translated into an objective event, i.e., action. The will is not free unless this translation takes place. "My purpose," Hegel writes, "so far as it is still only mine, is felt by me as a defect since freedom and will are for me the unity of the subjective and objective. Hence the purpose must be established objectively and thereby it attains not a new one-sided character but only its realization." (Add. to § 8) Implicit in this account of freedom is the belief that a will cannot be free unless it is conscious of itself, of its purposes, of what it wants to be. But this consciousness is impossible without self-understanding. By means of this understanding it discovers its concept *qua* individual, i.e., its potentialities. For only when it knows its true desires, interests, powers, weaknesses, and values as things peculiar to its individual nature can it project the right purpose and act on it intelligibly.

Besides, in order for an ego to act freely, to determine itself, three conditions should be fulfilled. *First*, it should choose or make a decision. Man is not given to the world as free but with the potentiality to be free; the ego is given with the capacity to will freely. This is what Hegel means when he says, "the will which is but implicitly free is the immediate or natural will." (§ 11) Being free, or the activity of freedom, is a function of action, and outside the domain of action freedom is an abstract possibility; it becomes actual only when there is a need to act. Prior to an action, however, the content of the will is a multiplicity of impulses — of inclinations, preferences, of interests. Each of these impulses presents itself as 'mine', as 'my desire', and "exists alongside other desires which are likewise all 'mine', and each of which is at the same time something universal and indeterminate, aimed at all kinds of objects and satiable in all kinds of ways. When, in this twofold indeterminacy, the will gives itself the form of individuality, this constitutes the resolution of the will, and it is only in so far as it resolves that the will is an actual will at all." (§ 12) In this state of indeterminacy my will is arbitrary; for I can choose this or that desire. But I cannot be free unless I make a choice, or unless I resolve. The reason some people are afraid to decide, to take a stand, is perhaps faint heartedness, which shows itself in one's inability to sacrifice the infinite for the sake of concrete achievement. Hegel is fully aware that choosing involves restriction; for when a person decides on a course of action he denies satisfaction to all the other possible desires which co — exist with the chosen one. But without such restriction no man can exist as a character; such a man would not be in a position to achieve something good in the world. "Whoever wills great achievement," Hegel quotes Goethe, "must be able to restrict himself." (Add. to § 13) Thus a man who for some reason or another cannot choose is impotent; he may enjoy the fact that he is always aware of a wide range of possible choices, but "possibility is still less than actuality. The will which is sure of itself does not *eo ipso* lose itself in its determinate volition." (*Ibid.*)

Second, in order for the ego to be free the act of choosing should be reflective, deliberative. In deciding a course of action the will assumes the position of a subject over its impulses, or desires. It cannot make an intelligent choice, i.e., determine itself, unless it reflects on the appropriateness and consequences of the various competing desires. It compares and evaluates the alternative courses of action and the impact of these courses on the well — being and future happiness of the ego. (Cf. § 20) In this activity the will acts first as arbitrary, for it can in principle choose any possible course of action; it can also choose not to act. But it is, moreover, determined; for the choice which it makes is in a strict sense limited by the sort of desires it encounters in its domain of reflection. This is why genuine self-determination is an activity in which I satisfy a desire which belongs to me and which I can acknowledge as mine. Although I am restricted to the desires which constitute the content of my will this restriction does not undermine the possibility of my freedom, because I *can* choose to act upon a certain desire and know that in choosing to perform the act I initiate it *sui generis*: "since it is possible for me to determine myself in this way or that, or in other words, since I can choose, I possess the arbitrary will, and to possess this is what is usually called freedom." (Add. to § 15)

But, *third*, the will is not free unless it chooses intelligently, rationally. Hence a merely arbitrary will is not truly free. Hegel is critical of the view which reduces freedom to random or capricious choice: "the idea which people most commonly have of freedom is that it is arbitrariness — the mean, chosen by abstract reflection, between the will wholly determined by natural impulses, and the will free absolutely. If we hear it said that the definition of freedom is ability to do what we please, such an idea can only be taken to reveal an utter immaturity of thought, for it contains not even an inkling of the absolutely free will, of right, ethical life, and so forth." (§ 15) When I act as I please I merely respond to the strongest or most insistent impules, or desire, without reflection on or assessment of the consequences and value of the prospective act; in other words, I give myself to the given desire. But in this act there is no guarantee that the satisfaction of the said desire is in my best interest as an individual and as a human being. (Cf. § 17) To will properly, I should classify, and evaluate the various impulses; this task requires a criterion on the basis of which I can carry on the classification and evaluation. This criterion is none other than my concept of myself as a rational being. The evaluation of the impulses in terms of this criterion is tantamount to the demand "that the impulses should become the rational system of the will's volition." (§ 19) For only when the impulses are assessed in terms of a rational perspective do the potentialities of the will become explicit. This is what enables the will to exist for itself as an object "in its sheer universality — a universality which is what it is simply because it has absorbed in itself the immediacy of instinctive desire and the particularity which is produced by reflection and with which such desire *eo ipso* becomes inbued." (§ 21) The means and the material of this activity is thinking: "here is the point at which it becomes clear that it is only as thinking intelligence that the will is genuinely a will and free. The slave does not know his essence, his infinity, his freedom; he does not know himself as human in essence; and he lacks this knowledge of himself because he does not think himself. This self — consciousness which apprehends itself through thinking as essentially human, and thereby frees itself from the contingent and the false, is the principle of right, morality, and all ethical life." (*Ibid.*)

Thus when the will succeeds in comprehending itself as a unity of explicit potentialities it frees itself from every dependence on anything else; it is "then true, or rather truth itself, because its self — determination consists in a correspondence between what it is in existence (i.e., what it is as objective to itself) and its concept; or in other words, the pure concept of the will has the intuition of itself for its goal and its reality." (§ 23) The will does not exist only as a potentiality for being free, but it is also aware of this potentiality and of its ability to realize it in actuality. It exists for itself, not only in itself. For example, in moral conduct, to will the rational means to act according to the universal and not according to my subjective or arbitrary desire. Here, "when I will what is rational, then I am acting not as a particular individual but in accordance with the concepts of ethics in general. In an ethical action, what I vindicate is not myself but the thing. But in doing a perverse action, it is my singularity that I bring on to the center of the state." (Add. to § 15) Put differently, the will is free when its subjectivity acquires an objective character, i.e., when its choice corresponds with, or reflects, its conception of itself as a free individual. When we speak of the subjective side of the will, however, we do not mean by 'subjective' an idiosyncratic end which exists exclusively to a certain subject, nor do we mean by it an arbitrarily chosen end, but rather "the will's self — conscious side, its individuality in distinction from its implicit concept." (§ 25) We mean the content, i.e., purpose, which the will has chosen consciously, rationally, and deliberatively as its end. We also mean the will's conception of itself as a possible individual. The subjectivity of the will, then represents the will's judgment of itself and the kind of individual it seeks to be in the actual world. Again, when we speak of the 'objective' side of the will we mean the content which the will *intends* subjectively: "the will is purely and simply objective in so far as it has itself for its determination and so is in correspondence with its concept and genuinely a will" (§ 26) Accordingly the will becomes objective when it presents its aim, its future being, viz., individuality, objectively and when it assents to realize this aim in its prospective act.

Thus freedom, for Hegel, is not a capacity or potentiality of the will, as if the will is a unique faculty existing in and by itself but the activity of the ego in an act of self — determination; it is the power of the mind to envision a course of action deliberately, rationally, consciously, to decide on that course of action, and to be ready to act on it in its concrete experience.

The Relationship Between Freedom and Personality

Now we should ask: under what conditions can the ego realize its freedom concretely? I ask this question because it is not enough for the will to choose freely; it should also *act* freely, and unless it acts freely its freedom remains one — sided, abstract, subjective. The will acts freely when it succeeds in realizing its aim objectively in concrete experience. But this freedom is not possible unless the act is right, i.e., unless it is the attainment of what is right: "an existent of any sort embodying the free will, this is what right is." (§ 29) Accordingly, right is not merely a claim as a duty prescribed by an established authority; it is rather the will's absolute demand to be itself, to realize itself according to the requirements of its essence, viz., rationality. Moreover, right is to be respected, it is sacrosanct, not because it is decreed by the state, or because it happens to be expressed in a positive law, but only because it embodies human freedom. Respect for this freedom is the foundation of our respect for a valid law. (Cf. § 30)

Hegel believes that, as a rational being man has an inherent capacity to bear rights. This capacity is the very meaning of being a person, or personality: "personality essentially involves the capacity for rights and constitutes the concept and the basis (itself abstract) of the system of abstract and therefore formal right. Hence the imperative of right is: 'Be a person and respect others as persons.'" (§ 36) Thus although a person has a right to pursue his ends freely he has one basic obligation: respect for the rights of others. But 'person' is an abstract concept. It refers to the self — conscious ego in an act of subjective self — determination. It is the will conscious of itself as immediate, universal, and free. The idea of personality exhibits three basic features:

First, being a person implies an ego conscious of itself as a self — determined will; as such the will is determined on every side in its "inner caprice, impulse, desire, as well as by immediate external facts;" consequently, it is finite. (§ 35) 'Person', Hegel points out, is not identical with 'subject'; on the contrary, being a subject provides the possibility of personhood. Hence a subject is a possible person. "A person, then, is subject aware of this subjectivity." (Add. to § 35) The capacity of self — consciousness is the basis of its freedom and power of self — determination. This is why, as a person I am essentially a free will aware of my freedom and independence: "a person is a unit of freedom aware of its sheer independence. As *this* person, I know myself to be free in myself. I can abstract from everything, since nothing confronts me save pure personality, and yet as *this* person I am something wholly determinate e.g., I am of a certain age, a certain stature, I occupy this space, and so on through whatever other details you like." (Add. to § 35) Thus as a person I am both finite and infinite, free and determined, yet I am the unity of this two — fold aspect. My will is abstract, for in this moment of self — consciousness it is contentless; it has not decided and acted on the basis of its decision. It merely confronts itself as a universal possibility of action.

Second, the abstract character of the ego implies that the rights it enjoys are likewise abstract. A person is a possible *particular* will, or ego. This possibility is realized when the ego determines itself subjectively and objectively, when it adopts a course of action on the basis of what is right or good. Prior to this determination right exists only as a possibility, "and to have a right is therefore to have only a permission or warrant." (§ 38) But in realizing any right whatsoever a person should observe one basic restriction: "Do not infringe personality and what personality entails." The point which merits special emphasis here is that, as a person the ego can be fully aware of its rights ideally; it can also articulate a certain kind of right as a general rule. But the crucial moment for the self — realized ego is the ability to translate the content of the rule into fact, i.e., to apply it concretely in its experience. This is why to restrict oneself to the general content or requirements of the rule without concern for the rights of others is a sign of 'cold heart': "it is uncultured people who insist most on their rights, while noble minds look on other aspects of the thing. Thus abstract right is nothing but a bare possibility and, at least in contrast with the whole range of the situation, something formal." (Add. to § 37)

Third, though abstract, personality has also the impetus to realize itself concretely in the world. For any decision it makes is related directly or indirectly to the external world of nature and people. In making such a decision it "stands over against this world as something subjective." (§ 39) This contrast, or rather confrontation, between its subjectivity and the objective character of the external world, creates in it a feeling of limitation, restriction, a feeling that it is, or may be, taken over by the web of external reality. It accordingly struggles "to lift itself above this restriction and to give itself reality, or in other words to claim the external world as its own." (§ 39) This struggle is prompted by its inner desire for freedom.

This freedom, however, cannot, as we saw, be achieved abstractly but concretely. It can be achieved only in realizing its claims to right in its socio — political reality. When we speak of right (*Recht*, i.e., *jus*) here we mean "not merely what is generally understood by the word, namely civil law, but also morality, ethical life, and world history." (Add. to § 33) It would accordingly be a grave mistake to think that a man can be truly free if he enjoys his basic rights in any one of these spheres alone. In the *Philosophy of Right* Hegel discusses in some detail the basic rights which are indispensible to the realization of freedom — rights in the domain of property, moral conduct, social ethics, the family, and the state. We have already seen how freedom is possible in the state in the preceding essays. In the remainder of this essay I shall be concerned with its possibility in morality and ethical life. I shall discuss this possibility with reference to work and family in the following essays.

III. *The Moral Point of View*

An important medium in which the ego *qua* person actualizes its freedom is morality. In this sphere the will is not free in relation to an external fact, whether the fact is natural or social, but in relation to itself as subjectivity, i.e., as a self — determined ego: "in this sphere the main thing is my insight, my intention, my purpose, because externality has now been established as of no purpose." (Add. to § 33) My goal is *the good*; this goal, which I choose and adopt as mine, should not remain within me as something subjective; it should be realized concretely in the world, "that is to say, the subjective will demands that what is internal to it, i.e., its end, shall acquire an external existence, that the good shall in this way be consummated in the external world." (*Ibid.*)

But how can the will make this demand? What warrants this demand? Put differently, how do we justify the claim that the subjective will has *the right* to realize its end — its moral end — concretely in the world? The will has the right primarily because it is, or can be, the author of its end; it is accordingly destined to be free. A subject can be aware of himself as a moral being; he can, in other words, understand and reflect on the principle (or concept) according to which he should act. However, what he takes to be moral, and therefore what he takes to be his true end, may be different from what the principle contains or dictates. But once he makes a decision, once he forms a conviction, the decision or conviction is his; and since the decision is a subjective fact and excluded from any social or physical or social embodiment none can compel or deprive him from this privilege. It is in a strict sense his, for it constitutes an integral element of his being. We may rob a man of his possessions or of his body but we cannot rob him of his ideas, insight, or sense of value. Again, in ordinary life we like to be judged or evaluated on the basis of personal initiative and achievement. But this judgment, or evaluation, is not possible unless we are free in projecting and realizing our moral ends. Without this freedom we cannot be held accountable for what we do. This is why Hegel insists that the inner moral conviction of a man cannot be infringed; "no violence can be done to it, and the moral will, therefore, is inaccessible. Man's worth is estimated by reference to his inward action and hence the standpoint of morality is that of freedom aware of itself." (Add. to § 106) Moreover, outside the domain of willing and self — determination freedom remains abstract; it remains a possibility awaiting realization. The medium in which it becomes actual is subjective experience. It becomes concrete when the will discovers the universal principle, which is its own principle given implicitly, and then proceeds to realize its content in the prospective act. In this activity the will is not at first aware of its independence; it exists for itself subjectively. In this state it is not aware of its universal nature or that it is "implicitly identical with the universal or the principle of the will." (§ 106) This identity, however, becomes explicit when the will "sinks deeper and deeper into itself" in a moment of critical self — examination. In this activity it discovers its principle and identifies itself with it: "what happens is that subjectivity, which is abstract at the start, i.e., distinct from the concept, becomes likened to it, and thereby the Idea acquires genuine realization. The result is that the subjective will determines itself as objective too and so as truly concrete." (*Ibid*)

But although my will determines itself objectively it retains its subjective character, and it should "continue to enshrine my subjectivity, and my act is to count as mine only if on its inward side it has been determined by me, if it was my purpose, my intention. Beyond what lay in my subjective will I recognize nothing in its expression as mine. What I wish to see in my deed is my subjective consciousness over again." (Add. to § 110) In an act of self — determination, then, the will translates the universal content of its principle into a concrete, objective content. This content reflects, and it is the realization of, the subjective aim or purpose of the will. It is, moreover, the judgment on which the will can act. But it cannot act in isolation or without regard to the well — being of others, because it cannot perform the act without their cooperation. In itself, the act is a mere event, or a natural occurence; it becomes moral only in so far as it is assessed or received in a certain way by others. But 'others' assess it in terms of its impact upon them. They judge it as moral if it promotes their well — being, immoral if it does the reverse. Accordingly, to be moral, the act should fulfill certain expectations which are expressive of the generally accepted sense of value. They reflect an identity or a harmony of will shared by all the members of the society. Thus in acting I am not only conscious of the impact of the act on myself but also on those around me: "the achievement of my aim, therefore, implies this identity of my will with the will of others, it has a positive bearing on the will of others." (§ 112)

Conditions of Moral Action

Now in order for an act to be moral three basic conditions should be fulfilled. First, the person who performs the act should be able to assume responsibility for it; second, the act should be intended; and third, the act should be good.

1. *Responsibility*. An act is not moral unless it issues from a responsible will. 'Responsibility' means, for Hegel, 'accountability'; it means one is ready to pay for what he has done in terms of reward and punishment. But it also means, or rather presupposes, that the act is 'mine' and that I as will have initiated and executed the act; for if it is not mine, if I am not its author, I do not have the right to be rewarded, or punished, for it. Thus if my act leads to certain consequences which were not part of my purpose, or of which I was ignorant, when I set to perform the act I cannot claim them as mine. I am responsible for an act only in so far as it reflects the purpose which I sought to realize in it. This is based on the assumption that the act is not a simple or straightforward activity; it is a complex event in the world: it is a "concrete external actuality which because of its concreteness has in it an indeterminable multiplicity of factors. Any and every single element which appears as the condition, ground, or cause of one of such factors, and so has contributed its share to the event in question, may be looked upon as responsible for the event, or at least as sharing the responsibility for it." (§ 115) Here one

may object: when I perform an act I must assume full responsibility for *all* the consequences of the act, because in performing the act, to begin with, I have initiated the act; consequently, I am in a strict sense its author. This implies that the act is mine, for without my initiative neither the act nor its consequences would occur. This line of reasoning is erroneous for it overlooks two basic assumptions.

First, I cannot claim an act as mine, and therefore I cannot be responsible for it, unless I *know* that the act is mine; put differently, in order for me to be responsible for an act, I must know what I am doing. This, for Hegel, is a fundamental right of the free will; it is the right " to recognize as its action, and to accept responsibility for, only those presuppositions of the deed of which it was conscious in its aim and those aspects of the deed which were contained in its purpose. The deed can be imputed to me only if my will is responsible for it — this is the right to know." (§ 117) My act is an objective event; as such it is an external fact and belongs to the furniture of the world. What entitles me to say it is 'mine' and not somebody else's is mainly the fact that it objectifies *my* purpose. But in order for something to be my purpose I must know it to be so, I must be conscious of it as my purpose. Consequently, anything which is not intended as part of my purpose cannot be imputed to me at least directly. Thus if an act cannot be imputed to me, unless I aim at it, and if I cannot aim at it unless I do so knowingly, it follows that I cannot be held responsible for the act unless I know that the act is mine and that I consciously sought to perform it. This is a main reason why we cannot hold children or insane people responsible for their action, and this is why Oedipus did not commit patricide, for he did not know the identity of his father when he killed him.[5]

Second, an act, or an aspect of an act, cannot be imputed to me, and therefore I cannot be responsible for it unless I freely execute it, or unless I cause it to happen. But "action is translated into external fact, and external fact has connexions in the field of external necessity through which it develops itself in all directions. Hence action has a multitude of consequences." (§ 118) But I am not always in a position to control the outcome of my action. Again, such consequences do not express or objectify my purpose; they are characterized as accidental or necessary. Thus it would be extremely difficult to be held responsible for those consequences which I have not chosen or which are beyond my power of control. We should not, however, view the act and its consequences as separate or independent of each other; on the contrary, "these consequences are the outward form whose inner soul is the aim *of the action*, they belong to the action." (*Ibid.*) This is why the utilitarian claim, "Judge actions by their consequences, and make these the criterion of right and good," and the de—ontological maxim, "Ignore the consequences of actions," are one — sided and abstract; they rest on the false assumption that the act and its consequences are separate and separable. For Hegel, the act becomes actual in and through its consequences: "the consequences, as the shape proper to the action and immanent within it, exhibit nothing but its nature and are simply the action itself; therefore the action can neither disavow nor ignore them. On the other hand, however, among the consequences there is also comprised something interposed from without and introduced by chance, and this is quite unrelated to the nature of the action itself." (*Ibid.*) I can, therefore, repudiate the consequences which come about contrary to my will or expectation primarily because I cannot claim them as mine. Accordingly, when we say 'responsibility' means 'accountability ', or that in order for one to be responsible for an act he has performed he should be the author of the act, we should mean that he is responsible for the consequences of the act only *in so far as* the said consequences are part of his purpose or aim and in so far as *he* causes them to happen.

2. *Intention*. But my act is not moral unless I also *intend* it, that is, unless I am aware of its general quality, the quality which gives it its identity as a specific act and which is the basis of my satisfaction or welfare as a particular individual. As an accomplished fact, the act may or may not correspond to my purpose. I have the right to refuse in it what was not in my purpose when I performed it. This only raises the question of my intention behind it — to what extent does the act reveal my intention, or to what extent do I intend the act? The principle which Hegel is anxious to emphasize here is that the free will has the right to know what it intends in its action: "the right of intention is that the universal quality of the action shall not merely be implicit but shall be known by the agent, and so shall have lain from the start in his subjective will. Vice versa, what may be called the right of the objectivity of action is the right of the action to evince itself as known and willed by the subject as a *thinker*. " (§ 120) For if he does not know what he intends, and if he does not thoughtfully realize his intention in his action, we cannot attribute the action to him or to his will; we cannot, in other words, be justified in saying that the action originates from his will.

We should not, however, make a sharp and fast distinction between intention as a subjective activity and the act as an external, objective event in the world. Intention is the content realized in the act as purpose; it is the general aspect, or universal, by which the act is distinguished, identified, as a specific, or 'this', act. Take, for example, murder. When someone kills a human being, the act of killing consists of injuring the flesh of the murdered man. Here the character of 'murdering', or what makes the act murder, is not the fact that a living lump of flesh is destroyed. Again, not every act in which a living body is destroyed is necessarily murder. In viewing the event of destroying the body one does not perceive the character of 'murder'. This character is not a sensuous content which belongs to the act as physical activity. To determine whether the act is murder we should ask the murderer: why did you perform the act? He does not, and cannot, murder for the sake of murdering; he usually has a reason, a purpose, for killing a human being; but if "we were to say that he murdered for the mere pleasure of murdering, then the purely positive content of the subject would surely be pleasure, and if that is the case then the deed is the satisfaction of the subject's will. Thus the motive of an act is, more particularly, what is called the 'moral' factor, and this has in that case the double meaning of the *universal* implicit in the purpose and the *particular* aspect of the intention." (Add. to § 121) Accordingly intention should not be viewed as an independent force, or motive, which causes a man to perform a certain act. What the man intends is, in a sense, a causal factor; it is a factor which causes him to act in a certain way. But it would be a mistake to consider this intention as separate or indifferent to the act; on the contrary, it is the soul of the act and what gives it its moral, social, or rational character; for in intending one declares explicitly a personal interest and then proceeds to seek it. Once the intention is declared it becomes an *end*; the end remains abstract, or universal, prior to its attainment; it becomes *actual*, concrete, in the activity of realizing it.

Now the attainment of personal ends is the basis of welfare, or happiness; it is consequently the basis of subjective freedom. We should not underestimate this sort of freedom, because the achievement of personal ends which relate to one's "needs, inclinations, possessions, opinions, fancies, &c.," is the content of his life. (§ 123) It is therefore essential to self — determination. This is why Hegel insists that subjective freedom is a basic right; it is the right to be satisfied, to be oneself. This right in its infinity is given expression in Christianity and it has become the universal effective principle of a new form of civilization. Amongst the primary shapes which this right assumes are love, romanticism, the quest for the eternal salvation of the individual, &c.; next come moral convictions and conscience; and, finally, the other forms, some of which come into prominence in what follows as the principle of civil society and as moments in the constitution of the state, while others appear in the course of history, particularly the history of art, and philosophy." (§124) This passage calls for the remark that subjective satisfaction is the basis of all meaningful endeavor in human life, not only because it is "part and parcel of the achievement of ends of absolute value," but also because without it one cannot know what it means to will the universal or objective ends. Only when a person pursues his ends does he discover that his welfare is at the same time the welfare of others; he also discovers that his true end, like the true end of others, lies in upholding and living according to the highest principle of justice, or right. This is why I cannot make moral claims for myself or for others contrary to the demands implicit in this principle. I cannot, in other words, posit the existence of a 'moral' intention which justifies wrong actions on the ground that they promote my welfare or the welfare of others. "It is one of the most prominent of the corrupt maxims of our time," Hegel writes, "to enter a plea for the so — called 'moral' intention behind wrong actions and to imagine bad men with well — meaning hearts, i.e., hearts willing their own welfare and perhaps that of others also." (§ 126) Thus if I steal leather, as St. Crispin did, to make shoes and other necessities for the poor my act may be characterized as moral but it is "wrong and so inadmissable." (Add. to § 126) If we locate the principle of moral distinction in 'moral' intention as something divorced from the act which a person intends the "result is that crime and the thoughts that lead to it, be they fancies however trite and empty, or opinions however wild, are to be regarded as right, rational, and excellent, simply because they issue from men's hearts and enthusiasms." (§ 126) As we shall see in the following section, the morality of an act cannot be determined merely by the intention behind the act but also by a thoughtful consideration of what is right, and also its impact upon those who will be affected by it. The point which we should here stress, though, is that an act cannot be moral unless the person who performs it intends in its performance to promote his welfare and the welfare of others.

3. *Moral Goodness* This last point leads us directly to the third condition of moral action: an act is not moral unless it is absolutely, or universally, good. This condition presupposes the preceding two, for an act cannot, as we shall presently see, be judged as good unless it is performed under the conditions of *responsibility* and *intention*; put differently, one's act cannot be moral, or good, if he does not know what it means for the act to be good or moral. One may intend an act thoughtfully, deliberately, and he may be in a position to assume responsibility for it, but it does not follow from this that the act is *eo ipso* good, or moral. In order for the act to be moral, or good, the person who performs it should also act on the basis, or principle, of goodness. Thus we should ask: what does Hegel mean by 'good'? What makes an act good?

"The good," writes Hegel, "is the Idea as the unity of the concept of the will with the particular will. In this unity, abstract right, welfare, the subjectivity of knowing and the contingency of external fact, have their independent self — subsistence superseded, though at the same time they are still contained and retained within it in their essence." (§ 129) This passage merits the following remark. 'Good' is not a simple quality, or aspect, which we can intuit directly or immediately when we confront a moral situation; it is not, moreover, a content contained or expressed in a clearly formulated principle; it is not, finally, a prescription dictated by an already existing voice or sentiment. 'Good' is, rather, a complex concept and consists of three basic elements: (1) the principle of the will, viz., what is right as such, objectively; (2) welfare, viz., what is beneficial to the person who performs the act; (3) the subjective activity of the will in which what is right and beneficial are unified and determined concretely.

What is truly good, for Hegel, then, is determined *creatively* in a concrete moral situation. I say 'creatively', for goodness is not a ready made quality, or content, but a task, a task to be achieved when a person faces a moral problem. But moral problems happen to particular individuals. Accordingly no two moral problems are alike, for no two individuals and what happens to them are exactly alike. Hence what is good in one situation is, broadly speaking, different from what is good in another situation. This difference, however, does not mean that 'good' is determined according to the whim or arbitrary feeling of the moral agent. On the contrary, 'good' is, for Hegel, an objective principle. What makes the act good is not merely the promotion of my personal welfare but also the welfare of others. In determining the welfare of others I am guided by the universal principle of right, or justice. Thus in order for an act to be good (1) it must promote welfare in general and (2) must be right: "welfare without right is not a good. Similarly, right without welfare is not the good; *fiat justitia* should not be followed by *pereat mundus*." (§ 130) Again, the good "is not something abstratly right, but something concrete whose contents are made up of both right and welfare alike." (Add. to § 129) Accordingly in acting good I do not merely obey the law — valid law, I mean — passively, for no such law contains what is right and consequently what is good in a specific situation, I should also seek my welfare, but I should seek my welfare in such a way that my act does not violate but accords with the principle of rightness. Now is this possible? I raise this question for two reasons: (1) in practical life there are many instances of irreconcilable conflict between right and personal welfare; (2) even though one may think that he has succeeded in resolving such a conflict there is no guarantee that his judgment is correct.

My subjective will, Hegel maintains, "has value and dignity only in so far as its insight and intention accord with the good. (§ 131) Thus in any given moral situation the good is at first given as an abstract ideal, as a possible achievement. The realization of this ideal is what makes the prospective act moral. Prior to its realization my will "stands in a *relation* to the good, and the relation is that the good *ought* to be substantative for it, i.e., it ought to make the good its aim and realize it completely, while the good on its side has in the subjective will its only means of stepping into actuality." (*Ibid.*) Thus, the ultimate basis, or ground, of moral action is not a capricious feeling, or force, but the universal principle of goodness; hence, no act is moral if it violates this principle. Moreover, the moral 'ought', or the feeling of moral obligation, does not originate from a supernatural power or from a subjective sentiment, nor is it given abstractly in a general principle; it originates, emerges so to say, in a concrete moral situation by the effort, insight, or wisdom of the moral agent, for, as Hegel says, the good steps into actuality on the hands of the subjective will. And the subjective will can do this primarily because the good it seeks to realize in its conduct belongs to its own essence: "the good is in principle the essence of the will in its substantiality and universality, i.e., of the will in its truth, and therefore it exists as simple and solely in thinking and by means of thinking. (§ 132)

Hegel makes here a sharp distinction between what the will actually is, as a particular individual, viz., as a given complex of desires, inclinations, attitudes, interests, and social outlook and what it ought to be. It exists as it ought to be when it actualizes its essence, the good, in its conduct. But since it cannot in fact realize its essence fully the good remains for it an ideal, and as such a duty; "since duty is thus abstract and universal in character, it should be done for duty's sake." (§ 133) Now what does Hegel mean when he says that duty should be done for duty's sake? I raise this question because it would seem that, on Hegel's view, one should do his duty for the sake of an abstract principle. If this were to happen the individual human being would in his moral conduct be subordinated to the law. This is not Hegel's intention or meaning. Like Kant, when he says that I should do my duty for duty's sake he means that the duty which I should do does not originate blindly from a principle imposed upon my will by an external power or institution, but rather the duty which expresses my will; thus "when I do my duty it is in a true sense my own objectivity which I am bringing to realization. In doing my duty, I am by myself and free. To have emphasized this meaning of duty has constituted the merit of Kant's moral philosophy and its loftiness of outlook." (Add. to § 133)

But even though the good is the essence and principle of the will it does not follow from this fact that the will cannot make mistakes in relating or translating the universal content of the good concretely. It may miss the mark, yet in spite of this possible error the subjective will has the right to assume full responsibility in determining what is absolutely good in a given moral situation. This is one of its fundamental rights: "the right of the subjective will is that whatever it is to recognize as valid shall be seen by it as good, and that an action, as its aim entering upon external objectivity, shall be imputed to it as right or wrong, good or evil, legal or illegal, in accordance with its *knowledge* of the worth which the action has in this objectivity." (§ 132) But although I have the absolute right to act on the basis of what I take to be good, and although I may believe that my moral conviction is sound, I may still err in my judgment. I may, in other words, act contrary to my true interest as a rational and responsible being. What I take to be good, or the way I make moral decisions, is determined by my past education and the way I conduct myself socially, intellectually, and professionally. I may be narrow minded and self — centered, I may be altruistic and wise, I may be active and ambitious, or I may be indolent or unmotivated. Accordingly, "I may demand from myself, and regard it as one of my subjective rights, that my insight into an obligation shall be based on good reasons, that I shall be convinced of the obligation even that I shall apprehend it from its concept and fundamental nature. But whatever I may claim for the satisfaction of my conviction about the character of an action as good, permitted, or forbidden, and so about its imputability in respect of this character, this in no way detracts from the right of objectivity." (*Ibid.*) Thus when the pursuit of my personal welfare conflicts with the objective demands of the principle of goodness, or when I err in my moral reasoning although I may believe otherwise, in these and similar situations the right of objectivity should be recognized: I should allow at least in principle that my judgment in moral matters may always be wrong, or partially wrong, and that absolute and universal good should prevail.

But how can absolute, or universal, good prevail? It is not enough, I may be told, that I acknowledge this good as the ultimate principle of moral action, or that this principle is the ground of our duties — we should also understand the framework, activity, or the procedure according to which the universal aspect of goodness is translated concretely in the experience of a particular individual. For unless this translation takes place the good remains abstract and therefore indifferent to the action; if this happens the action would not acquire a moral character, and would not consequently be the basis of freedom. Hegel is aware of this problem, for he writes: "because every action explicitly calls for a particular content and a specific end, while duty as an abstraction entails nothing of the kind, the question arises: what is my duty? As an answer nothing is so far available except: (a) to do the right, and (b) to strive after welfare, one's own welfare, and welfare in universal terms, the welfare of others." (§ 134) Thus in a moment of moral self — consciousness the will can know the universal content of duty only; it cannot discover what it ought to do in a *specific* moral situation. It cannot, in other words, discover its specific duties. The latter "are not contained in the definition of duty itself;" they cannot be derived, or deduced, from the principle of goodness alone.

But we should ask again: how can we determine specific duties in accordance with the principle of moral distinction, viz., the Good? For unless we establish criteria, or a framework within which duties may be determined concretely our theory or analysis of moral experience would be reduced to 'empty formalism'; it would tell us in general what is moral, but it would not instruct us on how to realize the moral principle concretely in social life. In spite of its greatness and novelty, Kant's moral theory provides such an example: "however essential it is to give prominence to the pure unconditioned self — determination of the will as the root of duty, and to the way in which knowledge of the will, thanks to Kant's philosophy, has won its firm foundation and starting —point for the first time owing to the thought of its infinite autonomy, still to adhere to the exclusively moral position, without making the transition to the conception of ethics, is to reduce the gain to an empty formalism, and the science of morals to the preaching of duty for duty's sake." (§ 135) Attributing 'empty formalism' to Kant's theory is a serious charge, and this charge has been debated by philosophers with unusual zeal for about two hundred years now. It would be useful to assess in detail Hegel's objections to Kant's moral philosophy in general. This goal is beyond the scope of the present work. I should, however, consider Hegel's main criticism of Kant's position in the *Philosophy of Right* with one end in view: to shed light on the relationship between law, morality, and ethical life. Put differently, why does Hegel find it necessary to formulate the concept of '*sittlichkeit*'? Does this concept allow, or restrict, the possibility of human individuality within the state?

Hegel's central objection to Kant's ethical theory is that, as a principle of moral evaluation or legislation the Categorical Imperative is a formal, abstract principle; it does not provide effective criteria, or guidelines, for the determination of moral duties concretely. It cannot, therefore, be adopted as a fruitful guide in moral conduct. Since this objection is serious and has been subject to intense controversy, I shall quote Hegel's line of reasoning without omission and then elucidate it in terms of recent criticism: "the proposition: 'Act as if the maxim of thine action could be laid down as a universal principle', would be admirable if we already had determinate principles of conduct. That is to say, to demand of a principle that it shall be able to serve in addition as a determinant of universal legislation is to presuppose that it already possesses a content. Given the content, then of course the application of the principle would be a simple matter. In Kant's case, however, the principle itself is still not available and his criterion of non — contradiction is productive of nothing, since where there is nothing, there can be no contradiction either." (Add. to § 135) This line of reasoning contains two basic arguments. First, the Categorical Imperative cannot be adopted as a useful principle of moral conduct because it does not contain a determinate content, or rules, of conduct. We do not have, to begin with, an established system of rules of moral conduct; if such rules exist, and if they are acknowledged as valid, it would be meaningful to speak of testing them by the Categorical Imperative. But their very existence is in question. Again, if we say that the Categorical Imperative is a principle of universal legislation, and that it is capable of determining duties concretely, we in effect hold that it has a content, but Kant repeatedly stressed that the said principle is formal, universal, a priori. The substance of this argument is sadly misinterpreted by M. Singer. He characterizes Hegel's objection to Kant as 'incredibly simple minded'; for it (Hegel's objection) "entirely ignores the fact that the maxim of an action, which is what the categorical imperative is designed to test, is itself a 'determinate principle of conduct' and 'already possesses a content'. Hegel assumes that the categorical imperative is supposed to be applied in a vacuum — or in other words, is not to be applied to anything, with the possible exception of itself — and it is this same assumption that vitiates the common charge that Kant's ethics is an 'empty formalism'. Given that someone proposes to adopt a certain maxim, or to act in a certain way in certain circumstances in order to achieve a certain purpose, then we 'already have a determinate principle of conduct,' to which the categorical imperative can be applied. Hence we are 'given the content,' but unfortunately 'the application of the principle' is not always a simple matter."[6] On the contrary, Hegel does not ignore the fact that the maxim which the categorical imperative is designed to test is a 'determinate content,' for he clearly says: "material may be brought in from outside and particular duties may be arrived at accordingly. (§ 135) He does not deny, in other words, that in concrete moral situations we do make moral decisions on the basis of specific rules of conduct, e.g., 'Keep your promise!' But what he means when he says the categorical imperative "is admirable if we had already determinate principle of conduct" is this: the categorical imperative is admirable if we have morally valid rules of conduct, rules whose validity is, or can be, established in accordance with the requirements of the categorical imperative. The question is not that we have determinate rules of conduct but whether the categorical imperative which is supposed to test them does allow for such a test. Hegel insists, like Kant, that the categorical imperative does not have any determinate content which relates to specific courses of action; this is why he insists: "to demand of a principle that it shall be able to serve in addition as a determinant of universal legislation is to presuppose that it already possesses a content." But Kant would not allow such a content to the categorical imperative. It would not help to say with Singer that, "given that someone proposes to adopt a certain maxim, or to act in a certain way in certain circumstances in order to achieve a certain purpose, then we 'already have a determinate principle of conduct, something that already possesses a content,' to which the categorical imperative can be applied." But Hegel's question which Singer does not seem to grasp is: how can we apply the categorical imperative which does not have a determinate content to this specific course of action, this course which is taking place for the first time in the world? When I propose to adopt a maxim or to act in a certain way the maxim, or the rule of my act, arises from my subjective will; the maxim is already a determinate content, but this content does not have its origin in the categorical imperative. My moral will, my good will, whose object, viz., the law, is the categorical imperative, is pure, universal, contentless.[7] But if the good will, the will which focuses its attention exclusively on the categorical imperative, is pure and free from determinate content, how can we then relate it to this specific maxim or rule of conduct? How, in other words, can we make a transition from the universal to the particular?

The criterion which Kant provides for the possibility of such a transition, i.e., for specifying particular duties, is non — contradiction, or consistency. In a given moral situation when I try to discover what I ought to do now I should ask whether the maxim of my proposed action can be willed as a universal, as a law applicable to all mankind. I shall take an example from the *Critique of Pure Reason* to illustrate this procedure: "I have, for example, made it my maxim to increase my property by every safe means. Now I have in my possession a deposit, the owner of which has died without leaving any record of it. Naturally, this case falls under my maxim. Now I want to know whether this maxim can hold as a universal practical law. I apply it, therefore, to the present case and ask if it could take the form of a law, and consequently whether I could, by the maxim, make the law that every man is allowed to deny that a deposit has been made when no one can prove the contrary. I immediately realize that taking such a principle as a law would annihilate itself, because its result would be that no one would make a deposit. A practical law which I acknowledge as such must qualify for being a universal law; this is an identical and therefore a self — evident proposition. Now, if I say that my will is subject to a practical law, I cannot put forward my inclination (in this case, my avarice) as fit to be a determining ground of a universal practical law. It is far from being worthy of universal legislation that in the form of a universal law it must destroy itself."[9] The point which we should here spotlight is this: I have received a deposit from a man who died without leaving a record of the deposit; consequently, I have the opportunity to increase my property. The question arises: can I increase my property by any safe means? No!

Why? If I universalize the maxim of my act, viz., "everyone is allowed to deny that a deposit has been made when no one can prove the contrary", I immediately discover that if my maxim becomes a universal law it would annihilate, i.e., destroy, itself. What does it mean for the maxim *qua* universal law to 'annihilate' itself? In other examples Kant used the term 'contradict' and 'consistent'. But regardless of which term we use, something happens to the maxim of a wrong action when the maxim is universalized — the action acquires the character of being morally wrong, and it acquires the character because it is presumably discordant with the demands of the categorical imperative. When a universal maxim annihilates itself the annihilation should here be viewed as a relation of contradiction or negation. This is the meaning suggested by all the examples which Kant gives for testing given maxims by the categorical imperative in *The Fundamental Principles of the Metaphysics of Morals* and the *Critique of Practical Reason,* and this is how Hegel understood Kant: "Kant's further formulation, the possibility of visualizing an action as a *universal* maxim, does lead to the more concrete visualization of a situation, but in itself it contains no principle beyond abstract identity and the 'absence of contradiction' already mentioned." (§ 135)[10] Thus let us suppose that I universalize the maxim, "every man is allowed to deny that a deposit has been made when no one can prove the contrary," we can ask Hegel's question: "where is the contradiction if there were no deposits? The non — existence of deposits would contradict other specific things, just as the possibility of deposits fits together with other necessary specific things and thereby will itself be necessary. But other ends and material grounds are not to be invoked; it is the immediate form of the concept which is to settle the rightness of adopting either one specific matter or the other. For the form, however, one of the opposed specifics is just as valid as the other; each can be conceived as a quality and this conception can be expressed as a Law".[11] The difficulty which we face here is not merely linguistic; it does not, in other words, hinge merely on whether Kant proclaimed contradiction as the criterion by which we determine specific duties. The crux of the issue is: if the maxim of my action annihilates itself when universalized, why should we judge the act as immoral? In the example under consideration, when I universalize the maxim of my action the "result would be that no one would make a deposit;" consequently we will live in a society which does not have a place for deposits or in which deposits are impossible.

Now suppose I have chosen to act on the principle that "every man is allowed to deny that a deposit has been made when no one can prove the contrary," suppose, to use Kant's language, I "put forward my inclination (in this case, my avarice) as fit to be a determining ground of a universal practical law," why should my act in this case be immoral?

How can I know merely by acting on a maxim that annihilates itself that my act is immoral? In a moment of self — reflection all that I can appeal to is the universal status of my maxim: "every man is allowed to deny that a deposit has been made when no one can prove the contrary." But from this principle, how can I discover that it is wrong to act accordingly? On Kant's view this principle should be consistent with the categorical imperative, but the latter is, as we saw, abstract; it does not contain within itself a determinate content which relates, or throws light on, the moral character of this specific case. Thus, to quote Hegel, "if the definition of duty is taken to be the absence of contradiction, formal correspondence with itself — which is nothing but abstract indeterminacy stabilized — then no transition is possible to the specification of particular duties nor, if some such particular content for acting comes under consideration, is there any criterion in that principle for deciding whether it is or is not a duty. On the contrary, by this means any wrong or immoral line of conduct may be justified." (§ 135) Kant is, it seems to me, aware of this problem, for after he tells us that we should not act according to a universal maxim which annihilates itself he adds: "it is so far from being worthy of universal legislation that in the form of a universal law it must destroy itself."[12]

Again, suppose that I have chosen to act on the principle that "every man is allowed to deny that a deposit has been made when no one can prove the contrary," suppose, to use Kant's language, I "put forward my inclination (in this case, my avarice) as fit to be the determining ground of a universal law,"[13] why should my act in this case be immoral? How can I know merely by acting on a maxim that annihilates itself that my act is immoral? Again, why should it be unworthy of "universal legislation that in the form of universal law it must destroy itself"? Kant does not give us an answer to this question. But this very answer is what Hegel tries to provide.

In the example under consideration the idea of returning, or declaring, a deposit presupposes that of property; i.e., it presupposes the rule that property must be respected. When I act on the maxim of not returning the deposit I in my act annihilate the whole institution of deposit. My act would not in this case contradict, or violate, anything if, of course, one assumes, with Kant, that the morality or immorality of the act is determined solely by reference to the categorical imperative. Again, the non — existence of deposits does not involve any contradiction; it is, also, a value free state, that is, we cannot assert, logically speaking, that a society which does not have a place for deposits is morally inferior to a society with such a place. But if we accept the principle, "property must be respected," as valid then violating this principle would render the act immoral. Contradiction, for Hegel, is contradiction of something, "i.e., of some content presupposed from the start as a fixed principle. It is to a principle of that kind alone, therefore, that an action can be related either by correspondence or contradiction. But if duty is to be willed simply for duty's sake and not for the sake of some content, it is only a formal identity whose nature it is to exclude all content and specification." (*Ibid.*)[14]

The question which led us to the preceding discussion of a basic concept of Kant's ethical theory is: how can we determine specific duties in accordance with the good as the highest principle of moral distinctions? We have so far found that Kant's answer to this question is inadequate. His conception of the categorical imperative does not provide a workable criterion, or guideline, which enables us to move from the universal principle of goodness to the determination of the moral character of specific actions. Before we proceed to Hegel's answer to our question we should consider one more concept — Conscience. The consideration of this concept is of vital importance not only because it throws ample light on the nature of moral decision and action but also because it constitutes an integral part of Hegel's answer to our question.

4. *Conscience.* Hegel makes a distinction between two senses (or types) of conscience, formal and true conscience. (A) "True conscience," he writes, "is the *disposition* to will what is absolutely good." (§ 137) I underline the word 'disposition' only to stress that conscience is not a faculty which can, readily and without reflection, dictate what is right or good in particular situations; it is a tendency, a power, *to will* what is good absolutely and to realize it concretely in a particular situation. This sort of good is achieved when the will recognizes and acts according to fixed and rational principles, and when "it is aware of these as its explicitly objective determinants and duties." (*Ibid.*) These principles constitute the basis of what Hegel calls *sittlichkeit*, or ethical life, which we shall study in the next section. They provide the content, *material*, whose realization in our conduct bestows a moral character upon our actions.[14]

Since the good is abstract and as such indifferent to the particular aspect of action its realization is, as we have seen, a task; it is a task to be achieved on the hands of the will in a moment of moral self — consciousness. The subjectivity of the will is the sanctuary where the good becomes actual, alive, determinate, and outside this sanctuary it remains abstract. "Subjectivity in its universality reflected into itself," Hegel writes, "is the subject's absolute inward subjectivity (Gewissheit) of himself, that which establishes the particular and is the determining and decisive element in him, his conscience (Gewissen)." (§ 136) In this task, when the will seeks to determine the good *concretely*, the moral agent is alone and completely responsible for his judgment and the consequences of his action. This is based on the assumption, as we have already seen, that the moral problem which a person faces is unique, and this not only because the person himself is an individual but also because the conditions under which the problem occurs are essentially different from any other conditions. No one is, therefore, in a position to assess or evaluate the elements, factual and psychological, of the moral situation adequately except the person who faces the problem. It is accordingly his bounden duty, first, to present the good to himself as "a particular will." But the good is universal; he should therefore see or will it according to rational principles, to principles that are already established and which are acknowledged to express the universal aspect of the good. Second, the moral agent should himself pronounce what the good is in that, or this, specific situation. The judgment on what the particular good is should spring from his will, from his volition. Third, he should proceed to realize it in his action primarily because it is the good, i.e., for its own sake. These three stages describe the activity, indeed the development, of conscience. They show that conscience is, for Hegel, a reflective, rational, and deliberative faculty. This faculty is sensitive to the factual, particular aspects of the moral agent — of his personal, social, and natural environment — and also to the supremacy of the good. But it is especially sensitive to the fact that conscience is one of the highest forms of self — expression and, consequently, self — determination. It is accordingly a privilege, a title, which cannot be contested or taken away: "conscience is the expression of the absolute title of subjective self — consciousness to know in itself what is right and obligatory, to give recognition only to what it thus knows as good, and at the same time to maintain that whatever in this way it knows and wills is in truth right and obligatory. Conscience as this unity of subjective knowing with what is absolute is a sanctuary which it would be sacrilege to violate." (§ 137)

I have the incontestable right to act on the basis of what I take to be right or good, and I have the right to assume responsibility for the consequences of my action; but from this two — fold right it does not follow that my judgment on what is good is necessarily correct. For the essence of conscience consists in disovering, articulating, the good, translating this good into a particular content, and then acting according to this content. But I may fail in this process even though I may think differently. Hegel insists that "what is right and obligatory is the absolutely rational element in the will's volitions and therefore it is not in essence the *particular* property of an individual, and its form is not that of feeling or any other private (i.e. sensuous) type of knowing, but essentially that of universals determined by thought, i.e. the form of laws and principles." (*Ibid.*) Thus what makes my act good, or obligatory, is not merely the fact that I choose it skillfully or intelligently, and that I act on the basis of my decision, but rather my success in bringing to life in moral reflection a concrete rational content of goodness. Good is the source of moral obligation: an act is obligatory inasmuch as it is a realization of the Good. But since the good is rational, objective, and can be determined in reflective thought the judgment of conscience is always subject to verification: "conscience is therefore subject to the judgment of its truth or falsity, and when it appeals only to itself for a decision, it is directly at variance with what it wishes to be, namely the rule for a mode of conduct which is rational, absolutely valid, and universal." (*Ibid.*)

(B) Conscience is 'true' when it succeeds in realizing the good concretely in a specific moral experience. Without this content conscience is only 'formal', abstract. Formal conscience, then, is the subjective activity of the will apart from any consideration or reflection on the good as a determinate content; it is nevertheless "both the power to judge, to determine from within itself alone, what is good in respect of any content, and also the power to which the good, at first only an ideal and ought — to — be, owes its actuality." (§ 138) Thus when Hegel characterizes conscience as formal what he really means is the will's power to withdraw into itself to reflect on its inner self as a knowing, willing, and acting agent, to understand its capacities, limits and rights, to discover and define the condition of its self — determination. This is one of the will's deepest moments of subjectivity which Socrates immortalized in his dictum: Know Thyself. In such a moment the will can be put to test, it can examine all the ideas and principles which are given as right and good and it can re — valuate its own stand in relation to what it should take as right or good. It may discover that the moral values which are upheld by its society are poor and that it cannot accommodate such a poverty. In this state the will has the right to withdraw into itself and search for the rational and true character of the principles of moral conduct, of those principles which are appropriate for that society at a given historical period.

This right should, however, be exercised with the utmost of care, for the established moral order, which is most likely the work of centuries, cannot be dismissed or overthrown overnight. This is why the total rejection of such an order must come as a last resort, i.e., when the normal channels of reform have become ineffective. Thus "it is only in times when the world of actuality is hollow, spiritless, and unstable, that an individual may be allowed to take refuge from actuality in his inner life. Socrates lived at the time of the ruin of the Athenian democracy. His thought vaporized the world around him and he withdrew into himself to search there for the right and the good. Even in our day there are cases when reverence for the established order is more or less lacking; man insists on having the authoritative as his *will*, as that to which he has granted recognition." (Add. to § 138)

But to discover the good is not enough; one should also act on the basis of the good. Thus if I happen to reject the existing principles of conduct and withdraw into myself in search of higher and richer values this activity would remain abstract, formal, unless I manage to transform my moral insight into moral convictions, i.e., principles, on which I can act and in acting determine myself as a human individual.

IV. *The Ethical Point of View*

The moral point of view poses, accordingly, a perplexing difficulty, for when the will attempts to determine itself, to actualize its freedom, or put differently, to do its duty, when it focuses its attention on the principles of its implicit concept, of its essence as a rational nature, viz., on the absolute good, it remains helpless, for this principle does not provide a specific content or prescription for the concrete determination of the good. The good as the principle of moral action remains an abstract universal, an ought to be; it simply states a general command: in your action do what is right and promote your own welfare as well as the welfare of others. But this command is formal, empty, therefore it cannot be an effective guide for moral conduct. This is why Hegel insisted that "good in the abstract evaporates into something completely powerless, into which I may introduce any and every content, while the subjectivity of mind becomes just as worthless because it lacks any objective significance." (Add. to § 141) The two basic elements — or unities, as Hegel calls them — of the moral experience, viz., conscience and the good, stand in direct opposition to one another without obvious unity or rapprochement. On the one hand, conscience as the disposition to will the good seeks, or should seek, to realize the universal objectively, and on the other hand, the good as a universal principle of action should be realized concretely and subjectively in a moral experience. Thus "if good and conscience are each kept abstract and thereby elevated to independent totalities, then both become the indeterminate which ought to be determined." (§ 141) But the unity or integration of these two elements is inherent in their very being or structure, for the good *qua* universal, rational principle is the concept, i.e., essence, of the will. The good *is*, and as such it is intelligible only to a will that wills it; the will is not a will unless it is capable of self — realization, of realizing itself as a rational nature: "but the integration of these two relative totalities into an absolute identity has already been implicitly achieved in that this very subjectivity of pure self — certainty, aware in its vacuity of its gradual evaporation, is identical with the abstract universality of the good. The identity of the good with the subjective will, an identity which therefore is concrete and the truth of them both, is Ethical life." (*Ibid.*)

The word '*sittlichkeit*' is, as Knox and Taylor rightly indicate, rather hard to translate precisely into English; the best expression which conveys the meaning of the term is 'ethical life', and when emphasis is placed on the principles of this life 'ethical order' or 'ethical realm' would, I think, be most appropriate to use.[15] Broadly speaking, *sittlichkeit* means the moral duties, or obligations, which a citizen is expected to perform in the state; it is "the concrete morality of a rational social order where rational institutions and laws provide the content of conscientious conviction."[16] 'Morality', or '*Moralität*', however, refers to the concept of morality which I have already discussed in the foregoing pages. The moral attitude, or consciousness, is the form of moral action; it is, as we saw, the will to seek the good as such but without a concrete content or translation of the good in action: "morality," writes Hegel, "is the form of the will in general on its subjective side. Ethical life is more than the subjective form and the self — determination of the will; in addition it has as its content the concept of the will, namely freedom." (Add. to § 141)

Let us now study in some detail Hegel's conception of ethical life. This study is urgent not only because this concept is notoriously misunderstood by many Hegelian critics and scholars but also because I wish to answer on a solid basis the objections which I pointed out in the introduction of this essay. As a concept, 'ethical life' is composed of two elements: (1) 'ethical order' which comprises the ethical principles, institutions, or values which are recognized and upheld in the state, and (2) 'virtue', which is the moral quality, or disposition, in the character and corresponds to the ethical principles or values as recognized moral ideals in the state. I shall begin my discussion with the first element.

1. *Ethical Order*

"Ethical life," Hegel writes, "is the Idea of freedom in that on the one hand it is the good become alive — the good endowed in self — consciousness with knowing and willing and actualized by self — conscious action — while on the other hand self — consciousness has in the ethical realm its absolute foundation and the end which actuates its effort." (§ 142) We should here ask: what does Hegel mean when he says that ethical life is the living reality of freedom, and that the ethical realm is the foundation of freedom? When Hegel says that ethical life is the living reality of freedom he means, broadly speaking, the activity of moral self — determination in which the will performs an act according to a clearly articulated principle of conduct, a principle which embodies, or expresses, the general essence of the good. In this activity the good does not stand against the will as an abstract but as a concrete universal: "the unity of the subjective with the objective and absolute good is ethical life, and in it we find the reconciliation which accords with the concept." (Add. to § 141) The point which merits special emphasis here, however, is that moral freedom is the activity of self — determination according to established, valid ethical principles or values; in this activity the will consciously, knowingly, and willingly realizes, lives, the good in its action. It is free not only because it authors the act and can be responsible for its consequences, and not only because the act is essentially good, but especially because the good realized in the act is expressive of its implicit concept, of its essence as a rational nature; put differently, because it is an objectification of its universal, rational nature, because the principle on which it acts is its own principle.

Thus the ground, foundation, of moral freedom is the existence of an ethical realm; this realm is the *raison d'être* of freedom, otherwise we would be thrown into the moral, or Kantian, point of view according to which the will confronts the good as an abstract principle. The ethical experience is thus composed, for Hegel, of two elements, or moments, the one subjective, viz., the will in its effort to realize the good in its experience, and the other objective, viz., the ethical principle *qua* embodiment of the good. Although these two elements are united in the ethical attitude this unity is not complete; the will remains conscious of itself as the subject which seeks to realize the ethical principle in its action. It remains, in other words, conscious of the distinction between its subjectivity and the principle which should determine this subjectivity. But this distinction is different from the one which we encounter in morality. In the latter the distinction is radical, irreconcilable; in the former each of the elements or moments, claims "the totality of the Idea and has that totality as its foundation and content." (§ 143) They make such a claim primarily because each one of them has been influenced, conditioned by the other — how? (1) The ethical order is dependent for its being on the citizens who constitute the state, and (2) the will which craves its freedom depends in this craving on the objective, universal character of this order, for only in living up to the promise of this order can it attain its freedom.

First, the objective element, or moment, of the ethical attitude consists of "absolutely valid laws and institutions;" these laws and institutions constitute the objective ethical order on which the will relies in the realization of its moral freedom. They are accordingly the foundation of this freedom. But although objective and free from the capricious emotions, whims, or idiosyncracies of particular individuals, they are not transcendent, because their articulation and recognition is made possible by the very people for whom they exist; they originate from their will, and consequently they are enshrined by their subjectivity: "the objective ethical order, which comes on the scene in place of good in the abstract, is substance made concrete by subjectivity as infinite form." (§ 144) We should here stress "as infinite form" only to obviate a possible misunderstanding; viz, the subjectivity which gives being to the ethical order might be viewed as capricious, selfish, or in some way relative, but it is not, because it is both infinite, i.e., universal and self — related, and also concrete; it is universal, on the one hand, and expresses the interests of the people, on the other. This point is made clear in the following sentence: "hence it (the ethical order) posits within itself distinctions whose specific character is thereby determined by the concept, and which endow the ethical order with a stable content independently necessary and subsistent in exaltation above subjective opinion and caprice. (§ 144) This is why in a given culture the people usually take their ethical laws and principles as final or as promulgated by a supreme being. In this connection Hegel refers to Antigone's proclamation that " 'no one knows whence the laws come; they are everlasting', i.e., their determinate character is absolute and has its source in the nature of the thing." (Add. to § 144) In as much as the ethical laws and institutions which give content to the ethical order are valid and universal they constitute the ethical substance of the people and consequently their freedom. It is this relation between the two — the ethical order and the people — which led Hegel to say that the individuals are related to the ethical substance as accidents are related to a substance: "since the laws and institutions of the ethical order make up the concept of freedom, they are the substance or universal essence of individuals, who are thus related to them as accidents only." (Add. to § 145) Does this mean that the individual is 'accidental', 'valueless', or that he is dependent, and therefore a means to an end? No, for three reasons: (1) the ethical order expresses the universal, yet concrete, interests, i.e., concrete good, of the people; (2) this order becomes actual, it comes to life, in the conscious self — determination of the individuals; (3) its very being, therefore, depends on the conscious decision and action of the individuals. The individuals come and go but not what is universally good, a good that embodies the universal interest of human nature as such: "whether the individual exists or not is all one to the objective order. It alone is permanent and is the power regulating the life of the individuals. Thus the ethical order has been represented by mankind as eternal justice, as gods absolutely existent, in contrast with which the empty business of individuals is only a game of see — saw." (*Ibid.*)

Second, unlike the basic principle of morality in Kant which remains an ideal, an ought — to — be — realized, the ethical order for Hegel is an established system of valid laws and institutions: "this ethical substance and its laws and powers are on the one hand an object over against the subject, and from his point of view they *are* — 'are' in the highest sense of self — subsistent being. This is an absolute authority and power infinitely more firmly established than the being of nature." (§ 146) This passage calls for two remarks: (1) when Hegel says the ethical order *is* he means, as we shall presently see, in the state the people recognize a body, or system, of 'moral' values and principles which are clearly acknowledged by the society and which are accepted as valid and binding upon everyone. Hegel is anxious to stress this point not only because he was dissatisfied with Kant's formalism which could not provide a practical guideline for moral conduct but also because he saw that the people *actually need* a rational ethical order, that this need is an expression of an inner urge for freedom and moral tranquility. When, for example, I face a moral problem I want, need, to know what is the moral thing to do in this specific case; if I do not have a clearly articulated system of what is good and right, or a system which applies to my life as a citizen, as a member of the state, I shall experience restlessness, if not moral anxiety. This sort of experience engenders a desire, a longing "for an objective moral order in which man gladly degrades himself to servitude and total subjection, if only to escape the torment of vacuity and negation." (Add. to § 141) Hegel refers to many Protestants in his day who had gone over to the Roman Catholic Church "because they found their inner life worthless and grasped at something fixed, at a support, an authority, even if it was not exactly the stability of thought which they caught." (*Ibid.*) It is not enough for man to know and feel that he *ought to be* moral; it is equally important for him to now *what* is moral.

(2) When Hegel says that the ethical order has an absolute authority and power over the individuals he means that the laws and institutions which make up this order are, or should be, objective and valid. I have already discussed in some detail in the first part of this essay the conditions under which laws can be viewed as valid for Hegel. Here I should only stress, though, that what makes a law valid for Hegel is neither the capricious power of the sovereign, or God, nor the fact that it already exists but its rationality and capacity to promote man's highest good as a human individual. Accordingly the ethical order does not stand in relation to the individual *qua* subjectivity as an alien authority but as the expression of the concept of his will, of his essence as a rational being: "they are not alien to the subject." Hegel writes, "On the contrary, his spirit bears witness to them as to its own essence, the essence in which he has a feeling of his selfhood, and in which he lives as in his own element which is not distinguished from himself." (§ 147) Thus the relation which holds between the ethical order and the individual who is supposed to submit his will to it is not one of opposition, faith, or trust, but of

identity. This is the main reason why in doing his duty a citizen does not abandon but indeed attains his freedom, and he attains his freedom because the law which he recognizes and observes is the law of his own nature, it is the law which expresses his nature as a rational and moral being. We should here understand freedom as a positive, not as a negative experience. As we have seen earlier, freedom for Hegel is not freedom *fom* certain mental states or social obligations; it is not, in other words, abstract freedom, but rather the activity in which a person attains to a higher level of human *being*. In this activity one is liberated, i.e., made free, in a two — fold sense: "first, liberation from dependence on mere natural impulse and from the depression which as a particular subject he cannot escape in his moral reflections on what ought to be and what might be; secondly, liberation from the indeterminate subjectivity which, never reaching reality or the objective determinacy of action, remains self — enclosed and devoid of actuality." (§ 149)

2. *Virtue*

A person is not virtuous, i.e., ethically good, unless his action originates from an ethical disposition, that is, unless the action expresses his will as a moral character: "to conform to the ethical order on this or that particular occasion is hardly enough to make a man virtuous; he is virtuous only when this mode of behaviour is a fixed element in his character." (Add. to § 150) Put differently, a person is virtuous when he already possesses a virtuous, i.e., ethical, disposition. And he possesses this disposition when the ethical order is 'reflected', i.e., ingrained, in his character, when his character is an interpenetration of the ethical values which are authoritative in the lives of the people as a whole: ethical life is a disposition, but one imbued with what is inherently right." (§ 141)

Hegel, I think, agrees with Aristotle that "moral virtue ... is formed by habit, *ethos*, and its name, *ethike*, is therefore derived, by a slight variation, from *ethos*. This shows, too, that none of the moral virtues is implanted in us by nature, for nothing which exists by nature can be changed by habit. For example, it is impossible for a stone, which has a natural downward movement, to become habituated to moving upward, even if one should try ten thousand times to inculcate the habit by throwing it in the air; nor can fire be made to move downward, nor can the direction of any nature — given tendency be changed by habituation. Thus the virtues are implanted in us neither by nature not contrary to nature: we are by nature equipped with the ability to receive them, and habit brings this ability to completion and fulfillment."[17] In a similar tone Hegel writes: "virtue is the ethical order reflected in the individual character so far as that character is determined by its natural endowment.' (§ 150) The medium in which virtue becomes actual in ethical life is two — fold: custom (*sitte*) and habit (*ethos*). The first refers to the "general mode of conduct" which is common to all the members of society. We may speak of honesty, friendship, justice, etc., as virtues. Corresponding to each of these virtues we encounter a rule, or a principle, which defines the meaning and scope of the virtue. In this way, although a rule prescribes a course of action, i.e., a duty, it is nevertheless viewed as a custom, the sort of behavior which every person is expected to observe: ethical conduct becomes a way of life. But observing such rules or customs is not enough; the individual should also cultivate, possess, these virtues in himself. They should exist in him as habits. Thus when a habit reflects an ethical rule or value it becomes the soul, élan, of custom. The ethical order outside does not anymore exist as an external but as a living principle which animates the mind in all its dimensions.

Again, like Aristotle, Hegel thinks that one becomes virtuous by doing, practising, virtuous actions. "The virtues," Aristotle writes, "we acquire by first having put them into action, and the same is also true of the arts. For the things which we have to learn before we can do them we learn by doing: men become builders by building houses, and harpists by playing the harp. Similarly, we become just by the practice of just actions, self — controlled by exercising self — control, and courageous by performing acts of courage."[18] Similarly Hegel writes: "education is the art of making men ethical. It begins with pupils whose life is at the instinctive level and shows them the way to a second birth, the way to change their instinctive nature into a second, intellectual, nature, and makes this intellectual level habitual to them" (Add. to § 151) Becoming virtuous, then, is achieved gradually in the process of social growth; in this process the growing child acquires a second nature, a nature regulated, or ruled, by the ethical order: "just as nature has its laws, and as animals, trees, and the sun fulfill their law, so custom (*sitte*) is the law appropriate to free mind." (*Ibid.*)

Now, if the ethical disposition which a person acquires in the family and the other major social institutions conforms to, or is a reflection of, the fundamental values which dominate the ethical order, are we not in a position to say that we have surpassed the abstractness and emptiness precipitated by the moral standpoint? For the question which has troubled us so far is: what is my duty? In raising this question we were not in search of an empty universal (like Kant's) which is impotent in prescribing the concrete moral content according to which the act should be performed but rather for a definite set of values or principles which are acknowledged as valid. Let us suppose that such values, or principles, i.e., the ethical order, is somehow present in a civilized society, should we not arm ourselves with enough courage to bring our children up according to the form and spirit of this order? And here I may be reminded that in most of the contemporary civilized societies we do this anyway, that is, we assume some faith, belief, or trust in a set of ethical values regardless of whether they are backed up by the church, our forefathers, the state, or society, and rear our children according to them, otherwise, how can we explain the various types of ethical character which fill the modern world around us? Whether this is the way we ethically educate our children at the present is not my concern here; what I am anxious to stress on behalf of Hegel is that if the character of a citizen is nourished by the ethical order of the state, an order which is acknowledged as rational and valid, then the possible clash between his subjective and natural will and between his private conscience and the ethical order would vanish; "for, when his character is ethical, he recognizes as the end which moves him to act the universal which is itself unmoved but is disclosed in its specific determinations as rationality actualized. He knows that his own dignity and the whole stability of his particular ends are grounded in this same universal, and it is therein that he actually attains these." (§ 152) A person so educated would not merely perform good deeds, he would not merely act virtuously, though he would certainly conduct himself in this way, no — *he himself* would be good and virtuous and his act or duty would be judged as good mainly because they issue from his good will. This is why, as I indicated in passing in the first essay, Hegel insisted that the achievement of goodness, virtue, or freedom is realized, properly speaking, in a good social environment. Let me quote once again Hegel's allusion to the answer of the Pythagorean to the father who was in search of "the best method of educating his son in ethical conduct:" *Make him a citizen of a state with good laws.* (§ 153)

V. *Evaluation*

Your discussion of ethical life in its entirety, my critic would here interject, confirms my fears and objection to Hegel's treatment of the relationship between law and morality, on the one hand, and the place of the individual in the state, on the other; for, as you have clearly shown, Hegel has reduced the moral to the legal: the moral law is replaced by the ethical order, and to express myself bluntly, he has replaced the categorical imperative by the Emperium of the state. The good citizen has turned out to be the individual whose soul — moral soul — is nurtured by the state law. This is why a person like this would appear to himself, and perhaps to Hegel, as free, but indeed he is practically a product fashioned in the most gradual, complex, and sophisticated manner by the various agencies, laws, and institutions of the state. Has not Hegel himself said in the page on which the last part of your discussion is based that when the ethical order prevails in the life of the state "the self — will of the individual has vanished together with his private conscience which had claimed independence and opposed itself to the ethical substance?" (§ 152) The trouble with Hegel's view, my critic would go on, is that he closed all the roads to any possible critical moral attitude or change of a given ethical order, for, to him, law is in the final analysis *positive* in character. Hegel has, as d'Entreves has argued, done away with the concept of natural law, of a law that is higher or more rational than any historical or existing law.[19] But if law as such is positive law, and if this law is both the principle of moral distinction and moral education, is there any more room left for political reform, moral reform, or human individuality? In short, the price which Hegel wishes us to pay in order to escape the abstractness of the Kantian moral point of view is rather dear; he wishes us to sacrifice conscience, moral freedom, and natural law at the altar of the state as a positive, historical institution.

The main charge in the preceding line of reasoning is that Hegel has reduced *the moral* to *the judicial*, to the Emperium of the state. But I say, on the contrary, that he sought to moralize the law of the state; he sought to provide a moral foundation for the constitution and consequently for the laws and institutions which determine human life both as an individual and as a society.[20] For him, the law which rules a nation should express the highest values, aspirations, or moral sentiments of the people; it should express their actual and rational, i.e., universal, interest as a concrete spiritual reality. It should, in other words, express their moral will.

Now when our critic complains that Hegel has reduced the moral to the judicial he is afraid that if the established, historical law — viz., the law of the state — is alien to the will of the citizen, or if it happens to be accidental, capricious, or expressive of the will of a ruthless ruler, then in obeying it the citizen will certainly be determined, or 'unfree'; he will be an instrument of the power that rules the social and economic life of society. A person is morally free, he would insist, only when the law on which he acts is that of his will. But why should we entertain this sort of fear? Are we justified in entertaining this fear? In view of the preceding analysis of Hegel's conception of law, morality, and ethical life my answer to both questions is in the negative — why?

Hegel repeatedly stressed that the essential character of the state as a human community is that it is an *ethical association*: "the state is the actuality of the ethical Idea. It is ethical mind *qua* the substantial will manifest and revealed to itself, knowing and thinking itself, accomplishing what it knows and in so far as it knows it." (§ 257) When Hegel says that the state is the *actuality* of the ethical Idea he means that the constitution in which the Idea of the state becomes immediate, actual, i.e., in which it acquires a concrete mode of economic and socio — political organization, is the basis of concrete freedom, and it is the basis of concrete freedom mainly because it embodies the spirit of the people *as a whole*, namely their ideals, values, interests, hopes, and general outlook upon life. (§ 264—265) I stress 'as a whole', for the constitution cannot, as we saw, be an abstract system of laws, nor can it be imported or devised according to the will or design of a powerful person or group of persons. On the contrary, it should be a concrete idealization, or better realization, of the will of the people as a historical reality, as a reality couched in a given geographical, cultural, religious setting, on the one hand, and a world or future outlook, on the other. Thus the constitution should express not merely the general temper or spirit of the people but especially their individuality. "We can understand," Hegel writes in *Natural Law*, "how all parts of the constitution and the laws, all specific details of ethical relationships, are entirely determined by the whole and form a structure in which no joint and no ornament has been independently present *a priori*, but each element has been brought about by the whole and is subservient to it."[21] Accordingly, the laws of a nation cannot, as Montesquieu has rightly argued, be deduced from reason or abstracted from experience, but, as we saw earlier, "legislation both in general and in its particular provisions is to be treated not as something isolated and abstract but rather as a subordinate moment in a whole interconnected with all the other features which make up the character of a nation and an epoch. It is in being so connected that the various laws acquire their true meaning and therewith their justification." (§ 3) The same argument is expounded in greater detail in *Natural Law*: "Montesquieu based his immortal work on the view of the individuality and character of nations, and while he did not rise to the height of the most living Idea, he did not merely deduce individual institutions and laws from so — called reason, nor merely abstract them from experience to raise them thereafter to some universal. On the contrary, he comprehended both the higher relationships of constitutional law and the lower specifications of civil relationships down to wills, marriage laws, etc., entirely from the character of the whole and its individuality."

In order for a constitution, then, to be valid it should express the character, spirit, or more accurately *ethos*, of the people. This is based on the assumption that the end of the state, in contrast to civil society, is not, for Hegel, *merely* the promotion of life but rather the *good life*. This kind of life is attained when every member of the state is, or can be, free, i.e., self — determined being: "the state," Hegel writes, "is the actuality of freedom." (§ 260) But this end cannot be achieved unless the foundation of the state, viz., its law, is ethical, or unless it provides a socio — political framework within which a person can exist as an ethical, or free human being: ethical life consists, as we have seen, in the living reality of the good, in exemplifying the good in concrete conduct. (§ 142) Accordingly if the state becomes actual in its laws and institutions, if these laws and institutions determine the life of the citizen, and if they are ethical in character, then it would be a mistake to view the state as an agency or power which oversees and directs or controls the lives of the people; it would be more correct to say that it is the realization of the ethical life. What makes this realization possible, and consequently the actuality of concrete freedom, is the fact that the ethical order expresses the universal moral sentiment of the people as an organic whole. The *good* which Hegel emphasizes is the *living* good, the good which unifies in itself the actual, historical wants, needs, desires, or interests of the people: only when a law expresses this sort of good can the citizen identify his will with it, and only then can he attain his freedom when he acts according to it. It is a grave error to think that a person, or a nation, becomes free if, or when, he, or it, acts according to a lofty yet abstract and arbitrarily conceived ideal; indeed such an ideal cannot be considered rational, for the rational is that which satisfies, fulfills, a person as a concrete, particular individual in a given geographical and historical setting: "like everything living," Hegel writes, "ethical life is a sheer identity of universal and particular, and for that reason is an individuality and a shape. It carries in itself a particularity, necessity, relation (i.e., relative identity), but these are identified with and assimilated to it, so that it is free in this identity."[22] That which is ethical is not, and cannot be, determined abstractly and without a thoughtful consideration of the actual spiritual and moral disposition of a people, of their needs and ideals, of what they hope to be. This is why "if, for example, the genius of a people is in general on a lower level and weaker, and the weakness of ethical life is at its most stubborn in barbarism and in formal culture; if the nation has allowed itself to be conquered by another and has had to lose its independence (i.e., if it has preferred misfortune and the disgrace of loss of independence, to battle and death); if it has sunk so crudely into the reality of animal life that it does not even rise to formal ideality, to the abstraction of a universal, and thus in determining relationships for physical necessities cannot bear the relation of law but only of personality; or, equally, if the reality of the universal and of law has lost all conviction and truth, and the nation cannot feel and enjoy the image of divinity in its own being, but must put that image outside itself and must make do instead with a dim feeling, or even the painful feeling of vast distance and lofty eminence: if all this occurs, then the feudal system and serfdom have absolute truth, and this relationship has one absolute form of ethical life and is therefore the necessary and just and ethical form."[23]

Hegel has replaced, as we can see, the Kantian standpoint of morality, in which the right and the good remain distinct and opposed to each other, by the concrete ethical order of the people *qua* state. He does this because he is anxious to provide an answer to our urgent question: what is my duty? What should I do here and now? "In an ethical community, it is easy to say what man must do, what are the duties he has to fulfill in order to be virtuous: he has simply to follow the well — known and explicit rules of his own situation." (§ 150) The duties which a person should perform are usually articulated in the laws and institutions of the society: it is expected that everyone should observe them (§ 148) They regulate the social conduct of the individual, on the one hand, and shape his moral disposition, on the other. When a person is born and grows up to be a member of the community he takes these laws, or values, as the established custom (*sitte*) of the land, a custom which repeats itself in the life of every citizen and constitutes his virtuous behavior. This is mainly why Hegel replaces *Moralität* by *Sittlichkeit*; the latter is similar in meaning to the Greek word *ethos*: "this Greek word for ethical life, like the German one (*Sitte*), expresses this nature admirably, while the newer systems of ethics, in making independence and individuality into a principle, cannot fail to expose the relation of these words."[24] The process of moral education is an activity in which the growing child abandons his subjective inclination and desires and acquires tendencies congruent with the universal content of the ethical order. The end of this activity is a unity between the ethical law and the virtue which reveals itself in action. Accordingly a virtuous person is one who knows what is right or good. Hegel points out that a main reason why certain men, e.g., Hercules, in the earlier times were distinguished, and were esteemed for their moral, virtuous behavior, was simply because virtue was not a custom and people were not normally expected to realize it in their conduct: "in the states of antiquity, ethical life had not grown into this free system of an objective order self — subsistently developed, and consequently it was by the personal genius of individuals that this effect had to be made good. It follows that if a 'doctrine of virtues' is not a mere 'doctrine of duties', and if therefore it embraces the particular facet of character, the facet grounded in natural endowment, it will be a natural history of mind." (§ 150) This perhaps accounts for Hegel's reluctance to construct or advance a 'doctrine' of duties, or of virtues; for, once more, 'moral' conduct consists in doing one's duty. Thus a person is virtuous inasmuch as he lives up to the ethical order, or, more concretely, inasmuch as he fulfills the duties of his position. "Each individual," Hegel writes in *Reson and History*, "has his position; he knows, on the whole, what a lawful and honorable course of conduct is. To assert in ordinary private relations that it is difficult to choose the right and good, and to regard it as mark of an exalted morality to find difficulties and raise scruples on that score indicates an evil and perverse will. It indicates a will that seeks to evade obvious duties or, at least, a petty will that gives its mind too little to do. The mind, then, in idle reflection, busies itself with itself and indulges in moral smugness."[25]

But, I may again be reminded, what if the existing ethical order is vague or for some reason does not express the people's sense of good or justice? On Hegel's view, the established ethical realm is prior, more superior to the individual; indeed, the individual is always at the mercy of the law, for as soon as he grows up and begins to acquire a sense of personal identity he submits to the will of the state, and he submits to its will the moment he receives what we termed earlier 'moral education'. But if he receives such education, if, in other words, he acquires his definitive conscience, how can he then deviate, rebel, or discover the shortcomings of the law which was internalized in him as a second nature? Again, is it really the case that a person who belongs to a given social position knows what is right and good every time he faces a moral problem? Is it not possible for one to encounter a problem whose solution resists the acknowledged ethical law or to find himself involved in a rather difficult or perhaps irreconcilable conflict? Is there any place for what we usually call 'natural' or 'universal' law as the final arbiter in times of moral crises?

When Hegel gives 'primacy', or 'priority', to the ethical order he does not in any way intend to subordinate the individual to the authority of the state as a final power or as an almighty emperium. He simply acknowledges the validity of the ancient principle that "to be ethical one should live according to the ethical principles of one's country."[26] This principle underlies Hegel's admiration of the Pythagorean's advice that in order for one to be a good citizen he should live in a state with good laws. The first aspect which we should recognize in this advice is that the goodness of the citizen depends on the quality or goodness of the laws which determines his social conduct and consequently his life. But this dependence is not a relation of literal subordination, primarily because the laws which the citizen should obey and according to which he should fashion his character are not, as I already argued, super — imposed on him and on the rest of the citizens but expressive of the general will of the people, of what they take to be good and right for them *qua* people (*Volk*). Although I discussed this point in the fourth section of this essay it would help if I cite a relevant passage from *Natural Law*: "the essence of the ethical life of the individual," Hegel writes, "is *the* real and therefore universal absolute ethical life; the ethical life of the individual is one pulse beat of the whole system and is itself the whole system." Again, "absolute ethical life is so essentially the ethical life of all that we can scarcely say of it that it mirrors itself as such in the individual."[27] But from the fact that it mirrors itself in the individual it does not necessarily follow that the individual is a passive mind completely at the mercy of the established order or those who administer its cultivation in the souls of the young, and this for three reasons: (1) man is a socio — political animal; his ethical life is therefore an integral element of the life of the whole. (2) Conscience is a living, dynamic faculty in Hegel. (3) The ethical order is not a static but a dynamic set of norms which grow with the spiritual, moral growth of a people. I shall now discuss these reasons in their present order.

First, like Plato and Aristotle, Hegel takes into serious consideration the principle that man is a socio — political animal. A man does not only depend on society for the satisfaction of his material means, i.e., for his survival, but especially for the attainment of his intellectual and human needs. Society is a medium in which a person actualizes the powers or forces which are peculiar to his growth as a human reality. In this medium he shares with others values, language, practices, beliefs, symbols, myths, duties, customs, major social and historical events, and a world outlook in general. The fabric of the experiences which move, indeed actuate, our individual lives is inconceivable apart from the communal, social structure within which the character — and therefore the destiny of the individual — is fashioned. What I hope, want, or feel ; what I plan, desire, or do; and what I dream, expect, or create is inconceivable if it does not relate to others: whatever I do, even if what is done is for myself, relates or points to another or to the social whole. When, for example, I vote, produce a work of art, complete a commercial bargain, or go to church my experience in any one of these or similar occasions involves the well — being of others in some way or another. Consider, for example, the idea of 'moral experience' or 'duty' — if I were alone on an island like Robinson Crusoe, what meaning can we attach to the idea of duty? Would such an idea come up in the first place? The consciousness of the idea of duty is at the same time a consciousness of the idea of right. A right I seek, or for which I am entitled, implies that someone else has a *duty* to respect my right. But what is right? A privilege, an entitlement? From whom? Under what conditions can it be attained? The very consciousness of right, or of duty, emerges in the social conditions of life when man faces, encounters, man, not as an animal but as a human reality, as a complex of spiritual potentialities awaiting realization. Consider again the idea of creation — what does it mean to create a work of art? Why? The very idea of creation, especially in art, implies communication, sharing; it implies that a human being, viz., the artist, has something to offer to someone, to someone who can grasp the *value* embodied in the created work. But if this someone does not exist, would the artist create his work? Would he in the first place exist *as artist*? The point which I wish to stress is that the *human* in man acquires its substance and meaning only in a social, i.e., communal, medium and outside this medium man remains a natural, i.e., animal, being. This, it seems to me, is the significance of Hegel's allusion to Aristotle's famous statement in *Natural Law*: "the state comes by nature before the individual; if the individual in isolation is not anything self — sufficient, he must be related to he whole state in one unity, just as other parts are to their whole. But a man incapable of communal life, or who is self — sufficing that he does not need it, is no part of the state and must be either a beast or a god."[28]

As human, a member of the state cannot, then, be viewed as numerically independent, i.e., discretely. His relationship to the world may be viewed as an organic relationship; he is an organ of a spiritual, cultural, yet living whole. This whole is not the physical, natural piece of land on which the people carry on their daily affairs where to an outside observer everyone seems to be pre — occupied with his own business, but rather the unity of the values, ideas, symbols, language, emotional dispositions, dreams, hopes, in short the spiritual tapestry which delineates the history of the people as a cultured unity, that is, as objective mind.

The ethical order plays an important role in the life of this mind, for it is the highest embodiment of the rational, ethical will of the people. It is the unity of what they take to be good and right. This is why Hegel calls it 'ethical totality' or 'ethical substance'. When a person is initiated into the ethical order of his society he acquires an ethical identity; he acquires an ethical substance which colors and conditions not only the way he looks upon other human beings but also the way he makes his ethical decisions. In receiving this identity he in effect participates in the ethical life of the state; he becomes a member of the ethical community. He reflects, mirrors, in his being the fundamental ethical values which are acknowledged as valid and in virtue of which he directs and structures his life. He becomes, in other words, an organ of the ethical whole. This is why Hegel says, as we have just seen, "the essence of the ethical life of the individual is *the* real and therefore universal absolute ethical life; the ethical life of the individual is one pulse beat of the whole system and is itself the whole system." We should here stress the last four words in the sentence, for the ethical nature which the individual acquires is not superior or higher either in content or in rank to the individual. This is why he (1) is not subordinate to it and (2) can transcend it. The relationship which holds between the individual and the ethical totality is, as I indicated, an organic relationship: the individual is not inferior to the totality, he does not receive his ethical instruction from it, he is an organ of it, and as such influences and is influenced by it. If therefore ethical life is (1) social in character, (2) universal, and (3) acquired in ethical practice it should then follow that the ethical life of the individual is an integral element of the whole. It would also follow that one attains his moral freedom only in so far as he lives the ethical in his personal life. It would be a sad, chaotic, in fact dreary, existence if the member of a society relies for what is right or good merely on the effort of a supposed personal moral insight or intuition without general regard for the well — being and rights of others, or without a rational pinciple which articulates the fundamental interests which define the human in man.

Second, in replacing the Kantian conception of morality by the concept of ethical life, or in attempting to bring about a union between what ought — to — be and is, or between right and good, Hegel does not in any way intend to ignore or undermine the being or importance of morality, or conscience. On the contrary, as I stressed in the second part of this essay, the individual has the incontestable right to subjectivity, to self — determination, and to act according to the judgment of his own conscience. His concept of *Sittlichkeit* relates specifically to social, objective duties which are entailed by the laws and institutions of the state. The domain of ethical life does not include or exhaust the moral domain nor does it exclude the Categorical Imperative. The realm of practical life in which people are related to each other as friends, husbands, wives, sons, daughters, neighbors, etc., may include vague situations or relations which are either unique or have escaped the normal run of custom. When such situations or relations arise the individual involved should rely on his moral conscience. But when we speak of conscience we should not understand by this term a vacuous or abstract faculty, on the one hand, or an already determined moral sentiment, on the other, but rather the unity of virtues which interpenetrate the moral character of the individual. Thus when one faces a moral problem he approaches it with a certain ethical disposition, or outlook; this disposition is, broadly speaking, the actuality of the values or norms which are upheld in the state. It would I think be helpful if I underscore a point I made earlier: viz., Hegel is vehemently critical of the notion that morality can be legislated: "in matters relating to marriage, love, religion, and the state, the only aspects which can become the subject of legislation are those of such a nature as to permit of their being in principle external . . . . Similarly, the legislation of the ancients in earlier times was full of precepts about uprightness and integrity which are unsuited by nature to legal enactment because they fall wholly within the field of the inner life. It is only in the case of the oath, whereby things are brought to conscience, that uprightness and integrity must be taken into account as the substance of the matter." (Add. to § 213)

When Hegel argues that a person is moral inasmuch as he does his duty

— viz., the duty prescribed by the established laws and institutions — his act does not have a moral character unless it is conscientiously done, i.e., unless it is intended, thoughtfully executed, and unless the agent can be held responsible for the act: "the moral man is not he who merely wills and does that which is right — not the merely innocent man — but he who has the consciousness of what he is doing."[29] What merits special emphasis here is that, for Hegel, an act of duty is essentially the same act which Kant, Fichte, and others have characterized as moral. What distinguishes Hegel's view from those held by these philosophers is that the content of the moral for him, viz., my duty or what *I* should do in the course of my daily life, exists as custom, *Sitte*, within the state as a rational social structure.

Conscience remains, for Hegel, "both the power to judge, to determine from within itself alone, what is good in respect of any content, and also the power to which the good, at first only an ideal and an ought — to — be, owes its actuality." (§ 138) This power remains effective in two types of circumstance: (A) when there is a clash between duties, and (B) when the existing ethical order becomes ossified, empty, or incongruous with the moral spirit of the people.

(A) Hegel is sensitive to the possible clash of obligations; but he is also aware that many a so — called clash is not genuine, mainly "because moral reflection can manufacture clashes of all sorts to suit its purpose and give itself a consciousness of being something special and having made sacrifices." (§ 150) It is accordingly imperative that before one falls a victim to an unreal conflict of duties he should determine within himself with the utmost of intellectual and emotional honesty that the conflict is real. But even if the conflict is real the person involved should not be at a loss, for his moral self — consciousness which is grounded in his ethical, i.e., virtuous, character should intuit what is right and good both in view of the universal moral law and the factual elements of the moral situation.[30] The conceptual moral and ethical apparatus which I discussed in the preceding pages provides, it seems to me, a viable framework within which one can settle situations of conflict of duties.

(B) The gist of the charge which seems to worry my critic is the possible subordination of the citizen to an ultimate, unquestionable, ethical order, for after all if the ethical 'second nature' which the individual acquires in the process of social growth reflects the fundamental values of the ethical order, what then inclines the citizen to criticize or reject the said order? Hegel is alive to this problem; he is quite aware that the legal systems of the world are not always expressive of the moral will of the people. He is also aware that a people may outgrow its legal code. The world scene at the present is a living example of how many a people feel the decadence, and in some cases irrelevance, of their legal codes to their lives as cultured human beings. For example, a movement was formed in the United States some years ago calling for the revaluation and re — writing of the constitution. The citizens which engineered this movement felt that the existing constitution is *dé modé* and does not suit the present values, aspirations, and interests of the American people. Thus it should be possible for the nation to have a public debate on the matter. I discussed the political aspect of this question in the first essay. Here I shall restrict myself to the moral aspect only.

The individual for Hegel is not under the mercy of the existing ethical order primarily because he is armed with a moral consciousness, or conscience; he is armed with the power to reflect not only on what is given as right and good but also on what ought to be right and good. Because of corruption, chaos, or necessary historical change, the established ethical order may fail to satisfy a man's desire for higher, freer moral life. If this happens, an individual has the right to search deep into his inner moral consciousness for a richer, deeper meaning of right or good; he has the right to intiut and articulate a richer, yet more rational, moral content. We may cite, with Hegel, historical figures like Socrates and Luther, but it seems to me that there is amongst us many a person who follows the pattern of these figures. This point is made clear in paragraph 138: "as one of the commoner features of history (e.g. in Socrates, the Stoics, and others), the tendency to look deeper into oneself and to know and determine from within oneself what is right and good appears when what is recognized as right and good in contemporary manners cannot satisfy the will of better men. When the existing world of freedom becomes faithless to the will of better men, that will fails to find itself in the duties there recognized and must try to find in the ideal world of the inner life alone the harmony which actuality has lost. Once self — consciousness has grasped and secured its formal right in this way, everything depends on the character of the content which it gives to itself." (§ 38)[31] What we should learn from this passage is that (1) the individual for Hegel is not a passive but a dynamic being capable of inwardness and the capacity to grasp the meaning of the right and the good not only in their concrete, determinate, but also in their universal being. He is therefore able to compare, evaluate, and judge whether an existing ethical order does satisfy the requirements of human freedom (Cf. § 279) (2) The individual is *inherently* capable of moral growth and development; for without this basic assumption moral education and progress would be inconceivable. Towards the end of the *Philosophy of Right* Hegel raises the question of the perfectibility and education of the human race. He believes that such education, or perfectibility, would not be possible unless we hold, as he did, that an individual is capable of moral change and reform. (§ 343)

Third, true moral growth and develoment of the individual is not possible unless the ethical order is itself dynamic, unless the state is structured in such a way that its laws can change with the spiritual change and progress of its people. But in order for a state to exist the people who compose it should enjoy a measure of moral and political consciousness; they should enjoy a sense of freedom, otherwise the whole political structure would become static. The state would then sink into the level of civil society or it would assume a despotic or oligarchical type of government.

The essence of the state which we are studying, however, is law, the rational will of the people; it is, as I have argued so far, an ethical order. As such, it is the unity of its actual, historical being, on the one hand, and its ideal of itself, on the other: spiritual activity is its fabric, or substance. This is why Hegel holds that the state as the actuality of the ethical Idea is a living reality. This doctrine is central to *The Philosophy of History*. Here we are told that the state is "a living, universal Spirit, but which is at the same time the self — conscious Spirit of the individuals composing the community."[32] In an earlier work, *System of Ethical Life*, we also read: "this ethical life is a living, independent mind (*Geist*); it appears as Briareus with myriads of eyes, arms and other limbs, each one of which is an absolute individual and absolute universal; by reference to the individual, every part of this universality, everything that belongs to it, appears as an object, an end."[33] And finally in the *Philosophy of Right*: "the state exists immediately in custom, mediately in individual self — consciousness, knowledge, and activity, while self-consciousness in virtue of its sentiment towards the state finds in the state, as its essence and the end and product of its activity, its substantative freedom." (§ 257) I draw on these works only to focus attention on an important issue which has been haunting us throughout this discussion, viz., the relationship between the *natural*, universal, law of reason and morality, or in Hegel's language the *ethical order*. We can begin our discussion with the following question: Does Hegel make a distinction between natural and positive law? I raise this question for three reasons: (1) a number of scholars are, as we saw, of the opinion that Hegel dismissed from his social and political philosophy the whole idea of natural law. (2) If Hegel does not acknowledge or take into serious consideration a certain concept of 'natural' law, if he admits only what is usually known as 'positive' law, or if he holds that the ethical order emerges necessarily in the course of historical progress, then all my labor in the preceding pages would be rendered helpless, for if a universal, rational, basis of morality is not admitted it is useless, indeed meaningless, to discuss intelligibly any aspect of moral life or experience. (3) If we hold that ethical life is dynamic, if it is capable of growth, then we need a higher principle or criterion not only as the guideline of the growth but also as its measure or standard.

Hegel makes a distinction, to begin with, between natural and positive law. His concept of abstract law (Recht) with which he begins his analysis of the state and on which his conception of the state and political reality is based is what is usually known as 'natural law', *jus naturale*. "The subject matter," he writes, "of the philosophical science of right is the Idea of right, i.e., the concept of right with actualization of that concept." (§ 1) Accordingly Hegel's interest in the *Philosophy of Right* is not restricted merely to the concept, i.e., essence or universal nature of law, Recht, as such but also includes the way this essence becomes actual in the history of mankind. Again, in the first addition to the Preface he clearly states: "laws are of two kinds — laws of nature and laws of the land. The laws of nature simply are what they are and are valid as they are; they are not liable to encroachment, though in certain cases man may transgress them." The laws of the land, viz., positive laws, are "something posited, something originated by men." (*Ibid.*) The diversity "at once draws attention to the fact that they are not absolute; on the contrary, they are relative. What is right or good in one society differs from what is right or good in the other societies of the world. Moreover, we may in general articulate universal laws, laws that are judged by reason as valid, like: "in your action do what is right and promote your welfare and the welfare of others," or, "be a person and respect others as persons." In other words, it may seem easy to see how a specific society translates to its own satisfaction the meaning of right or good or for a philosopher to pronounce the universal principle of right and good according to the highest intuition of reason; but Hegel is not interested in justifying this or that positive or universal law but in how a society can articulate that constitution in accordance with its highest achievements and values. He sought to obviate early in his study "at once any possible supposition, let alone demand, that the outcome of its systematic developent should be a code of positive law, i.e., a code like the one an actual state requires." (§ 3) His main concern was to provide a rational framework within which the universal content of the natural law may become concrete in the positive law of a nation and as such actualize the highest degree of freedom in the lives of its people.

In characterizing the relationship between the universal and the particular in *Reason in History*, Hegel writes: "the first thing we notice — something which has been stressed more than once before but which cannot be repeated too often, for it belongs to the central point of our enquiry — is the merely general and abstract nature of what we call principle, final purpose, destiny, or the nature of the concept of spirit. A principle, a law, is something implicit, which as such, however true in itself, is not completely real (actual). Purposes, principles, and the like, are at first in our thoughts, our inner intention. They are not yet in reality. That which is in itself is a possibility, a faculty. It has not emerged out of its implicitness into existence. A second element must be added for it to become reality, namely, activity, actualization. The principle of this is the will, man's activity in general. It is only through this activity that the concept and its implicit ("being — in — themselves") determinations can be realized, actualized; for of themselves they have no immediate efficacy. The activity which puts them in operation and in existence is the need, the instinct, the inclination, and passion of man. When I have an idea I am greatly interested in transforming it into action, into actuality. In its realization through my participation I want to find my own satisfaction."[34] I quote this important passage at length to stress that, for Hegel, in the philosophical study of the state we should concentrate our efforts not only on the universal but especially on how the universal should become concrete and relevant in the life of a people. It is easy to speak of ideals, utopias, or universal principles, but the main question should be: given a society in a certain spot on the earth and in a certain historical period of development, what is the best constitution for this society? What sort of constitution would create the best conditions for the realization of human freedom? To espouse beautiful or noble ideals, ideals approved by the abstract taste of reason alone, is naive: "these ideals, which in the voyage of life founder on the rocks of hard reality, may be merely subjective to begin with and belong to the peculiarity of an individual who regards himself as supremely wise. Such ideals do not belong here. For what an individual fancies for himself in his isolation cannot be the norm or universal reality. The universal law is not designed for individuals, as such, who indeed may find themselves very much the losers."[35] It is designed, as I argued earlier, for the whole people as a living historical reality. Thus the task of the legislator, which is the main interest of the political philosopher, is: how is a positive law to be derived from natural law? We should consider this question for at least two reasons: (1) natural law is not a law in the ordinary sense of 'law'; accordingly the activity of deriving a rule or a principle from it requires both clarification and justification. (2) What counts in fact is the positive law, the law which regulates the actual life of a people, or the way the natural law is understood or interpreted concretely; accordingly we should examine the criteria according to which a positive law is enacted.

I have already discussed in some detail Hegel's view of how right in general becomes positive and the conditions under which a positive law may be considered as valid. Here I should add two more observations: (1) in formulating a law, the legislator should be sensitive to the practical reality of society — to its economic, religious, artistic, and social needs;

he should fashion (or modify) a law that can relate and apply "to the material of civil society (i.e., to the endlessly growing complexity and subdivision of social ties) and the different species of property and contract within the society." (§ 213 (2) The legislator should be sensitive to the moral sentiment and values of society; the law which he enacts should be consistent with its moral ideals — indeed it should embody these ideals. The law should not violate or undermine the moral customs (*Sitten*) and principles which are cherished by the people; on the contrary, it should ennoble and uplift them. (*Ibid.*) In advancing this criterion Hegel does not at all mean to say, as I argued earlier, that morality can, or should be, legislated. He does mean to say, though, that a valid law should express the moral sentiment and aspirations of the people (Cf. L. Fuller) and the fundamental obligation of justice: "a lack of skill in formulating the true ethical principles as laws, and the fear of thinking these principles, of regarding them, as one's own, and acknowledging them, is the sign of barbarism".[36]

It does not necessarily follow, however, that once a law is enacted it is therefore absolute or cannot be questioned. Hegel repeatedly stressed that positive law is something created by men, that it can always be distorted or one — sided. What is right and rational is not the exclusive specialty of the legislator. Every human being has within him the power to reflect and to intuit what is right; he can therefore judge a certain law as bad or unjust: "in nature, the highest truth is that there is a *law*; in the law of the land, the thing is not valid simply because it exists; on the contrary, everyone demands that it shall comply with his private criterion. Here then an antagonism is possible between what ought to be and what is, between the absolutely right which stands unaltered and the arbitrary determination of what is to be recognized as right." (Add. to Preface, p. 4) It is this antagonism between the inner sense of right and the right posited in the written law which creates an occasion and need for legal reform.[37]

Thus a law is valid in the state inasmuch as it is ethical, and it is ethical inasmuch as it is rational, and it is rational inasmuch as it expresses the interests and moral values of the people, i.e., inasmuch as it is conducive to human freedom. Only when this condition is fulfilled does the good which the law embodies become a living good; i.e., the good which the ethical Idea intuits. Accordingly this sort of law is not static but dynamic, for it remains a living expression of the will of the people. The political structure which Hegel develops in the *Philosophy of Right* and which I discussed in the first two essays provides an exemplary machinery for the modification, deletion, or institution of laws in general.

The crux of the issue which occupied our attention in this essay is the *identity* of *the ethical*, or the content of my duty here and now. A concrete yet intelligible answer to this question is at the same time a concrete and intelligible answer to the question of moral freedom. I become morally free when I do my duty and when the maxim of my act is legislated by my will, or when the maxim on which I act expresses the moral value which I can claim as mine. Hegel's concept of *Sittlichkeit* which I discussed and defended in the foregoing pages is an attempt to remedy the abstractness of the Kantian moral point of view, on the one hand, and to provide a reasoned account of a rational basis of ethical conduct, on the other. The essential feature of this concept is: the law of the state, the genuinely organized state, expresses the highest moral and rational values of the people as an organic whole, as a *human community*; they express, in other words, my moral will as a member of the state. Hence in acting on these laws I do not only realize my ethical nature as a human being but I also attain my moral freedom, and I attain this freedom primarily because these laws are the laws of my will as a self — determined being.

FOUR
LOVE AS THE BASIS OF THE FAMILY

Let us grant, for the sake of argument, my critic would object, that Hegel has made a distinction between a universal or natural law and a human law, let us also grant that the universal law is, for him, superior to the human, or state, law, in other words, let us grant that Hegel upholds the being and integrity of *moral conscience* as a faculty capable of knowing and revolting against a bad law or social practice — does Hegel allow for the growth of this conscience? Does he account for a social structure within which conscience can develop as a rational, autonomous faculty aware of the universal moral demands, on the one hand, and the practical, factual conditions of individual life, on the other? In raising these questions, my critic is certainly anxious to focus our attention on the family as a fundamental building block of society within which the character of the citizen is nourished or, perhaps, fashioned.[1] This point merits special attention, for if the family is the basic social institution in which the ethical order of the state becomes concrete and living in the life of the people, if it is the institution in which the growing child is initiated into citizenship, then we must ask whether this institution is based on a rational foundation, i.e., whether it is in its very structure conducive to human freedom. Again, if the family is the main arena and guardian of the ethical order, if this order is given as a supreme authority in the life of the society, and if it is the principle according to which the ethical, virtuous disposition of the youth is to be cultivated, how can one develop, or acquire, a critical moral faculty? How can one escape the ultimate will or authority of the state as a positive historical reality? Does the family as Hegel envisions it allow for the gowth of critical moral conscience? Does it allow for the growth of *human individuality*. I say 'human individuality' primarily because only an *individual* can know what it means to have a conscience and can act according to it. In its very essence, conscience is a critical, thoughtful, valuative, and deliberative faculty. One cannot have it, or live by it, unless he is free. Again, conscience is not a passive but active, creative power in human nature. Making a sound moral judgment requires insight, intelligence, skill, and virtuous disposition. These characteristics cannot be acquired by theoretical study, lecturing, or mere imitation but by experience — i.e., by suggestion, emphasis, counsel, rational direction, and creating an atmosphere in which the growing child is aware of the dignity and validity of moral values. One becomes good, virtuous, by doing good, virtuous, deeds. But the actual conditions of human life are always variable and changing. Thus acting, or being moral, requires a creative moral attitude, an attitude in which a person translates wisely and responsibly the universal content of the moral law concretely. The development of this attitude is a *sine qua non* for the art of making sound moral judgments and, consequently, of moral freedom.

Now, where can one acquire this attitude? For Hegel, mainly in the family. This institution is essential for the cultivation of human individuality as such, for it is the medium in which the ethical substance, or order becomes concrete, effective, and relevant to the actual life of a people: "ethical life is not abstract like the good, but is intensely actual". (Add. to § 156) This is why he insisted that a family cannot perform this function properly unless its basis is rational or ethical, or unless it is a sanctuary of human freedom. The assumption which underlies my discussion in this essay is: one learns how to be free — morally, socially, politically, or intellectually — by doing, practising free action. Family is the first, indeed most basic, sphere in which one learns the art of being free. Thus only in a *free family* can a child learn how to practice this art. By 'free family' I here understand what is now known as a 'nuclear' family, a social structure in which every member exists under the conditions of freedom. The propositions which I intend to elucidate and defend in this essay are: (1) love is, for Hegel, the basis of the family. On this premise he erects the family on an ethical foundation. (2) The family is an essential sphere of human freedom. (3) In the family parents and children actualize their ethical nature. I shall retain Hegel's titles in my discussion of these propositions.

I. *Marriage*

The foundation, or basic principle, of the family is, for Hegel, love: "the family, as the immediate substantiality of mind, is specifically characterized by love, which is mind's feeling of its own unity." (§ 158) That is, an association of two or more human beings (viz., husband, wife, and children) acquires the character of 'family' when these human beings are related to one another by a tie, nexus, of love. This nexus *relates*, or gathers, the members of the association into a *unity* in which each individual does not exist as an independent person but as a member. "In a family," Hegel writes, "one's frame of mind is to have self — consciousness of one's individuality within this unity as the absolute essence of oneself, with the result that one is in it not as an independent person but as a member." (*Ibid.*) Accordingly, in order to understand the meaning, or being, of the family *qua* family we should analyze or explore the essential features of love as it exists between its various members, first between husband and wife and then between parents and children.

The first dimension of love which is the source and *raison d'être* of the family is marriage. Marriage is a relationship in which man and woman become at first husband and wife and later on parents. What is the basis of this relationship? What is its end? Hegel rejects, to begin with, three views on the basis or end of marriage. According to the first view, usually found in theories of natural law, "attention was paid to the physical side of marriage or to its natural character. Consequently, it was treated only as a sex relationship, and this completely barred the way to its other characteristics." (Add. to § 161) Hegel characterizes this view as crude, for it reduces man to a natural object, to an object motivated in his endeavors by instinct or impulse. But man is a spiritual being; thus the bond which relates two huan beings for the sake of mutual existence and the creation and promotion of life should be spiritual, it should reflect and embody the higher spiritual demands of human nature. According to the second view, the basis of marriage is love alone; but this view, Hegel insists, must be rejected, "since love is only feeling and so is exposed in every respect to contingency, a guise which ethical life may not assume." (*Ibid.*)

According to the third view, which was propounded in Kant's *Philosophy of Law*, marrige is a civil contract. The parties "are bound by a contract of mutual caprice, and marriage is thus degraded to the level of a contract for reciprocal use." (*Ibid.*) But a human being cannot be 'used'; he is not a thing or an entity that can be used by another human being under any conditions whatever and for any purpose whatever. As a rational, self — conscious, self — determined being man is an end in himself. On more than one occasion Hegel points out this weakness in Kant's conception of the family. Early in the section on Abstract Right Hegel stresses that "the object about which a contract is made is a single external thing, since it is only things of that kind which the parties' purely abitrary will has it in its power to alienate." Accordingly, "to subsume marriage under the concept of contract is thus quite impossible; this subsumption — though shameful is the only word for it — is propounded in Kant's *Philosophy of Law* " (§ 75) Again, "the reason I can alienate my property is that it is mine only in so far as I put my will into it. Hence I may abandon (*derelinquere*) as a *res nullius* anything that I have or yield it to the will of another and so into his possession, provided always that the thing in question is a thing external by nature . . . . Therefore those goods, or rather substantative characteristics, which constitute my own private personality and the universal essence of my self — consciousness are inalienable and my right to them is imprescribable. Such characteristics are my personality as such, my universal freedom of will, my ethical life, my religion." (§ 65—66)[2] This is the main reason why human beings cannot be owned as slaves, treated as objects, or subordinated to the will of another person or ruler. Although it begins, as I shall presently indicate, in contract, marriage, for Hegel, is not a contractual relation; "it is precisely a contract to transcend the standpoint of contract, the standpoint from which persons are regarded in their individuality as subsistent units." (§ 163) In the marital relationship a partner does not give up an aspect of his or her personality, or an object of possession, but the whole personality: one surrenders himself unto the other. This activity undermines the very meaning and being of contract.

The ground on which a man and a woman give themselves to each other in marriage is love; that is, the tie which holds them together, and thereby the whole family, is not a physical, legal, social, or emotional tie, but a spiritual one: "Love means in general terms the consciousness of my unity with another, so that I am not in selfish isolation but win my self — consciousness only as the renunciation of my independence and through knowing myself as the unity of myself with another and of the other with me." (Add. to § 158) In this statement Hegel provides an answer to one of the most difficult quesions which was raised by Plato sometime ago, viz., what is the reason of love? What underlies its thrust, or urge? Love is an urge for union, or better *being*, with another person. In this union I abandon my independence as a selfish, or atomistic, existence and share the world of another person. Like Plato, Hegel assumes that on his own, an individual is incomplete, dependent. One knows and becomes essentially complete in and through another person. Although Hegel discusses this point in detail in early fragments and *First Philosophy of Spirit* it does not escape his attention in the *Philosophy of Right*. Here he writes: "the first moment in love is that I do not wish to be a self — subsistent and independent person and that, if I were, then I would feel defective and incomplete. The second moment is that I find myself in another person, that I count for something in the other, while the other in turn comes to count for something in me. Love, therefore, is the most tremendous contradiction; the Understanding cannot resolve it since there is nothing more stubborn than this point (*Punktualität*) of self — consciousness which is negated and which nevertheless I ought to possess as affirmative. Love is at once the propounding and the resolving of this contradiction. As the resolving of it, love is the unity of an ethical type." (*Ibid.*)[3] I should here make two remarks: (1) love is a complex feeling; its richness resists conceptual or discursive articulation. Yet it is an essential urge, or demand, in human nature. It underlies our sensitive, cognitive, and affective nature and is perhaps the ultimate source of passion and drive for the higher attainments in human life. (2) As a cry for union with the other, love is the realization of a basic type of freedom — social freedom. How? *Sociality* consists in with — ness, or being with another person, or sharing the being of another person, not externally as it happens in civil society but internally on a spiritual level. In love I entertain the being of the other into me, while my being is entertained wholly by the other. I am also conscious of this mutual interchange, in which a third type of consciousness emerges, the consciousness which gathers my and the other's consciousnesses into a higher unity, in which although the two are united they nevertheless remain individuals; indeed their individuality is, on the level of being or feeling, attained in this consciousness or unity. This very attainment is an attainent of freedom. For to be free is, as we saw, to exist as an individual, or as a self — conscious, self — determined being. It means to exist for and from oneself; but in love this mode of being is achieved in and through the other.

As an ethical union, marriage contains two elements, or moments; the first is physical and the second is spiritual. (1) In a marriage the physical life of the individual is created and nourished. Sexual union is the activity, or practice, in which this end is achieved. We should accordingly grant that, from this standpoint, marriage is essential to the preservation of the human species; its unity and integrity underlie the unity and integrity of the race as such. (2) But man is not only body; he is also a mind. The sexual union is momentary, one — sided; it leaves the man and the woman external to each other, i.e., with a feeling that they are separate from each other. Hence it is not a genuine union. To become genuine, the sexual union must be "changed into a union on the level of mind, into self — conscious love." (§ 161) How does this change occur? Under what conditions does love become the *ethical tie* of marriage?

First, in order for love, and consequently for marriage, to acquire an ethical character the man and the woman must seek and consumate it *freely*. The objective source of marriage, Hegel states, "lies in the free consent of the persons, especially in their consent to make themselves one person, to renounce their natural and individual personality to this unity of one with the other. From this point of view, their union is a self — restriction, but in fact it is their liberation, because in it they attain their substantative self — consciousness." (§ 162) To what extent is this condition possible, especially if we take into serious consideration the awkward, and in some cases irrational, historical structure of the family both in the West and in the East? Hegel is aware of this aspect; he is aware that marriages were in many cases arranged by parents or members of the immediate family, while in others by the particular inclination of the partners. How a man and a woman are related to each other in love is, for Hegel, a contingent, external matter; "it depends on the extent to which reflective thought has been developed. At one extreme, the first step is that the marriage is arranged by the contrivance of benevolent parents; "the appointed end of the parties is a union of mutual love, and their inclination to marry arises from the fact that each grows acquainted with the other from the first as a destined partner. At the other extreme, it is the inclination of the parties which comes first appearing in them *as these* two infinitely particularized individuals. " (*Ibid*.) The question as to which of these two methods is more rational or ethical should here be raised. One can advance objections to both of them. If we espouse the first we would certainly ignore the will of the man or woman, and if we espouse the second we would run the risk of capricious or arbitrary decision — making. Hegel is aware of both defects. He cites societies in which the female sex, e.g., was given away in marriage without her will or knowledge. The woman in such societies lacked a sense of individuality. Marriage, for her, "is only a matter of getting a husband," while for the man, "of getting a wife." "In other social conditions, considerations of wealth, connexions, political ends, may be the determining factor. In such circumstances, great hardships may arise through making marriage a means to other ends. Nowadays, however, the subjective origin of marriage, the state of being in love, is regarded as the only important originating factor. Here the position is represented to be that a man must wait until his hour has struck and that he can bestow his love only on one specific individual." (Add. to § 162) But the hour may never strike! And even if it strikes, there is no absolute certainty that the marriage will be the highest example of love. In our own day we witness some of the saddest consequences of this method in building a marriage. The view that romantic love, or the mere presence of romantic passion in the young lovers, as the basis of marriage does not seem to lead to successful marriages. The high divorce rate and the spread of marriage clinics is enough to show the validity of this remark. This is I think the main reason why Hegel stressed the role of parents in selecting a marriage partner. The parents are older, more experienced; therefore they are supposed to know more about the practical aspect of human life and its problems. They should accordingly bring with their opinion, or counsel, a measure of wisdom. But regardless of what method one employs in establishing a marriage, what counts for Hegel is whether the partners have consented to marry each other willingly, freely.

Second, in order for love as the basis of marriage to be an ethical tie the partners should be conscious of their unity "as their substantative aim, and so in their love, trust, and common sharing of their entire existence as individuals." (§ 163) Thus marriage is a union of two minds. Subjectively, this union becomes concrete, actual, in the daily activities which husband and wife undertake for the sake of their life. It is in this medium of actual conduct that love assumes its spiritual actuality: sharing implies trust, for what is shared is not an object or an event but *human life*, the concrete lives of individuals. In this activity what is shared is given as a free gift. But in giving one receives: to give oneself, or of oneself, to the other means to receive the other unto oneself. Only in this way can love exist as a bond, for bond establishes, if it truly exists, a union between the elements of which it is a bond, otherwise the elements would remain external to each other. Thus a family based on love is a person with one mind: "the identification of personalities whereby the family becomes one person and its members become its accidents (though substance is in essence the relation of accidents to itself), is the ethical mind." (*Ibid.*) When Hegel characterizes the family as mind or person he does not mean to deny its physical, material, or even psychological basis. Physical desire, sexual or otherwise, does have its place in the family life, but within this sphere it acquires a spiritual character. Thus love cannot be viewed as something divorced from sex or the material, social domains of life. The attempt to relegate it to the life of the mind as if this faculty exists in and by itself apart from the body is a mistake: "it is a further abstraction still to separate the divine, or the substantative from its body, and then to stamp it, together with the feeling and consciousness of mental unity, as what is falsely called 'Platonic love'." (*Ibid.*) As a bond, then, love is onmipresent in the whole being of the family. Two consequences follow from this premise. In the first place, marriage cannot, or should not, be dissolved: "the spiritual bond of union secures its rights as the substance of marriage and thus rises, inherently indissoluble, to a plane above the contingency of passion and the transience of particular caprice." (*Ibid.*) We should here stress 'inherently indissoluble', because Hegel does not mean to say that once a man and a woman are married they cannot under any conditions whatever be separated; he allows, for example, that when the heart has become hard divorce may be granted. (Cf. § 176) What he means to say, however, is that marriage cannot be dissolved *in principle*, since "the end of marriage is the ethical end, an end so lofty that everything else is manifestly powerless against it and made subject to it." (Add. to § 163) Romantic, passionate affairs, internal disorders, or material misfortunes should not be viewed as valid causes of divorce; and since love exists as a feeling, and since this feeling is not always rational or mature, the state should prohibit, or discourage, divorce as much as possible: "legislation, however, must make its dissolution as difficult as possible and uphold the right of the ethical order against caprice." (*Ibid.*) In the second place, marriage is monogomous. Accordingly a partner cannot participate or allow himself, or herself, to participate in the being of another. It would indeed be contradictory to say that a person in love with one person can establish a similar relation with a second person, because the act of love is, inasmuch as it involves the surrender of the total personality, an exclusive act. Thus if I give my person to some one in exchange of the one's person it would be inconceivable for me to do the same with another person simultaneously. This is why Hegel holds that "in essence marriage is monogamy because it is personality — immediate exclusive individuality — which enters into this tie and surrenders itself to it; and hence the tie's truth and inwardness (i.e., the subjective form of its substantiality) proceeds only from the mutual, whole — hearted, surrender of this personality. Personality attains its right of being conscious of itself in another only in so far as the other is in this identical relationship as a person, i.e. as an atomic individual." (§ 167)

Third, in order for love as the basis of marriage to be an ethical bond it should be declared and agreed upon legally and socially: "the solemn declaration of the parties of their consent to enter the ethical bond of marriage, and its corresponding recognition and confirmation by the family and the community, constitutes the formal completion and actuality of marriage. The knot is tied and made ethical only after this ceremony, whereby by the use of signs, i.e. of language (the most mental embodiment of mind — see paragraph 78), the substantial thing in the marriage is brought completely into being." (§ 164) Accordingly marriage is an *ethical contract*. What makes it ethical is not merely the verbal or written agreement to proceed with it, nor the presence of the social or official witnesses during the event, but mainly the fact that it is the concretization of love or union between the parties concerned: it is, or should be, binding legally, but the ground of this binding is the ethical content of the contract; this is why Hegel characterizes it, contra Kant, as ethico — legal in nature. Its legal aspect gives the marriage stability and endurance and eliminates from it " the transient, fickle, and purely subjective aspect of love." (Add. to § 161) This aspect, however, cannot be exhausted or reduced to one single factor of the whole phenomenon of marriage: love, legal contract, ceremony. All these factors are organically constitutive of the ethical foundation of marriage: "if with a view to framing or criticizing legal enactments, the question is asked: what is to be regarded as the chief end of marriage?, the question may be taken to mean: which single facet of marriage in its actuality is to be regarded as the most essential one? No one facet by itself, however, makes up the whole range of its implicit and explicit content, i.e. of its ethical character, and one or other of its facets may be lacking in an existing marriage without detriment to the essence of marriage itself." (§ 164) Thus if, on the one hand, the wedding ceremony is viewed as an external formality, or as a 'civil requirement', the marriage would be "stripped of all significance except perhaps that of serving the purpose of edification and attesting the civil relations of the parties." (*Ibid.*) It would be reduced to "a mere *fiat* of a civil or ecclesiastical authority. As such it appears as something not merely indifferent to the true nature of marriage, but actually alien to it." (*Ibid.*) And since it is not an expression of their will it becomes an external imposition on their hearts to care or be loyal to each other; "as such it appears to bring disunion into their loving disposition and, like an alien intruder, to thwart the inwardness of their union." (*Ibid.*) If, on the other hand, the wedding ceremony is discarded as something superfluous on the ground that love is the substance of marriage (Schlegel), marriage would be placed under the sway of passion; sexual satisfaction, not love, becomes the basis, indeed test, of marriage. But, Hegel objects, if sensual impulse is considered "necessary to prove the freedom and inwardness of love," marriage would certainly lose its ethical character — its depth and sanctity; but the ethical character, Hegel contends, " consists in this, that the consciousness of the parties is crystallized out of its physical and subjective mode and lifted to the thought of what is substantative." (*Ibid.*)

Hegel holds that man and woman are polar in nature; one of the poles is masculine and the other is feminine in nature. This polarity is, as we saw, essential to the continuation of the race. But it also reveals an "intellectual and ethical significance," (§ 165) Accordingly, although both sexes are essentially mind, the man is in virtue of his physical and intellectual make — up suited to pursue ends which are peculiar to the public, objective world, i.e., to the state: "man has his actual substantative life in the state, in learning, and so forth, as well as in labour and struggle with the external world and with himself so that it is only out of his diremption that he fights his way to self — subsistent unity with himself. In the family he has a tranquil intuition of this unity, and there he lives a subjective ethical life on the plane of feeling." (§ 166) The woman fulfills herself as an individual, she has "her substantative destiny," in the family. She is not "made for activities which demand a universal faculty such as the more advanced sciences, philosophy, and certain forms of artistic production. Women may have happy ideas, taste, and elegance, but they cannot attain to the ideal." (Add. to § 166) When Hegel says that she cannot attain to the universal, or ideal, he does not mean that woman cannot comprehend its meaning or significance; woman is "mind maintaining itself in unity as knowledge and volition of the substantative, but knowledge and volition in the form of concrete individuality and feeling." (§ 166) Thus although the woman does not pursue the universal discursively or philosophically she is nevertheless the living reality of its meaning and being. In her actual life she represents the highest actuality of the universal. This is the main reason why she should arm herself with family piety the way it is delineated in Sophocles' *Antigone*. This piety is here depicted "as principally the law of woman, and as the law of a substantiality at once subjective and on the plane of feeling, the law of the inward life, a life which has not yet attained its full actualization; as the law of the ancient gods, 'the gods of the underworld'; as 'an everlasting law, and no man knows at what time it was first put forth'. This law is there displayed as a law opposed to public law, to the law of the land. This is the supreme opposition in ethics and therefore in tragedy; and it is individualized in the same play in the opposing natures of man and woman." (*Ibid.*) Thus while man is the power which safeguards the external welfare and unity of the family the woman safeguards its internal welfare and unity; accordingly, they do not rule but complement one another as individual members of the family.

II. *Property*

Implicit in the preceding discussion is the assumption that, as a social institution, the family is an essential domain of freedom. As Plato and Aristotle stressed repeatedly, man is a socio — political animal; he is naturally inclined to cooperate with others for the sake of self — realization. When this inclination is for some reason ignored or restricted the individual feels defective, insufficient as a human being. He can accordingly be himself only when he fulfills his social nature; and when this aspect of his is realized he enjoys a feeling of freedom. In this feeling he is at home with himself; he is what he should be, or to put it in Hegel's language, he exists according to the concept of his will, i.e., essence. But 'social life' is not possible in the abstract. 'Sociality' is a bond, a relation between two or more human beings. Etymologically, the term, which comes from the Latin, *socius*, means companion. Thus to be social, or to enjoy social life, means to be with or share the companionship of another human being. Accordingly a social experience is an experience of 'with — ness', of 'together — ness'. In this experience there is an interchange of ideas, mutuality of feelings, and cooperation in achieving things and ends. Sociality, however, does not happen simply or 'naturally'; one does not receive his social nature the way he receives his eyes or hands. Sociality is not, in other words, a ready made faculty or function; it is a potentiality awaiting realization. It requires a rational order within which it can be cultivated and realized. But its realization is an on — going process primarily because it is an inherent, essential demand of human nature. This is why inasmuch as man is a social being he is destined to cherish some of his highest moments of freedom in the family; and this is why Hegel stressed that a citizen in the state has a right to be a family member. This right, "which the individual enjoys on the strength of the family unity and which is in the first place simply the individual's life within this unity," (§ 159) "consists in the fact that its substantiality should have determinate existence." (Add. to § 159)

Marriage is the first step, or moment, in which the family acquires a determinate existence. In this event a social bond, a bond of love, is established between two human beings. But this is not enough; the inner being of the family must assume an external, objective structure. This structure is what Hegel calls Capital, or estate, *Vermogen*: "the family, as person, has its real external existence in property; and it is only when this property takes the form of capital that it becomes the embodiment of the substantial personality of the family." (§ 169) In this paragraph Hegel states an important principle: capital, or material possession, is a necessary condition for the unity and personhood of the family. It is accordingly necessary for the integrity of the family as the most fundamental institution of the state. Why? First, capital is necessary to secure the livelihood or material survival of the family. Human survival is not a gift, but an achievement; one has to work to earn a living. This principle is implicit in the very meaning of self — determination. I am self — determined, i.e., free, not only when I realize myself as a complex of *human* potentialities but also when I secure the means of my survival. Thus if a family *qua* person is to be free, if it is to be a social milieu within which its members can exist as free agents, it should be self — sufficient materially, that is, it should possess a permanent and secure material basis, i.e., capital (*Vermogen*). Thus the right to capital is grounded in the family's right to exist; it is strictly the right to survive. In Hegel's words, "it is a right against externality and against secessions from the family unity." (Add. to § 159) Second, capital is necessary for the satisfaction of one's personal, or rather *particular*, needs; it is accordingly an essential factor in human self — determination. But the acquisiton of capital, which I shall study in the next essay, is a social, cooperative activity; it takes place in a social order of laws, institutions, customs, expectations, etc. What one does or achieves influences and is influenced by what others do or achieve. Thus one's good, or quest for self — determination, is integrally related to the good or self — determination of others or of the state as such. In this way capital ceases to be merely a means for the satisfaction of selfish desire; it acquires an ethical character and becomes a factor in promoting the general good: "the arbirariness of a single owner's needs is one moment in property taken abstractly; but this moment, together with the selfishness of desire, is here transformed into something ethical, into labour and care for a common possession." (§ 170) Capital, then, is not only a means for the survival of the family; it is also a means for its integrity as a human, ethical association.

Now, as a person, or unity, the family is a legal entity; it has certain rights and duties in relation to the state and to itself. And as a legal entity, the family should, for Hegel, be represented by the husband; the latter is its head and is accountable for its general well — being: "it is his prerogative to go out and work for its living, to attend to its needs, and to control and administer its capital." (§ 171) In giving the husband such a privilege, though calling it a privilege is questionable, Hegel does not, I think, mean or intend to grant him absolute power over the family, for the capital of the family "is common property so that, while no member of the family has property of his own, each has his right in the common stock." (*Ibid.*) Put differently, the husband is not superior to his wife and children because he secures the capital of the family or because he has legal authority over them. Why?

First, the material possession of the family is common to all its members. The assumption which underlies Hegel's view on this point is that property and material possessions are means to self — realization, not to the exercise of selfish or abnormal authority. When the husband works and accumulates capital he does so *as a member* of the family, not as a particular, self — seeking individual. Certain things in life have to be done, and they have to be done for a certain purpose. Securing the family capital is one of these things. Hegel thought that, given the socio — economic structure which was available to him at that historical period of human history the husband was the one who was qualified to achieve this purpose. Thus securing the family capital does not, and should not, make the husbnd necessarily superior, or 'better', than the other members of the family. Second, since the basis of the marriage is not legal or material contract, but love, and since this relation is established freely and knowingly, it follows that the relationship in which husband and wife stand towards each other is ethical relationship; it is one in which both partners respect and uphold the being of each other. In this sort of relationship it is meaningless to speak of superiority or superior authority. Hegel is, however, aware that husbands and wives do not usually live up to this ideal or expectation — hence the constant recurrence of injustice or mistreatment within the members of the family. The husband may be ignorant, weak, or narcissitic; accordingly, what he takes to be right, or his right, may conflict with the rights and well — being of the other members of the family: "this right, however, may come into collision with the head of the family's right of administration owing to the fact that the ethical temper of the family is still only at the level of immediacy (See § 158) and so is exposed to partition and contingency." (*Ibid.*) This is why Hegel insists that the law should take situations like this into consideration to protect the right, or what is just, for every member of the family. In paragraph 172 he remarks that "the significance of marriage settlements which impose a restriction on the couple's common ownership of their goods, of arrangements to secure continued legal assistance for the woman, and so forth, lies in their being provisions in the case of the dissolution of the marriage, either naturally or by death, or by divorce, &c. They are also safeguards for securing that in such an eventuality the different members of the family shall secure their share of the common stock."

It is important to remark here that the sort of family which Hegel has in mind is what is now known in sociological circles as the 'nuclear family', which is composed of husband, wife, and children. (Cf. add. to § 172) The essential reality of this family is a nexus of love between the parents, on the one hand, and the parents and children, on the other. This nexus underlies the being of the family as an organism, or person, and gives it its ethical character. This is based on the assumption that love is a concrete relation between two or more human beings. Since this relation is subtle, personal, and requires a long period of time, indeed a life — time, to build, the nuclear family is the ideal social institution within which it can be realized. This is why Hegel insisted that when a man and a woman marry each other to form a new family they should love their families, 'houses', or clans; and bring with them their personal possessions: "the tie between these and the new family has a natural basis — consanguinity, but the new family is based on love of an ethical type. Thus an individual's property too has an essential connexion with his conjugal relationship and only a comparatively remote one with his relation to his clan or 'house'. (*Ibid.*)

III. *Education of Children*

As the basis of the family, love is a feeling; and since feeling is a subjective experience or mode of being, love exists between husband and wife as an active, responsive consciousness in which each lives subjectively the being of the other: each lives in the consciousness of the others. Although one, in the sense that each exists in, for, and through the other, each partner is an organism, an individual. Their unity does not shatter but preserves their individuality. And precisely because in this union each partner surrenders himself or herself as an individual to the other the bond which exists between them is sacred and cannot be articulated or reduced to a contract. Thus externally, objectively, husband and wife exist as separate, unrelated; each seems to move and live in a different social or physical world. Their unity becomes concrete, actual, for the first time when they become a legal entity and acquire a home, possessions, or, as I indicated earlier, capital (*Vermogen*). The unity of their love and the consciousness of this love assumes actual embodiment in their capital, for their love for each other, which is an activity of sharing, giving, taking, achieving, or feeling the being of each other, becomes concrete, and therefore actual, in this medium for the first time.

This dimension is, however, only one moment, or element, of the complete objective reality of their love: here the unity of husband and wife "is embodied only in an external thing." (Add. to § 173) The other moment is the creation of child (or children).

The child is, for Hegel, the actual fruit or embodiment of the spiritual dimension of love, of the unity between husband and wife: "in substance marriage is a unity, though only a unity of inwardness or disposition: in outward existence, however, the unity is sundered in the two parties. It is only in the children that the unity itself exists eternally, objectively, and explicity as a unity, because the parents love the children as their love, as the embodiment of their own substance. (§ 173) The bond of love, then, becomes complete, whole, when it is objectified in the children: here the love which is the basis of marriage acquires both objectivity and validity. The parents recognize themselves and their love, or unity, for each other in their children; in this recognition their separateness is cancelled. I say 'recognition' because their unity and its objectification in their children exists exclusively on the level of consciousness, and outside this consciousness they exist for each other as separate domains of consciousness. Thus only in their children, in the recognition of them as their children, do the parents transcend their separateness and become conscious of their unity, i.e., of themselves as husband and wife, i.e., as lovers. But the mere recognition, consciousness, or intuition of the fact that their children are the embodiment of their love is not enough; this consciousness becomes concrete and a living objectification of this love only in supporting their life as human beings, that is in educating them. Husband and wife are parents only when they become conscious of the need to educate their children.

"Children," Hegel states, "have the right to maintenance and education at the expense of the family's common capital." (§ 174) One may wonder: why do children have the right to education by their parents? Because they (the children) are related to the family as members; they are essential to its structure, to its being. Therefore, their welfare is equal in value to the welfare of the other members of the family: "the welfare of the whole means the welfare of its members and the converse. To know this and to be loyal to it is the mutual *trust* which is the substantial core of social ethics. It implies that freedom for all and freedom for each are inseparable."[4] But since the child is a potential individual, since he is not born as a self — determined will, but as a potential for such a will, and since this will needs skill, cultivation, in the art of self — determination, it is the duty of the parents to provide such a skill or cultivation: "man has to acquire for himself the position which he ought to attain; he is not already in possession of it by instinct. It is on this fact that the child's right to education is based." (Add. to § 174) Thus during the process of education the child should not be exposed to situations or experiences which are not conducive to his development as a human individual. And when he is exposed to such an experience he would be deprived of a major right — the right to education: "the services which may be demanded from children should therefore have education as their sole end and be relevant thereto; they must not be ends in themselves, since a child in slavery is in the most unethical of all situations whatever." (*Ibid.*) Beside the right to education, the child has the duty to obey and respect his parents. When this duty is absent the parent has the right to punish the child. This punishement cannot, however, be imposed in order to attain or realize justice but only to improve the moral character of the child: "the punishment of children does not aim at justice as such; the aim is more subjective and moral in character, i.e. to deter them from exercising a freedom still in the toils of nature and to lift the universal into their consciousness and will." (§ 174)

My critic would at this point of my discussion object: yes, the child has the right to education by its parents; it has the right to grow up in the path of human individuality. But if this education is the responsibility of the parents, if the parents as the main pillars of the family live according to the established order of the state, if their moral, social, political, in short, spiritual consciousness, is the outcome of the existing ethical forces which rule the life of the people (Volk), how can they transcend their own subjective ethical standpoint, or the ethical standpoint of the state? It is one thing, my critic would go on, to claim that the end of education is the cultivation of human individuality and another to provide an adequate account for how this sort of cultivation is at all possible. For, on Hegel's view, the state becomes actual in its laws and institutions. The family is the most basic institution in which the central values, virtues, or ethical principles of the state are lived and transmitted to the future generations. The parents in a family may feel that they are right in what they do or believe, and that in acting according to their ideas and values they are free; but from the fact that they believe they are right or free it does not necessarily follow that their belief is true.

Before I respond to this objection I should first remark that by 'education', *Bildung*, Hegel does not simply, or only, mean the formal course of instruction which one receives in school during the early years of his life but rather the insight, knowledge, and understanding which one acquires in and through the rich spectrum of daily activities, practical or theoretical, which engage his will, or mind, in knowing the world, solving the problems which face him as a growing individual, and appreciating the beauty, mystery, order, and divinity which permeate man's experience of the world. *Bildung* is the activity which leads to the highest fruition of the potentialities which are peculiar to the human essence and whose realization, maturing (*bildet*), underlies the being of human individuality.[5]

We may focus our attention on the objection posed to us by our critic by raising the following questions: under what conditions can a child grow up as a rational, free, individual for Hegel? How does Hegel view (1) the end of education and (2) the method according to which this end can be achieved? I raise this two — fold question because it is not enough to envision a noble ideal; what matters in practical life is how the noble ideal may become a living reality in the life of the individual or society at large. Thus we should demand from Hegel an answer to two questions: (1) what is the end of education? (2) Under what conditions can this end be achieved? I assume in articulating these questions that a noble, rational end cannot under any conditions be achieved by a base, irrational method; for the method which leads to the end is an integral part of the end; the former is immanent in the latter. Accordingly if the method is base, or irrational, the end would necessarily be infested with this baseness or irrationality.

Hegel rejects, to begin with, the play theory of education, which was expounded in Rousseau's *Emile* and made popular in Germany at the end of the eighteenth century by J. H. Basedow, according to which what is childish is *inherently* important; thus emphasis should be placed on innocence and "simplicity of manners". The model of this sort of conduct is the so — called 'state of nature' in which life is supposed to be simple, natural, spontaneous. The assumption which underlies this view is that, if left alone, unobstructed by the complex, and perhaps superfluous fabric of civilization, human nature would on its own and under the ordinary condition of nature find its highest growth and fulfillment. Against this theory Hegel advances two major objections: (1) this theory "implies treating education (*Bildung*) as something purely external; the ally of corruption." (§ 187) But, as I shall emphasize, the human element in man is not a spontaneously self — actualizing power; on the contrary, what is human is an achievement, something to be learned in a cultural medium, in a complex order of values, principles, ideas, practices, customs, and past achievements. The human world, i.e., culture, is a creatively fashioned domain by and for the spirit. Such a domain does not simply grow the way trees or flowers grow in nature. (2) The play theory underestimates the serious aspect of human pursuits and endeavors, indeed of human life as such; its advocates "represent the child, in the immaturity in which he feels himself to be, as really mature and they struggle to make him satisfied with himself as he is. But they corrupt and distort his genuine and proper need for something better, and create in him a blind indifference to the substantial ties of the intellectual world, a contempt of his elders because they have thus posed before him, a child, in a contemptible and childish fashion, and finally a vanity and conceit which feeds on the notion of its own superiority." (§ 175)

The second theory of education which Hegel rejects holds that education is a means to a practical end. This end is viewed differently by different thinkers: while some hold that it consists in acquiring a career, hence the purpose of education is to provide a skill for securing one's survival, others argue that the end is pleasure or comfort. But this theory, like the preceding one, Hegel argues, "implies treating education as a mere means to these ends. Both these views display lack of acquaintance with the nature of mind and the end of reason." (§ 187) Accordingly, an adequate theory of education should proceed from a comprehensive, sound conception or understanding of the human mind, or of human nature. This proposition is based on the assumption that education is not merely a skill, or an instrument, to achieve a certain end, but primarily an activity — skillful activity, if you wish — in which the individual actualizes the powers, or potentialities, which are essential to his being as a human individual. But in order for one to be skilled in managing this activity he should know himself and the world around him, he should be armed with a sense of value, facility in making a sound judgment, an ideal of personal life, and an imagination which enables him to see himself as he is and as he ought to be in the scheme of things. Hegel had this notion of education in mind when he wrote: "the multiplicity of objects and situations which excite interest is the stage on which theoretical educaion develops. This education consists in possessing not simply a multiplicity of ideas and facts, but also a flexibility and rapidity of mind, ability to pass from one idea to another, to grasp complex and general relations, and so on. It is the education of the understanding in every way, and so also the building of language." (§ 197) Thus if I am to express succinctly the ultimate end of education for Hegel I can say: the nourishment of human individuality. This statement is, however, broad and requires a measure of elucidation, for one can ask: what does 'individual' mean? What makes one an individual? An individual is, as we saw, and as we shall see in the next essay, a self — determined being, a being who authors his ideas, values, emotions, desires, actions, a being who, in short, authors his life, i.e., is free. In stating this as the end of education Hegel assumes that a child is not born free but with the potentiality for being free: "children are potentially free and their life directly embodies nothing save potential freedom." (§ 175)

Education, then, is an activity, an exercise, of realizing, i.e., bringing forth, or helping to mature certain potentialities in human nature; the actualization of these potentialities, which is an on — going process of achievement, is the activity and being of freedom. In this activity one acquires and lives the meaning and content of culture. In order for this end to be achieved three principles, or goals, should be realized.

First, the educator should nourish the rational powers of the mind. The nourishment of this faculty is a necessary and basic condition for learning how to be free not only because one cannot be free unless he knows what it means to be free, or that he is free, but especially because knowledge is itself a power, a power which enables one to understand in general and to control oneself in the path of freedom. Again, reason is the faculty which enables a person to overcome and surpass himself as a particular, discrete being and exist on the level of universality and individuality. As we saw earlier, one is free when one acts according to the concept, i.e., essential, universal principle, of his will. Thus in education the growing child should be oriented in the art of discovering and living the universal in his personal, subjective life. The universal should, in other words, be the actuating principle of his subjectivity, i.e., will; it should accordingly appropriate the external conditions of its existence to its universal mode of deciding and acting: "by this means alone does mind become at home with itself.... There, then, mind's freedom is existent and mind becomes objective to itself in this element which is implicitly inimical to mind's appointed end, freedom; it has to do there only with what it has itself produced and stamped with its seal. It is in this way then that the form of universality comes explicitly into existence in thought, and this form is the only worthy element for the existence of the Idea." (§ 187)

Second, the educator should nourish the ethical disposition, or character, of the child. "Education," Hegel writes, "is the art of making man ethical. It begins with pupils whose life is at the instinctive level and shows them the way to a second birth, the way to change their instinctive nature into a second, intellectual, nature, and makes this intellectual level habitual to them." (Add. to § 151) Thus one cannot learn to grow in freedom unless he possesses an ethical, virtuous, disposition. But this disposition cannot, as we already saw, be acquired by means of lectures, sermons, or threats, but in and through experience, and the ideal place of this experience is the family, for on this social level the child enjoys the most intimate, lasting, and profound relations with individuals, viz., his parents, who care for him and who are in a position to provide for him an occasion for ethical growth and development: "in respect of his relation to the family, the child's education has the positive aim of instilling ethical principles into him in the form of an immediate feeling for which differences are not yet explicit, so that thus equipped with the foundation of an ethical life, his heart may live its early years in love, trust, and obedience." (§ 175) Acting in a special way, especially when the acting is restrictive, hard, and involves an effort, requires love and trust; these values cannot be easily shown and furnished except by paretns. This is why Hegel insists that "as a child, a man must have lived with his parents encircled by love and trust, and rationality must appear in him as his very own subjectivity." (Add. to § 175) Again, being ethical is not merely a matter of obeying the law, or custom (*Sitte*), passively the way a Pharisee would do it; to be ethical an act should spring from the heart; it should be willed; it should, in short, be *felt* and *lived*. And when it is not felt and lived the act's character of being 'mine' would be absent. But ethical feeling cannot be injected into our souls the way penicillin is injected into our bodies; it has to grow and later on form the structure of the ethical character of the individual. But in order for this growth to proceed normally and effectively its environment should inspire love, trust, and a feeling of confidence: "in the early years it is education by the mother especially which is important, since ethical principles must be implanted in the child in the form of feelings." (*Ibid.*)[6] We may here disagree with Hegel as to whether the mother is the major educational factor in the ethical growth of the child, and I do not think he would quibble over who is more qualified in this regard, the mother or the father; what matters for him is that the child should receive early in his life an ethical disposition. And since the mother seems, at least in his time, to be the one entrusted with the early life of the child, and since she, *qua* woman, is the living reality or embodiment of the universal ethical law, she would be the most effective choice in implanting this disposition. Hegel does not rule out either the suitability or the need for the father to participate in this undertaking, especially as the child begins to advance in age.

The cultivation of an ethical disposition, however, is not enough; education should aim at a higher level of ethical growth, namely, the capacity to think, espouse, and translate the universal character of the ethical law concretely, for only when this translation is achieved successfully, i.e., when the universal content of the law becomes a living fact in conduct, does the individual attain his freedom: "The final purpose of education, therefore, is liberation and the struggle for a higher liberation still; education is the absolute transition from an ethical substantiality which is immediate and natural to the one which is intellectual and so both infinitely subjective and lofty enough to have attained a universality of form. In the individual subject, this liberation is the hard struggle against pure subjectivity of demeanour, against the immediacy of desire, against the empty subjectivity of feeling and the caprice of information." (§ 187)[7] This is based on the assumption that one becomes ethical, and therefore free, only in so far as he acts not on the basis of instinct, impulse, or natural inclination but rationally, i.e., on the basis of a universal principle. Thus education has a negative aim, to raise "children out of the instinctive, physical, level on which they are originally, to self — subsistence and freedom of personality." (§ 175; Cf. also § 20) But this aim is impossible outside the domain of an ethical community, a community which upholds and lives the ideal in all the spheres of its life.

The family is, for Hegel, the paradigm of this community; this is why he considers it, with civil society, as an *ethical root* of the state.

Third, the educator should nourish in the child discipline, or the capacity of self — control. This capacity is a necessary condition for the cultivation of rationality and ethical conduct: "one of the chief factors in education," Hegel writes, "is discipline, the purpose of which is to break down the child's self — will and thereby eradicate his purely natural and sensuous self." (Add. to § 174) Natural impulses, or desire, is a power that seeks to assert or satisfy itself blindly without any consideration of the rational or ethical well — being of the individual or society at large. In order therefore for rational or ethical conduct to prevail the individual should arm himself with a greater measure of power to refrain from satisfying the natural impulse, or desire, and this on the basis of a promise, of attaining a valued ethical or rational satisfaction. In any concrete ethical situation which requires decision and action the individual usually confronts a number of competing preferences which are dictated by various impulses, inclinations, or desires. If he does not deliberate or evaluate the worth of these preferences the strongest impulse, inclination, or desire will certainly assert itself. Again, the agent may theoretically see that a certain preference is worthy of satisfaction, but if he does not have the power to restrict, or control himself, again he would succumb to the strongest impulse, inclination, or desire. Any moment of decision requires restriction and a faith in a goal projected and approved by reason. This faith, whose content is an intuition of the universal, i.e., of what is right, good, or true, arouses, indeed *generates* the needed power to overcome impulse or instinct and act according to the universal: "when reflection is brought to bear on impulses, they are imaged, estimated, compared with one another, with their means of satisfaction and their consequences, &c., and with a sum of satisfaction (i.e., with happiness). In this way reflection invests this material with abstract universality and in this external manner purifies it from its crudity and barbarity. This growth of the universality of thought is the absolute value in education." (§ 20) Accordingly if the ultimate end of education is freedom, and if this end is achieved when the individual lives the universal in his action, it should follow that the educator should seek to free the child from the sway of impulse or instinct and direct its energy and interest towards the universal. This task is not easy, and we must not expect to achieve it "by mere goodness, since it is just the immediate will which acts on immediate fancies and caprices, not on reasons and representative thinking. If we advance reasons to children, we leave it open to them to decide whether the reasons are weighty or not, and thus we make everything depend on their whim. So far as children are concerned, universality and the substance of things reside in their parents, and this implies that children must be obedient. If the feeling of subordination, producing the longing to grow up, is not fostered in children, they become forward and impertinent." (Add. to § 174) This whole line of reasoning is based on the Aristotelian principle which we already discussed, viz., one becomes good, or virtuous, by doing good or virtuous acts. Accordingly the child should first acquire a disposition and a training in the art of acting according to the universal and later on, when his reason develops its full powers, reflect on and understand its being and end.

Your last principle of education, my critic would argue here, brings into clear focus the crux of our problem: if the family as the most basic social institution is entrusted with the task of nourishing the child rationally and ethically in the early period of his development, which is considered by most psychologists as the formative period of human character, if, moreover, the ethical or rational principles which they follow are the established principles of the state, and, finally, if the child is at their mercy, how can this child grow to be a critical mind, a mind enlightened by the power of universal reason and morality? This sort of objection which we have already encountered on more than one occasion is in essence a request to show, or somehow establish, that Hegel's view of the education of the child is both human and rational, that is, truly conducive to the growth of human individuality, or freedom. Thus, we should ask: what are the rational criteria, or conditions, of education for Hegel? This question is important, for if we can show, at least in principle, that the meaning and end of education are rational then we should undermine the force of the objection once and for all.

If put in a nut shell, a conception of education is rational, it is sound or adequate, if, according to this conception, (1) the end of education is human freedom and (2) the conditions under which it is realized are conducive to this end. What I am here stressing in the Hegelian framework of thinking is the following principle: it is not enough to espouse in the actual arena of human life lofty ideals; we should also see to it that the ideal espoused can be realized in the life of a people, or a person, in a given region and historical period. Accordingly, given the nuclear family as a basic social institution within which the child receives the substantial nourishment of his character, under what conditions, rational conditions, is education possible?

We should emphasize at the outset that, if it is to be rational, education should aim at the cultivation of human individuality, i.e., the capacity of the person to exist as a self — determined being. The preceding discussion has, I hope, made this point amply clear. We should, therefore, restrict ourselves in the remainder of this discussion to the conditions under which education is possible.

First, the education of the child in the family is, for Hegel, a purely spiritual activity in which the parents assist in the formation, i.e., actualization, of the character of the child. As I insisted earlier, the end of education is not external to the soul or mind of the child, in which the latter acquires a skill, a set of ideas, interests, or a certain inclination, but rather internal, viz., the actualization of those powers, or potentialities, which constitute the very essence of the mind. Thus the child as a possible human individual is the end of the educational process. And *he* is the end primarily because he is the objective embodiment of the parents' love for each other. The parents see for the first time the unity of their love objectified in the child: "in the child, a mother loves its father and he its mother. Both have their love objectified for them in the child. While in their goods their unity is embodied only in an external thing, in their children it is embodied in a spiritual one in which the parents are loved and which they love." (Add. to § 173) But this unity is a union of two individuals: the husband and wife exist for each other as self — determined beings, as beings in an on — going process of self — realization. But they are also mutually conscious of this relationship between each other and of their desire to promote it for ever. Thus if the child is a concrete objectification of their love he must be a living example of this love; he must reflect in his conduct the fundamental features of union with each other: trust, care, cooperation, mutual respect, and a drive for freedom. This is why Hegel holds that the parents feel a need to educate him: their desire to see their love embodied concretely is at the same time a desire to educate their child.[8] And in educating him they instill in him their achieved consciousness of their love for each other. In other words, what the child receives in education is a consciousness which later on becomes self — consciousness, he receives the capacities of reflection, valuation, and judgment, he receives, in short, the capacity of self — determination. Thus in education the parents give, or rather transmit, to their children their most important asset or possession — their humanity, or put differently, the art of being free.

I have elucidated the preceding point only to stress that in family education the child is, for Hegel, treated as an end in himself, and he is treated as such mainly because he is destined for freedom: "children are potentially free and their life directly embodies nothing save potential freedom. Consequently they are not things and cannot be the property either of their parents or others." (§ 175) This clearly shows that the relation which holds between the parent and the child is not contractual, legal, or material, but ethical; for as I argued in the first part of this essay, the basis of the family is an ethical tie of love, and if the child as a spiritual being is an expression of this love, it should follow that the child must be treated as a possible human being.[9]

Second, in educating their child the parents should not assume a final, or dogmatic, attitude regarding the ideas, values, or experiences to which the child should be exposed as he grows up. Hegel avers that the parents may be ignorant, one — sided, or arbitrary, or even fanatic in the sort of education they provide for their children. This is why they should not be viewed as the ultimate authority in deciding the content or means of their education: "in its character as a universal family, civil society has the right and duty of superintending and influencing education, inasmuch as education bears upon the child's capacity to become a member of society. Society's right here is paramount over the arbitrary and contingent preferences of parents, particularly in cases where education is to be completed not by the parents but by others." (§ 239) The same principle is stressed again by Hegel: "parents usually suppose that in the matter of education they have complete freedom and may arrange everything as they like. The chief opposition to any form of public education usually comes from parents and it is they who talk and make an outcry about teachers and schools because they have a fadish dislike of them. None the less, society has a right to act on principles tested by its experience and to compel parents to send their children to school, to have them vaccinated, and so forth." (Add. to § 239) I quote these two passages at length because I am anxious to impress upon my critic Hegel's sensitivity to the need for a rational basis for education. Even though the family, the school, or some other social institution is a crucial factor in shaping the character of the child this institution does not have the final say in what and how the child is to be educated. The educational principles which should be fostered must be tested; they must be shown to be valid, i.e., rational. This premise is based on the assumption which was defended in the preceding paragraph, viz., the child is not, and cannot be owned by any person or institution but exists as an end in himself, i.e., as a possible individual.

Hegel's emphasis on the principles of education must be spotlighted because they are formative factors of the human character: a man grows up to be a good citizen in a state with good laws. But who is to decide what laws are good, or bad? This question has been answered in detail in the first three essays. Here I should only remark that in speaking of 'good laws' Hegel has in mind laws that promote the good of the people, express their highest values as an organic whole, and have withstood the vicissitudes of the historical turmoil of the nation. Yet the existence of good laws is not enough, for Hegel, because it is quite possible for one to acquire or develop a character consistent with the established ethical order without the capacity of self — conscious self — determination; we can, in other words, envision a human being who mirrors the values and expectations of society in a passive, unreflective manner. Such a human being is usually called a 'conformist'; he is, to express myself briefly, a creature of habit, a social product. His will is an extension of the social will. Society feels, thinks, and acts through him. But a person who has fallen a victim to habit is not, and cannot be, free: "it is true that a man is killed by habit," Hegel writes, "i.e., if he has once come to feel completely at home in life, if he has not attained his end and wills to develop his potentialities and vindicate himself in struggling to attain it. When this has been fully achieved, activity and vitality are at an end, and the result — loss of interest in life — is mental or physical death." (Add. to § 151) Thus as an activity, education should take place in an atmosphere of critical thinking, of open enquiry, feeling, and imagining, in an atmosphere conducive to creative existence and self — realization.[10]

Is there an atmosphere more conducive to this end than one built on, and permeated by, love, trust, sharing, spiritual quest, and respect for the being and individuality of others?

FIVE
SELF — REALIZATION AS THE END OF WORK

One may develop a character skilled in the art of loving, self — determination and respect for the being of others, and one may cherish some of the warmest moments of freedom in the family, my critic would at this point of my discussion point out, but this sort, or dimension, of freedom is limited, subjective: it is restricted to family life. The problem with Hegel's account of the relationship between the state and the individual is that the 'individual', which is supposed to be the foundation and building block of the state, remains an abstract being, a part, or a means to the 'will' of the state as a historical institution. "Hegel," he would argue, "rejected the fundamental truth of political philosophy, which is that the body politic (by him perniciously confused with the state) is a Whole made up of parts which are themselves wholes, a Whole composed of wholes. His State is a Whole whose parts are nothing but pure parts, that is, parts which are not persons, and which only acquire personality insofar as they are and wish themselves to be integrated into the supra — individual Self of the State. Then they cease to be mere clouds of atoms, and are recognized and dignified, invested with authentic morality and personality (that is, for Hegel, with rational necessity) *as members and uniquely* as members of an organic whole or concrete universal which is the State. There is no place here for the freedom of autonomy which on the level of social life we attain to as persons in the body politic of which we are members, or as individual wholes possessing their own rights within the political whole and surpassing it by virtue of that which is eternal in them, bound to that whole by mutual relations of justice and by civic friendship, obeying its laws because their personal conscience commits them to the common good, which flows back upon or is redistributed among them as members of the community."[1] I quote this lengthy passage from my critic without omission not only because it reveals the thrust and logic of his line of reasoning but also because it brings into clear focus the ultimate meaning and being of human individuality in Hegel's conception of the state.

The heart of the objection which we now face is that Hegel has reduced the citizen to an abstract individual, to a being that is nourished and destined for the final cause of the state: "for Hegel the individual as a particular individual, or as a human atom, is a whole or a person only in a purely abstract and formal sense; but the individual renounces even this and then goes beyond it. In the family he exists "not as an independent person but as a member (*Phil. of Right*, § 158); it is the same, and for all the more reason, in the State."[2] Accordingly a so — called individual who exists as a passing, and perhaps expendable, 'moment' in the life of the state does not owe his life — ideas, feelings, emotions, values, desires, etc. — to himself but to the social and political institutions and forces which are consciously designed for his mission and satisfaction in life: he achieves his happiness by living up to the norms and expectations of the social whole of which he is a part. Thus as a part, the citizen does not, indeed cannot, exist as a self — determined being; he cannot accordingly claim or enjoy his most fundamental right, the right to *human* individuality.

We have already seen that an individual (1) is a self—determined being, a being who owes the content of his being, i.e., his life, to himself. In acting, that is living, his action originates from his will: the action is an expression of his will, an objectification of what he takes to be right, good or beautiful. If I am to express this point briefly, I can say: an individual is a conscious self — determined unity of thought, feeling, and action. A corollary to this premise is the need for self — realization. An individual is a self — realized person, a person who seems to know and make, i.e., form, his self or identity. Accordingly, (A) an individual is a particular man with definite goals, wants, and aspirations. One is not an individual simply because he possesses the power or capacity to determine his life but who also actualizes or achieves the ends which are the content of his life. (B) Individuality is a task; it is an achievement: one is not born as an individual but with the potentiality to be one. The aim of education is, as we saw in essay IV, to learn the art of how to grow as an individual, i.e., as a self — determined being. (2) An individual is a person who exists as an end in himself; he respects himself and others not merely as means but always as ends in themselves. Respecting oneself or others here means safeguarding, upholding, the rights or privileges which constitute the essence of personality; for, as we saw, 'personality' means the capacity to bear rights: e.g., the right to life, belief, association, conscience, work, the pursuit of happiness. A corollary to this basic feature of individuality is *self - assertiveness*, viz., the demand to be recognized or acknowledged by others, or the state, as an individual. Accordingly if an individual is a person who claims and pursues certain rights in actualizing himself then others, or the state, should recognize him as the subject of such rights; they should recognize him for what he is or achieves, i.e., he should be 'honored', respected, for his achievements as a human being.

Now let us ask: does Hegel take into serious account the value of human individuality in his analysis of the state, especially of the place of the individual in the state? Can the citizen within his political scheme exist as an individual, that is, as a whole within a Whole? In order for a citizen to exist as an individual in the state the private and public life — put differently, his subjective and objective life — should be an expression of a value or law which originates from his will, otherwise, he would be determined, conditioned, or somehow controlled by the Social Whole.

My concern in the preceding essays has been to show that the law which rules the public life of the citizen in the realm of ethical and political conduct originates from the will of the individual or the people as a unity of purpose and aspiration. I should now discuss the conditions under which the citizen actualizes himself as a *particular* or concrete person. In this discussion two propositions will be defended: (1) a member of the state is, for Hegel, a particular person. The fundamental character of particularily is work, or the satisfaction of personal human needs. (2) The end of work is self — realization.

I. *Man as a Particular Person*

The most fundamental institution (beside the family) in which the state becomes actual is civil society, and the building block of this society is what Hegel calls the concrete, particular person who, as we saw earlier, seeks his own personal or selfish ends. This political sphere is a web of economic relationships; in it men are not related to each other as ethical or religious beings, nor as family members, but as men in quest of particular satisfaction. What makes a person particular, concrete — indeed a man — is the fact that he is a bundle of desires, interests, aspirations, in short, *needs*: "in (abstract) right, what we had before us was the Person; in the sphere of morality, the subject; in the family, the family — member; in civil society as a whole, the burgher or *bourgeois*. Here at the standpoint of needs what we have before us is the composite idea which we call *man*. Thus this is the first time, and indeed properly the only time, to speak of *man* in this sense." (§ 190) Accordingly as a member of the state, a citizen is not, contrary to our critic's claim, merely a part of an abstract entity but a specific identifiable being composed of flesh, bone, and blood, a being conscious of needs in a certain way and whose life and satisfaction depend on the attainment of these needs.

Left to himself, alone, a particular person tries to satisfy his needs without regard to the being or well — being of others; but since others try to do the same, and since one's needs are frequently capricious, unstable, and hard to limit, a collision between the members of civil society is bound to occur. A power, viz., government, is accordingly necessary to create an atmosphere of harmony and cooperation, so that each person pursues his ends without obstructing or undermining the pursuit of others: "particularity by itself, given free rein in every direction to satisfy its needs, accidental caprices, and subjective desires, destroys itself and its substantive concept in this process of gratification. At the same time, the satisfaction of needs, necessary and accidental alike, is accidental because it breeds new desires without end, is in thorough — going dependence on caprice and external accident, and is held in check by the power of universality." (§ 185)

Particularity is, for Hegel, an essential power, drive, in human nature. Man has all sorts of needs, passions, fancies, etc., with which he identifies himself and which he can claim as 'mine': "men are willing to be *active* in pursuit of what interest them, or should interest them, as something which is their own." (§ 123) The attainment of these needs is the basis of (1) subjectivity and (2) human happiness, or welfare. This is, I think, why Hegel considered, as we saw, subjective satisfaction, or welfare and happiness, as a right: attainment of this right is the attainment of particularity. What Hegel means when he says that every man is entitled to be happy is that every man has the distinctive, inalienable, right to pursue his personal ends, ends which express his will as a specific, concrete human essence existing in a specific society during a specific period of history. One cannot, however, pursue this right capriciously or without regard to the welfare of others: "the demand that such an end alone shall appear as willed and attained, like the view that, in willing, objective and subjective ends are mutually exclusive, is an empty dogmatism of the abstract Understanding." (§ 124) This is based on the assumption that a man is what he does: one reveals his being, his identity, in what he does. Accordingly if what he does is silly or worthless then he would be a silly or worthless person. Thus in order for subjective satisfaction to be meaningful and conducive to freedom it should seek to realize the universal concretely: "but in developing itself independently to totality, the principle of particularity passes over into universality, and only there does it attain its truth and the right to which its positive actuality is entitled." (§ 186) Possession, knowledge, and devotion to the universal, however, is not an easy task. This task is the over — riding goal of education. It begins, as we saw, early in childhood, in a family atmosphere where a young soul is nourished in the art of thinking, feeling, and valuing that which is true, right, and good.

Hegel dismisses, then, once and for all the notion that one achieves his happiness by pursuing arbitrary or capricious interests, not only because such pursuit is contrary to the demands of freedom but also because it ignores the most fundamental side of human nature: viz., the demand for spiritual satisfaction. But the realm of the spirit is the universal, and as such it has to be sought, espoused, and realized. It should accordingly be adopted as a subjective principle, and only when such adoption takes place can the individual achieve the happiness which becomes him as a man. In saying this Hegel does not at all mean to reduce man in the state to a universal thinking machine so that whatever he does conforms to some prescribed abstract rational rule; what he wishes to stress is that in the realm of civil society in which people seek their personal ends one is entitled to carry on any activity he wishes inasmuch as that activity is not detrimental to his well — being or the well — being of others: "in civil society each member is his own end, everything else is nothing to him. But except in contact with others he cannot attain the whole compass of his ends, and therefore these others are means to the end of the particular member. A particular end, however, assumes the form of universality through this relation to other people, and it is attained in the simultaneous attainment of the welfare of others. Since particularity is inevitably conditioned by universality, the whole sphere of civil society is the territory of mediation where there is free play for every idiosyncrasy, every talent, every accident of birth and fortune, and where waves of every passion gush forth, regulated only by reason glinting through them. Particularity, restricted by universality, is the only standard whereby each particular member promotes his welfare." (Add. to § 182)

We should now ask: what kind of needs does, and should, man seek? Hegel makes a distinction between two types of need, natural and social, or human, needs. Attainment of the first secures physical well — being and survival, and attainment of the second secures human satisfaction or well — being. Man shares with the animal the necessity of satisfying only the first kind of needs; in this sense it is restricted exclusively to particularity; its "needs and its ways and means of satisfying them are both alike restricted in scope." (§ 190) The animal has, again, "its instincts and means of satisfying them, means which are limited and which it cannot overstep. Some insects are parasitic on a certain kind of plant; some animals have a wider range and can live in different climates." (Add. to § 190) Although man is in principle subject to the same kind of restriction he is nevertheless able to transcend it and assert himself as a universal being, and this for two reasons: "first by the multiplicaton of needs and means of satisfying them, and secondly by the differentiation and division of concrete needs into single parts and aspects which in turn become different needs, particularized and so more abstract." (§ 19) When needs and the means of multiplying them are multiplied and, gradually refined "taste and utility become criteria" in determining them. Accordingly "it is no longer need but opinion which has to be satisfied, and it is just the educated man who analyses the concrete into its particulars. The very multiplication of needs involves a check on desire, because when many things are in use, the urge to obtain any one thing which might be needed is less strong, and this is a sign that want altogether is not so imperious." (Add. to § 190) It is also a sign that the relations which hold between needs and the means of their satisfaction have become abstract, universal, i.e., social; "this abstract character, universality, is the character of being recognized and is the moment which makes concrete, i.e., social, the isolated and abstract needs and their ways and means of satisfaction." (§ 192) How does this happen? When I seek ends I do so with regard to the being and well — being of the needs of others. My needs and what I have to offer is intertwined with their needs and what they have to offer: "it is from others that I acquire the means of satisfaction and I must accordingly accept their views. At the same time, however, I am compelled to produce means for the satisfaction of others. We play into each other's hands and so hang together. To this extent everything private becomes something social." (Add. to § 192)

When we speak of social needs, however, we do not only mean those needs which are conducive to the physical safety and well — being of the individual; we also mean the mental needs, those needs which are peculiar to man as mind or spirit. Because of their universal character the latter type of needs are more preponderant: "since in social needs, as the conjunction of immediate or natural needs with mental needs arising from ideas, it is needs of the latter type which because of their universality make themselves preponderant, this social moment has in it the aspect of liberation." (§ 194) That is, the more a particular person participates in social life, the more he immerses himself in the culture of his society, and the more he contributes to the vitality and richness of this culture, the *freer* he is. This is only an application of the basic dictum that man is a socio — political animal. Accordingly to withdraw from society, and *human* society comes to life in the medium of culture, constitutes a limitation, a restriction on one's attainment of freedom. This is why Hegel was critical of Rousseau's emphasis on leading a simple, or 'natural', life. "The idea has been advanced," he writes, "that in respect of his needs man lived in freedom in the so — called 'state of nature' when his needs were supposed to be confined to what are known as the simple necessities of nature, and when he required for their satisfaction only the means which the accidents of nature directly assured him." (*Ibid.*) But this idea is one — sided, indeed erroneous, first, because it does not take into consideration the fact that man, in addition to being social, political, rational, is essentially a *maker*, a worker; he does not, as we shall presently see, only make things, he also makes himself — actually he makes himself in making things, and the sort of self he makes depends on the sort of things he makes. Second, if man withdraws from society and returns to the so — called state of nature he would reduce himself to the level of animals: "to be confined to mere physical needs as such and their direct satisfaction would simply be the condition in which the mental is plunged in the natural and so would be one of savagery and unfreedom, while freedom itself is to be found only in the reflection of mind into itself, in mind's distinction from nature, and in the reflex of mind in nature." (*Ibid.*) Yet, Hegel warns, it would be a grave mistake for one to devote all his powers and talents to what we call social needs, for as the modern economic system has clearly shown, society can produce all sorts of objects which, though attractive and may excite one's desire or taste, may not be so crucial to one's true satisfaction: "when social conditions tend to multiply and subdivide needs, means, and enjoyments indefinitely — a process which, like the distinction between natural and refined needs, has no qualitative limits — this is luxury." (§ 195) When a society becomes extreme in emphasizing and producing luxuries it is bound to create a class who cannot afford such luxuries — hence the ground for some social discontent. This tendency is certainly demoralizing. Hegel makes reference in this connection to the rise of Diogenes and the cynical school in Athena in the fourth century B.C. as a critical reaction to the extravagant way of life led by the elite of Athena at the time. His remark is, I think, instructive, and since it has a direct bearing on our contemporary social scene, I shall quote it in its entirety: "the entire Cynical mode of life adopted by Diogenes was nothing more or less than a product of Athenian social life, and what determined it was the way of thinking against which his whole manner protested. Hence it was not independent of social conditions but simply their result; it was itself a rude product of luxury. When luxury is at its height, distress and depravity are equally extreme, and in such circumstances Cynicism is the outcome of opposition to refinement." (Add. to § 195)

II. *Self-Realization as the End of Work*

"The means," Hegel writes, "of acquiring and preparing the particularized means appropriate to our similarly particularized needs is work. Through work the raw material directly supplied by nature is specifically adapted to these ends by all sorts of different processes." (§ 196) In this activity man bestows, confers, value on the means, viz., work, and consequently on the product of work. Thus in what he does or consumes man is "mainly concerned with the products of men. It is the product of human efforts which man consumes." (*Ibid.*) The arena in which this effort and consumption take place is civil society, the sphere where man confronts his fellow man as an economic being. In this sphere man actualizes himself as a *particular person*, as a working animal: "it is by the sweat of his brow and toil of his hands that man attains the means to satisfy his needs." (Add to § 196)

It would be reasonable here to say that man is, for Hegel, destined for work and that his true happiness as a particular person is achieved and felt in the course of fulfilling his calling or vocation in life in and through which he promotes his well — being as well as the well — being of society in general. Hegel repeatedly stressed the need to be proficient in one line of activity as a necessary condition for the realization of particularity (Cf. § 13, Add. to § 189, 297) This point is articulated clearly and forcefully in the smaller *Logic*: "character is an essential in conduct, and a man of character is an understanding man, who in that capacity has definite ends in view and undeviatingly pursues them. The man who will do something great must learn, as Goethe says, to limit himself. The man who, on the contrary, would do everything, really would do nothing, and fails. There is a host of interesting things in the world: Spanish, poetry, chemistry, politics, and music are all very interesting, and if any one takes an interst in them we need not find fault. But for a person in a given situation to accomplish anything, he must stick to one definite point, and not dissipate his forces in many directions. In every calling, too, the great thing is to pursue it with understanding."[3] This passage merits two remarks. (1) There is in man a drive to be a particular person with a specific identity uniquely different from the identity of everyone else; there is, in other words, an inherent desire in man to be somebody and to be recognized for what he is. This drive is, as I shall explicate presently, the basis of subjectivity and subjective satisfaction. (2) The drive for particularity is also a drive for being *actual*. As I indicated earlier, man is not given at birth as a finished product but as a complex of potentialities awaiting realization. We were instructed, advised, some time ago *to be ourselves*. I am myself only when I actualize the potentialities which are peculiar to me not only as a universal human nature but also as a particular nature, and I actualize myself when I do, achieve that which is within my powers as posibility. When this possibility remains dormant in my given being I lack actuality and thereby the inner tranquility and satisfaction which I crave as a human being. To remain on the level of possibility is to remain 'empty' as a human being and therefore groping in all my endeavors. Thus self — realization is an activity of achievement. This activity, however, is not given; accordingly self — realization entails another feature: self — discovery — therefore the need for education. One should know what sort of being he is and what he can do, namely, his strengths, weaknesses, desires, passions, interests, tastes. He should also know his social environment and the work possibilities which are consonant with his inclinations and potentialities; for as we saw earlier any activity is human and worth seeking inasmuch as it is social in character. Regardless of the role he plays in his life, man, as Hegel repeatedly stressed, is the child of his age. The value of what he does, even his self — esteem or dignity as a person, implies a human community which understands and appreciates his product.

While education at home and in the school aims at the nourishment of character, primarily the cultivation of the rational and ethical sides of the mind, or as Hegel would put it, at making the child "actually and for himself what he is at first potentially,"[4] practical education, which takes place in civil society, aims at the nourishment of a skill, or vocation, in and through which a person actualizes himself as a *particular individual*: "practical education, acquired though working, consists first in the habit of simply being busy; next, in the strict adoption of one activity according not only to the nature of the material worked on, but also, and especially, to the pleasure of other workers; and finally, in a habit, produced by this discipline, of objective activity and universally recognized aptitude." (§ 197) It is I think important to stress this passage not only because it enunciates Hegel's firm belief that there is in man a need (1) to work, to be productive and (2) to learn a skill according to recognized and established general, rational principles and to be proficient in this skill, but especially because it shows that one's real happiness is attained in and through work; put differently, the sphere of work is a sphere of human freedom: the activity of work, or working, is an activity of human liberation, not of killing time, and not merely as a means to earn a living for the sake of survival or meeting some immediate instrumental need. This point is made amply clear in the addition to § 197: "the savage is lazy and is distinguished from the educated man by his brooding stupidity, because practical education is just education in the need and habit of being busy. A clumsy man always produces a result he does not intend; he is not master of his job. The skilled worker, on the other hand, may be said to be the man who produces the thing as it ought to be and who hits the nail on the head without shrinking (*keine Sprödigkeit in seinem subjektiven Tun gegen den Zweck findet.*") He performs, in other words, his task with understanding: he knows what he is doing and why he is doing it: "understanding, too, is always an element in thorough training. The trained intellect is not satisfied with cloudy and indefinite impressions, but grasps the objects in their fixed character: whereas the uncultivated man wavers unsettled, and it often costs a deal of trouble to come to an understanding with him on the matter under discussion, and to bring him to fix his eye on the definite point in question."[5]

This understanding, this grasp, is a necessary condition for the attainment of particularity and, consequently, happiness; for without it one cannot, to use Goethe's words, 'collect his energies', master his emotions and impulses, and act on the basis of a consciously projected purpose or end. Adoption of an end, however, i.e., end grounded in the universal, is the basis of true happiness; only when this universal becomes the living principle of subjectivity — of thinking, feeling, willing, acting — can a person free himself from enslavement to impulse or given emotion and actualize himself under the conditions of rationality and universality. Like Aristotle, Hegel believes that happiness is not a momentary feeling or experience but a quality of action, of the whole man as a creative and productive being, as a being who acts on principle and lives for a cause. "In happiness," Hegel writes, "thought has already a mastery over the natural force of impulses, since the thinker is not content with the momentary but requires happiness in a whole. This requirement is connected with education in that it is education which vindicates the universal." (Add. to § 20) The aim of practical education, then, is not simply to acquire a skill to perform an assigned task in society, or to 'serve' the state, but to create the conditions under which a person can grow in the art of human living. Acquiring a skill is only a means, a framework within which one can learn to be a self — realized being, and only when a person is truly self — realized can he be productive on the human level.

III. *Conditions of Work*

We should now investigate the conditions under which a citizen can realize himself as a particular individual. This investigation is important for two reasons: (1) it sheds further light on Hegel's view of work; (2) it helps us to come to grips with our critic's charge that the citizen for Hegel remains an abstract person or a *part* of the state; he cannot consequently exist as a self — determined whole. For if a citizen conducts his life *as a part*, i.e., as a dependent being, then he cannot choose his vocation; he will remain under the mercy of the economic structure which serves the highest end of the state. The question which we should now ask is: does Hegel's conception of the state provide or allow for an economic framework, or atmosphere, within which a citizen can choose a vocation and realize himself as a particular person?

An essential feature of the economic life of the modern state is the unusual, sophisticated, multiplication and complexity of human needs and the means of satisfying these needs, i.e., work. This life is an intricate system of relations in which men are dependent on one another for their work and the objects which they need in order to live and fulfill themselves as individuals. The objective and universal element of work in this system "lies in the abstracting process which effects the subdivision of needs and means and thereby *eo ipso* subdivides production and brings about the division of Labour." (§ 198) Hegel here begins with civil society in which every man is independent and seeks his own interest and subjective satisfaction; he begins, in other words, with the necessity of economic freedom: the economic system of the state should reflect the needs of the people, on the one hand, and the means the people choose in satisfying these needs, on the other. The division of labor and the distribution of economic privileges and opportunities are determined by what the people desire as particular persons, the natural resources available at their disposal, and the technical means by which they appropriate these resources for their satisfaction. The economic system of the modern state à la Hegel should reflect, as we shall presently see, the *economic will* of the people.[6]

When the division of labor is effected, "the work of the individual becomes less complex, and consequently his skill at his section of the job increases, like his output. At the same time, this abstraction of one man's skill and means of production from another's completes and makes necessary everywhere the dependence of men on one another and their reciprocal relation in the satisfaction of their other needs." (*Ibid.*) In this interdependence of work and cooperation the subjective satisfaction or self — seeking of the individual "turns into the mediation of the particular through the universal, with the result that each man in earning, producing, and enjoying his own account is *eo ipso* producing and earning for the enjoyment of everyone else. The compulsion which brings this about is rooted in the complex interdependence of each on all, and it now presents itself to each as the universal permanent capital which gives each the opportunity, by the exercise of his education and skill, to draw a share from it and so be assured of his livelihood, while what he thus earns by means of his work maintains and increases the general capital." (§ 199)[7] From an economic standpoint, then, civil society is a domain which consists of (1) capital and (2) possibility of work and production. Capital is not the result of a singular effort or the effort of a specific group in society but rather the cooperative effort of society as an organic whole; as such, it has a social character. This is why it provides a medium in which every citizen can work and fulfill his needs as a particular individual. The economic opportunity of a person is, however, determined by a number of factors, "partly by his own unearned principal (his capital) and partly by his skill; this in turn is itself dependent not on his capital, but also on accidental circumstances whose multiplicity introduces differences in a development of natural, bodily, and mental characteristics, which were already in themselves dissimilar. (§ 200) In this passage Hegel is careful to stress the aspect of particularity as a necessary condition for self — realization. This is based on the assumption that people differ in their physical and mental powers and endowments; they are *particular* persons. Every man is a unique world of ideas, emotions, interests, desires, hopes, habits, and problems. "Men," Hegel writes, "are made unequal by nature, where inequality is in its element, and in civil society the right of particularity is so far from annulling this natural inequality that it produces it out of mind and raises it to an inequality of skill and resources, and even to one of moral and intellectual attainment. To oppose to this right a demand for equality is a folly of the Understanding which takes as real and rational its abstract equality and its 'ought — to — 'be'. (*Ibid.*) Thus the right to self — realization is a right to personal satisfaction, or happiness, as a particular individual — as a *this* or *that* rational, cultured lump of flesh. But my particularity, which consists in the unique blend of my emotions, ideas, habits, etc., which determines the uniqueness of my character, remains abstract, indeed impossible, outside a social context; it shows itself in the ideas and values on which I act, in the political demeanor I adopt, in the religious beliefs I publicly espouse, in the sort of family life I lead, and in the vocation in and through which I become a functional citizen in society. Thus to be a particular person means to occupy a certain place, to assume a certain role, or to enjoy certain rights and duties in the social structure which make up the heart of the state.

But society is divided into three classes: the agricultural, business, and governing class. This division is, as we saw, effected by the division of labor, by the types of needs sought and by the means of satisfying these needs, on the one hand, and as Prof. Taylor rightly indicates by the "life — styles and hence values" of the people who compose these classes, on the other.[8] Thus as a particular person, a citizen should necessarily belong to a social class: "a man actualizes himself only in becoming something definite, e.g. something specifically particularized; this means restricting himself exclusively to one of the particular spheres of need." (§ 207) Belonging to such a class should only mean commitment to a specific vocation in and through which a person distinguishes himself as a unique individual. I make this assertion only to stress that Hegel does not in any way espouse, or even imply, a rigid class system or that he determines the value and dignity of a man on the basis of class membership, for he clearly states that "the question of the particular class to which an individual is to belong is one in which natural capacity, birth, and other circumstances have their influence, though the essential and final determining factors are subjective opinion and the individual's arbitrary will, which win this sphere their right, their merit, and their dignity." (§ 206) The concept of social class in Hegel, then, is a dynamic concept. Each class constitutes a domain of human activity and productivity, a sphere of action in which a citizen can pursue an idea or a purpose with which he identifies himself in his life; "but when subjective particularity is upheld by the objective order in conformity with it and is at the same time allowed its rights, then it becomes the animating principle of the entire civil society, of the development alike of mental activity, merit, and dignity." (*Ibid*.) Accordingly the fundamental principle of civil society as a domain of economic activity is the will of the people. In this domain one is not, and cannot be, free if the system within which he works is not an expression of his will. This is what Hegel means when he says: "the recognition of the right that what is brought about by reason of necessity in civil society and the state shall at the same time be effected by the mediation of the arbitrary will is the more precise definition of what is primarily meant by freedom in common parlance." (*Ibid*.)[9]

But how can subjective particularity, and consequently individual freedom, my critic would here object, be upheld by the objective order if this order is *inherently* indifferent to the will of the citizen as a particular person? We may grant for the sake of argument that man actualizes himself as an individual in and through work, and that work is a necessary condition for the being of human freedom. But on Hegel's view this condition is superior to the will or welfare of the particular person. Do these laws not represent the authority of the universal, or perhaps the cunning of reason in its own way to make the universal actual in the modern state?[10] The work, or livelihood, of every citizen remains for Hegel a possibility, and this possibility depends on the existing economic conditions with all their contingencies, caprices, and human frailties. Thus if, or when, civil society expands both in population and production profit and capital would necessarily increase, but so would poverty. To be poor means to be deprived of the right to subjective particularity. Indeed poverty, I may be told, is a necessary consequence of Hegel's view of civil society and political economy. Although he was intensely concerned about it, Hegel was unable to provide an adequate solution to it, and his inability to provide such a solution is a clear indication of the helplessness of the particular person in the face of the economic system which imposes on rather than reflects the will of the people in their attempt to work and meet their needs for the sake of self — realization.[11] Thus *in principle* at least the citizen remains in Hegel's political scheme dependent, i.e., part, hence an abstract individual.

But does the citizen in Hegel's scheme remain dependent, helpless in the face of an abstract, or indifferent, economic system? And does Hegel fail to provide a solution to the problem of poverty or perhaps means to cope with it consistently with his political ideal, viz., freedom? My answer to both questions is in the negative. In defending this claim I shall argue that although poverty in Hegel's theory of the state is a possibility which can be actuated by empirical, contingent factors this possibility can be checked, primarily because the laws which govern the citizens both on the level of civil society and the state are in the final analysis rooted in the will of the people as a whole. From an economic standpoint, the state which Hegel espouses is a *welfare state*.

Hegel admits, to begin with, that the economic sphere of the modern state is vitiated by caprice and contingency: "in the system of needs, the livelihood and welfare of every single person is a possibility whose actual attainment is just as much conditioned by his caprices and particular endowment as by the objective system of needs." (§ 230) Accordingly the work opportunities of the citizen are neither predetermined nor automatically guaranteed, nor arranged on a personal level. The quest for work is a task. What one does and how he should secure and maintain his work is the responsibility of every member of civil society. This premise is consistent with the principle of particularity, according to which a man adopts a line of vocational activity on the basis of a conscious and thoughtful decision in such a way that *he* actualizes his potentialities as an individual. This is why Hegel insists that in the economic domain the state has the singular duty of providing and guarding the possibility of work for everyone. This possibility is of course determined in its richness and extent by the natural, material, and political resources of the nation as a whole. But since in this domain what happens is conditioned by the qualification of the people — by their mental, physical, and social endowments — and by the state of the given economic opportunities it is quite possible for some persons to be ignored or to be treated unjustly. Hegel does not, however, think that this should be allowed to happen, because every citizen has, as we saw earlier, the right to particular satisfaction. This right is the basis of social justice: "the right actually present in the particular requires, first, that accidental hindrances to one aim or another be removed; and secondly, that the securing of every single person's livelihood and welfare be treated and actualized as a right, i.e., that particular welfare as such be so treated." (§ 230) The same point is elucidated with greater force in the addition to § 229. Here Hegel acknowledges the primacy of the law which governs the economic sphere of civil society, but this primacy is conditional, not absolute. What is absolute is the need to protect and promote justice, namely, the citizen's right to his welfare. "In civil society," Hegel writes, "universality is necessity only." When we are dealing with human needs, it is only right as such which is steadfast. But this right — only a restricted sphere — has bearing simply on the protection of property; welfare is something external to right as such. This welfare, however, is an essential end in the system of needs. Hence the universal, which in the first instance is the right only, has to be extended over the whole field of particularity. Justice is a big thing in civil society. Given good laws, a state can flourish, and freedom of property is a fundamental condition of its prosperity. Still since I am inextricably involved in particulars, my particular welfare too shall be promoted." (§ Add. to § 229) Thus although work, or human labor, is for Hegel the foundation of civil society, this work, or the way it is organized and administered, should not determine, influence, or condition the basic structure of the state; it should not, in other words, dictate or determine the rights or privileges of the citizens as members of the state. On the contrary, the economic or social reality of the state should evolve and develop up to the ideals which express the will of the people. This is why, Hegel maintains, the economic sphere should be controlled with an eye on the integrity of social justice. This element of control is effected by two institutions: (1) the public authority and (2) the corporation.

1. *Public Authority*

In addition to the protection of property and the prevention of crime (cf. § 232 — 234) the public authority has an obligation to oversee and care for the welfare of every person in his attempt to satisfy his needs. This obligation, however, cannot under any conditions whatever infringe upon the will of a person in choosing this or that particular end but only to safeguard the realm of possibility within which he can make his choice. This is why the public authority should remain "in the first instance, (a) restricted to the sphere of contingencies, and (b) an external organization.' (§ 231) In other words, it should act as a "middle term between an individual and the universal possibility, afforded by society, of attaining individual ends." (Add. to § 236) In undertaking this task the public authority should oversee two types of contingencies, (a) objective and (b)subjective.

(A) The objective contingencies relate to trade and the public's right to be treated by the business class honestly and fairly. Hegel admits at the outset that "the differing interests of the producers and consumers may come into collision with each other; and although a fair balance between them on the whole may be brought about automatically, still their adjustment also requires a control which stands above both and is consciously undertaken." (§ 236) This control may be exercised in two domains. The first includes specific objects and services which directly affect the well — being of the people; e.g. "street — lighting, bridge — building, the pricing of daily necessaries, and the care of public health." (Add. to § 236) The right of the public authority to exercise control in this domain "depends on the fact that, by being publicly exposed for sale, goods in absolutely daily demand are offered not so much to the individual as such but rather to a universal purchaser, the public; and thus both the defense of the public's right not be be defrauded, and also the management of goods inspection, may lie, as a common concern, with a public authority." (§236) The second domain in which the public authority can exercise control includes large industries or corporations; and the need for control here is greater than in the first domain, "because these are dependent on conditions abroad and on combinations of distant circumstances which cannot be grasped as a whole by the individuals tied to these industries for their living." (*Ibid.*)

This conception of economic control is an attempt by Hegel to reconcile two major theories of economics. According to the first, the public authority should superintend all the activities of civil society. But this view should be rejected mainly because it undermines the very being of human individuality. According to the second, the public authority should stay out of the economic sphere, not only because "everyone will direct his conduct according to the needs of others," but also because a person "has a right to work for his bread as he pleases." (Add. to § 236) This view should also be rejected because (1) there is no guarantee that business will have the public good as its over — riding goal, (2) the public "has a right to insist that essential tasks shall be properly done," (*Ibid.*) and (3) "control is also necessary to diminish the danger of upheavals arising from clashing interests and to abbreviate the period in which their tension should be eased through the working of a necessity of which they themselves know nothing." (§ 236) Thus although the business man has a right to produce, distribute his goods, or fix his prices the way he sees fit, although, put differently, he should enjoy freedom of trade, this freedom "should not be such as to jeopardize the general good." (Add. to § 236) Accordingly the principle which should govern the economic sphere is not the 'invisible hands' of Adam Smith nor a public authority as a final power but the general good, the universal which springs from the will of the people and is intended for their own well — being.

(B) The subjective contingencies relate to the conditions under which a person is prepared in the family and the school to work and satisfy his needs as a particular person. It is quite possible for civil society to provide a resourceful realm of possibility for work, but if the growing youth is not prepared to take advantage of this possibility he would remain dependent, and as such he would not enjoy his right to subjective satisfaction which is due him as a human being. Thus although the family has a right to educate its children and prepare them for life this right is not, as we saw in the preceding essay, the exclusive responsibility of the parents, for the child has the right to receive not merely *any* type of education but the right education in which he grows in mind and moral stature, or character. This is why the public authority should oversee the educational process in society to make sure that the principles adopted in this process are rational and conducive to human growth and development. This is based on the assumption that a child is not an object which can be owned or used by any person or institution merely as a means to an end. As a person, or as a potential person, he has the right to become himself, i.e., to actualize the potentialities which constitute his being as something human. Thus whether it is the family, civil society, the school, or the church, a social institution has an obligation to nourish in the youth one art, the art of self — realization.

Moreover, the public authority has the right and duty to protect the members of civil society from themselves; it acts in this way as a "trustee to those whose extravagance destroys the security of their own subsistence of their families. It must substitute for extravagance the pursuit of the ends of society and the individuals concerned." (§ 240) This claim may seem strange or unwarranted especially in our present day in which most people exist independently, discretely, and think that they can do with their lives whatever they please. This way of thinking is, for Hegel, erroneous, because a person does not have a right to harm or destroy himself. Why?

As a member of civil society, a person has the right to live, to pursue his personal ends and fulfill himself as an individual. Corresponding to this right is society's duty to protect all its members from any possible harm regardless of its source; "of course every individual is from one point of view independent, but he also plays his part in the system of civil society, and while every man has the right to demand subsistence from it, it must at the same time protect him from himself." (Add. to § 240) Again, if the public authority does not take the initiative in protecting the members of civil society from themselves the outcome would not merely be hungry people but a 'pauperized rabble', a dehumanized society; this would constitute an insult not only to moral conscience but also to the meaning and being of human dignity as such: what is at issue, Hegel argues, is not simply starvation, "the further end in view is to prevent the formation of a pauperized rabble. Since civil society is responsible for feeding its members, it also has the right to press them to provide for their own livelihood." (*Ibid.*)

The Question of Poverty

Now it is quite possible for the public authority to exercise proper control of the application of the law, it is quite possible for the family to function smoothly and according to generally accepted standards, and it is quite possible for the business class to proceed assiduously in production and the accumulation of wealth — yet, even though these institutions may seem to be in a healthy state of affairs, still some members of society may be affected adversely or may be deprived of their right to work. When this happens a class of poor people will be generated. This phenomenon may be caused by two types of reasons, the first contingent and the second necessary.

First, people may be reduced to poverty because of natural caprice and "also contingencies, physical conditions, and factors grounded in external circumstances." (§ 241) *Second*, people may become poor simply because they cannot find jobs. This happens when civil society is in a state of 'unimpeded activity' and when it expands "internally in population and industry." In this expansion it increases its wealth or output but it also creates negative working conditions; the amount of particular jobs would necessarily be restricted; "this results in the dependence and distress of the class tied to work of that sort, and these again entail inability to feel and enjoy the broader freedoms and especially the intellectual benefits of civil society." (§ 243)

Hegel recognizes, as we saw, that the modern state, with which we presently live, is not 'an ideal work of art' but "stands on earth and so in the sphere of caprice, chance, and error, and bad behavior may disfigure it in many respects." (Add. to § 258) The existence of poverty is a testimony to this recognition. One does not choose or desire to be poor; one is somehow made or led to be poor. His poverty is usually precipitated by natural and social causes. But from the fact that a man finds himself poor, that he is stuck in a certain social predicament, it does not necessarily follow that he does not have the right to exist as a particular individual. This is why the public authority should assist on behalf of the state in overcoming their poverty. "The poor," Hegel argues, "still have the needs common to civil society, and yet since society has withdrawn from them the natural means of acquisition and broken the bond of the family — in the wider sense of the clan — their poverty leaves them more or less deprived of all the advantages of society, of the opportunity of acquiring skill of education of any kind, as well as of the administration of justice, the public health services, and often even of the consolations of religion, and so forth." (§ 241) But how?, my critic would here interject. Should the public authority act as a paternal agency? If so, what guarantee do we have that this agency does not slip into despotic power? Should the wealthy assist the poor on the basis of philanthropy? Should charitable organizations be allowed to feed, console, and care for the poor as a class by themselves? The question which we should consider, my critic would insist, is: under what conditions — human conditions, that is — can Hegel provide a solution to the problem of poverty? This is an important question primarily because poverty seems to be a necessary phenomenon within his political scheme. But if the central principle of this scheme is the principle of human dignity, or self — respect, then how can we organize society in such a way that poverty can be overcome rationally?

Hegel is acutely alive to this problem. His concern in the analysis of this issue is not simply to find a way to 'feed' the poor — to appease, pity, or quiet their discontent — but mainly to alleviate the whole problem, to provide a socio — political mechanism by which the poor person can overcome his poverty and live under the conditions of human dignity. Poverty is a serious evil not only because it deprives certain members of society from the opportunity to acquire an education and to work but especially because it necessarily leads to the creation of a rabble of paupers: "when the standard of living of a large mass of people falls below a certain subsistence level — a level regulated automatically as the one necessary for a member of society — and when there is a consequent loss of the sense of right and wrong, of honesty and the self — respect which makes a man insist on maintaining himself by his own work and effort, the result is the creation of a rabble of paupers." (§ 244) We cannot, Hegel insists, take this matter lightly because a rabble of paupers are *not merely* a group of poor people; they are people who have lost their identity as human beings: they have lost the meaning of dignity and self — respect, sociality, and respect for the being of others, for truth and the meaning of human values, and of creativity and the drive to be free: "poverty in itself," Hegel writes, "does not make men into a rabble; a rabble is created only when there is joined to poverty a disposition of mind, an inner indignation against the rich, against society, against the government. A further consequence of this attitude is that through their dependence on chance men become frivolous and idle, like the Neapolitan *Lazzaroni* for example. In this way there is born in the rabble the evil of lacking self — respect enough to secure subsistence by its own labour and yet at the same time of claiming to receive subsistence as its right." (Add. to § 244) When a society condones the existence of such a rabble, as Hegel saw happening in Britain, its wealth will necessarily be concentrated in the hands of a few economically powerful people: "at the same time this brings with it, at the other end of the social scale, conditions which greatly facilitate the concentration of disproportionate wealth in a few hands." (§ 244)[12]

Poverty cannot, however, be allowed or condoned primarily because it is immoral and contrary to the very ideal of the state, viz., promotion of human freedom. But how are we to check or undermine this social evil? We may, *first*, argue that the existence or non — existence of poverty is a moral question: it is our duty to help the poor. This is a fundamental obligation of love and human sympathy. Hegel is aware of this obligation. "Poverty," he writes, "and, in general, the distress of every kind to which every individual is exposed from the start in the cycle of his natural life has a subjective side which demands similarly subjective aid, arising both from the special circumstances of a particular case and also from love and sympathy. This is the place where morality finds plenty to do despite all public organization." (§ 242) But this way of solving the problem is unsatisfactory because it is subjective and contingent, therefore unreliable. What is needed is not simply to help this or that person, or family, at a specific time or place but to create social and economic conditions in which the members of civil society do not have to be poor: "subjective aid, however, both in itself and in its operation, is dependent on contingency and consequently society struggles to make it less necessary, by discovering the general causes of penury and general means of its relief, and by organizing relief accordingly." (*Ibid.*)

We may, *second*, argue that the burden of assisting the poor "might be directly laid on the wealthier classes, or they might recieve the means of livelihood directly from other public sources of wealth (e.g. from the endowments of rich hospitals, monasteries, and other foundations.)" (§ 245) Like the first, this argument rests on a plea of charity, according to which the poor man *receives* his means of living or is enabled to maintain a certain standard of living. This argument, Hegel holds, should be rejected mainly because the poor man remains poor and as such deprived of his privilege to self — realization. The needy would, according to this argument, "receive subsistence directly, not by means of their work, and this would violate the principle of civil society and the feeling of individual independence and self — respect in its individual members." (§ 245) Again, "public social conditions are on the contrary to be regarded as all the more perfect the less (in comparison with what is arranged publicly) is left for an individual to do by himself as his private inclination directs." (§ 242) And these public social conditions should be emphasized mainly because working, and consequently self — realization, is not a favor but a right which should be protected and upheld by the state.

We may, *third*, argue that the poor should be assisted "indirectly through being given work, i.e., the opportunity to work." (§ 245) That is, the government should create work opportunities for all those who happen to be unemployed. The assumption which underlies this argument is that since charity or charitable acts towards the poor violate the principle of human dignity, and since a respectable human being should earn his own living, the government should accordingly create the needed work opportunities. But, Hegel observes, this line of reasoning is inadequate because if extra work positions are created production will necessarily increase; this will in turn lead to unemployment, for, to begin with, it was excess production in the first place which has led to unemployment; "in this event the volume of production would be increased, but the evil consists precisely in an excess of production and in the face of a proportionate number of consumers who are themselves also producers.... It hence becomes apparent that despite an excess of wealth civil society is not rich enough, i.e., its own resources are insufficient to check excessive poverty and the creation of a penurious rabble." (*Ibid.*)

The problem of poverty cannot, then, be solved by the efforts of charitable agencies or by contriving work opportunities for the poor but by creating a socio — political structure and conditions under which every person should be able to pursue his personal ends as a particular individual. This is based on a two — fold assumption: (1) work, and consequently self — realization, is a basic human right which should be safeguarded and uncompromised by the state. (2) Economic growth is not *necessarily* contrary to, or incompatible with, the prevalence of social justice; that is, it is reasonable to envision a society which enjoys the highest state of economic health and in which every person works productively and contributes to the general welfare.

The proposition which I should underscore in view of the foregoing discussion is that poverty, or any economic deprivation, should be alleviated not by charitable persons or organizations but by the state and this on the basis of economic planning. This point is made amply clear in § 249 where Hegel states that the primary purpose of the public authority is to actualize and maintain the universal contained in the particularity of civil society: "while the public authority must also undertake the higher directive function of providing for the interests which lead beyond the borders of its society, its primary purpose is to actualize and maintain the universal contained within the particularity of civil society, and its control takes the form of an external system and organization for the protection and security of particular ends and interests *en masse*, inasmuch as these interests subsist only in this universal. This universal is immanent in the interests of particularity itself and, in accordance with the Idea, particularity makes it the end and object of its own willing and activity."

2. *The Corporation*

In addition to the public authority, a necessary condition for the realization of particularity, i.e., self — realization, is what Hegel calls the Corporation. While the former supervises the well — being of economic activity in civil society and makes certain that every person is able to work and satisfy his personal needs, the latter, viz., the corporation, creates the *actual conditions* of work; it is the 'medium' in which a member of civil society acquires his vocation and fulfills himself as a working animal.

It should here be remarked that when I speak of the corporation as the medium of work I do not at all mean that what a farmer or a civil servant does is not work; what a person does in these socio —

economic spheres is work *par excellence*. But since the business class, which corresponds in our times to the middle class, is the largest class discussion of work would essentially revolve on this class.

"The labour organization of civil society," Hegel writes, "is split, in accordance with the nature of its particulars, into different branches. The implicit likeness of such particulars to one another becomes really existent in an association, as something common to its members. Hence a selfish purpose, directed towards its particular self — interest, apprehends and evinces itself at the same time as universal." (§ 251) Civil society, then, is composed of corporations. As an economic unit, a corporation is an association of particular individuals who are alike in their interests and who are devoted to a specific type of socio — economic activity. They cooperate together in meeting their needs as well as the needs of others. Accordingly the corporation is the concrete sphere in which the life of the individual unfolds as a particular person; within this sphere he attends to his potentialities and actualizes them by producing an object with a universal character, an object which can be used and consumed by society at large: "a member in civil society is in virtue of his own particular skill a member of a Corporation, whose universal purpose is thus wholly concrete and no wider in scope than the purpose involved in business, its proper task and interest." (*Ibid.*)

A corporation the way Hegel conceives it must be distinguished from a twentieth century labor union, cooperative, or workers' association. These types of organizations are grouped formally for the sake of a political end, securing a job, or promoting a cause of some kind. The personal or professional ends of the members remain external, irrelevant, to the over — all purpose of the organization. For Hegel, a corporation is a substantial economic and social institution within which a person functions as a citizen, i.e., as a member of the state. The essential nature of this institution can be understood if we examine the functions which it performs; "(a) to look after its own interests within its own sphere, (b) to co — opt members, qualified objectively by the requisite skill and rectitude, to a number fixed by the general structure of society, (c) to protect its members against particular contingencies, (d) to provide the education requisite to fit others to become members." (§ 252) The corporation is, as we can see, not merely an expedient or convenience but a *human association*; it does not only educate and prepare its members to be proficient, skilled, and effective in a certain area of work but also protects their economic interests. It provides, in short, a secure social and material foundation which is a *sine qua non* for spiritual accomplishments and satisfaction. This is why Hegel characterizes it as a kind of family: "Its right is to come on the scene like a second family for its members, while civil society can only be an indeterminate sort of family because it comprises everyone and so is farther removed from individuals and their special exigencies." (*Ibid.*) Thus unlike the day laborer or the man who chooses his career or job casually, the member of the corporation is, first "a master of his craft, he is a member of the association not for casual gain on single occasions but for the whole range, the universality, of his personal livelihood." (*Ibid.*) The value entailed by his livelihood is a function of the totality of his life as it becomes actual in his daily work; it gives a special meaning and adds richness to the inner satisfaction which work should yield. Second, the member of a corporation enjoys special rights, or more concretely privileges (from *privilegium*), which originate from the unique activities or achievements of the corporation; these rights are "distinct in meaning from privileges proper in the etymological sense. The latter are casual exceptions to universal rules; the former, however, are only the crystallization, as regulations, of characteristics inherent in an essential branch of society itself owing to its nature as particular." (*Ibid.*)

I am certain that one cannot but question the usefulness or viability of the corporation as a basic institution in a society like ours which seems to increase in complexity, on the one hand, and to stress more and more the value of independence, of 'each to his own', on the other. One can also wonder whether this sort of institution does not promote a tendency towards social regimentation. We should therefore ask: why should Hegel introduce this institution in his political scheme? Is he justified in this introduction?

Hegel is, *first*, aware of the possible tendency towards social regimentation; he is aware that if a corporation is left to itself as an independent economic unity unrelated to the life of the state as a whole it would tend to become a closed system within which the member is reduced to a number, a cog in a machine, and lose his capacity for self — determination. This is why in § 252 he declares that the corporation should remain "under the surveillance of the public authority." And in the addition to § 255 he writes: "of course the corporations must fall under the higher surveillance of the state, because otherwise they would ossify, build themselves in, and decline into a miserable system of castes. In and by itself, however, a corporation is not a closed caste; its purpose is rather to bring an isolated trade into the social order and elevate it to a sphere in which it gains strength and respect."

Second, Hegel is conscious of the need to justify the introduction of the corporation as a basic social institution in his political scheme. Its formulation is his answer to the atomism which began during his lifetime to sweep the European states. Beside the family, in the corporation an individual actualizes himself as a socio — political being. Here he fulfills himself both as a particular individual and as a member of the state.

There is, as we have seen, a drive in man to be recognized, accepted, and appreciated as a human being. But what a person is depends on what he does or achieves; his value as an individual is commensurate with the value of his accomplishments in the community. But if a person works and produces in a society where people are indifferent to each other or are inter — related on the basis of self — interest his product will go either unnoticed or used casually to satisfy a personal need; the product will not be related or associated with its producer, and the latter will go about in society as an 'atom' unrecognized for his accomplishments. In the corporation, however, the whole scene changes. In this institution, Hegel writes, the nexus of capability and livelihood of a corporation member "is a *recognized* fact, with the result that the corporation member needs no external marks beyond his own membership as evidence of his skill and his regular income and subsistence, i.e., as evidence that he is somebody." (§ 253) This is of course based on the assumption that a corporation is a legally and socially recognized institution, and that this recognition depends on acknowledged standards of integrity and accomplishment.[13] To be a member of a corporation is to be a person with a specific set of qualifications both professionally and ethically. Thus when a person is accepted as a member he *eo ipso* assumes a certain social and professional identity which becomes the basis of his dignity and respectability.

Moreover, as a corporation member, a man does not work in isolation or only for himself, on his own, but with others and for the sake of others, i.e., society. In his work he does not have an eye merely on an immediate outcome or satisfaction but on the whole. He knows, in other words, that his work is valuable because it is conducive to the well — being of society; but this knowledge is not exclusive to him: it is also recognized by society "that he belongs to a whole which is itself an organ of an entire society, and that he is actively concerned in promoting the comparatively disinterested end of his whole. Thus he commands the respect due to one corporation in his social position." (*Ibid.*) But his contribution in his capacity as a member has a two — fold character: (1) economically, he contributes to the material welfare of society; (2) politically, he declares his interests within the corporation; these interests will, as we saw in essay II, be incorporated by the efforts of the elected members in the legislative process, i.e., in the enactment of the law. In this way he functions in society as a self — determined being because the political and economic laws by which he lives express and are consonant with his will.

Even though the preceding arguments may seem plausible one may still ask: why complicate socio — economic life by corporations or similar associations? Why should every member of society not pursue his ends on his own? This sort of objection is really an attempt to endorse the atomism I mentioned above, and Hegel sees a place for it (i.e., the objection) in the area of socio — political criticism, for he writes: "the consideration behind the abolition of corporations in recent times is that the individual should fend for himself. But we may grant this and still hold that corporation membership does not alter a man's obligation to earn his living." (Add. to § 255) The point which Hegel is trying to emphasize is not *that* one should work but *under* what *working conditions* can he fulfill himself as a particular individual and function as an effective member of the state as a whole, as a member that counts! In response to the defenders of atomism Hegel advances the following complaint: "under modern political conditions, the citizens have only a restricted share in the public business of the state, yet it is essential to provide men — ethical entities — with work of a public character over and above their private business. This work of a public character, which the modern state does not always provide, is found in the corporation." (*Ibid.*) Hegel admits that in fending for himself a man does make a contribution to society, but he makes this contribution indirectly, unconsciously, and therefore indifferently. This sort of contribution does not have an ethical character, for it is neither intended as such nor deliberate. Thus "unless he is a member of an authorized corportion (and it is only by being authorized that an association becomes a corporation), an individual is without rank or dignity, his isolation reduces his business to mere self — seeking, and his livelihood and satisfaction become insecure. Consequently, he has to try to gain recognition for himself by giving external proofs of success in his business, and to these proofs no limits can be set. He cannot live in the manner of his class, for no class really exists for him, since in civil society it is only something common to particular persons which really exists, i.e. something legally constituted and recognized. Hence he cannot achieve for himself a way of life proper to his class and less idiosyncratic." (§ 253)

Concluding Remarks on Poverty

I hope I have said enough to show that the state which Hegel advocates is a welfare state. Briefly formulated, the fundamental principles of the state are:

1. Law is the foundation of the state.
2. The ultimate source of political authority is the people; the law which the citizen should obey expresses his interest as a rational being and as a member of the state.
3. The government represents the will, viz., the interests, of the people; therefore its main function is to create a socio — economic structure within which the common good can be realized.

4. The capital of the state is, or should be, owned by the people, not the government.

5. Economic health and growth within a system of private enterprise is not incompatible with social justice. For Hegel, the common good, or the law, is the highest principle according to which the political, social, and economic activities should be organized.

If we take the fifth premise into serious consideration we should then hold that there is no need within Hegel's political scheme for poverty as a basic social issue either to exist or to grow beyond the bounds of control. This state of affairs is, as I have just explained, guaranteed by the institution of the public authority and the system of corporations as organs of the state. I should here add that Hegel does not mean to say that poverty will be absolutely, and once for all, eliminated; perhaps the poor will always be with us. What he is anxious to accomplish, though, is a socio — political framework based on just principles, and concern for the well — being of every member of society, a framework which guarantees *in principle* work opportunities for every person who can and has the will to work.

But has he accomplished this framework, my critic would object? What happens, for example, if economic production increases, if the wealthy grow in power and become indifferent to the masses, and if consequently many people find themselves unemployed? Can, in a situation like this, the public authority interfere? If so, how?

The formulation of this objection is misleading, for it is based on the assumption that the business class exists in Hegel's system independently, that it operates on its own discretely without concern for the well — being of the people or the state in general. But, as we saw in the first two essays, Hegel rejects this assumption. He views the various spheres of the state as organically inter — related, in which these spheres cooperate rather than antagonize each other. Thus although the capital should, for him, remain in private hands, i.e., owned by the people, we should not automatically assume the people are necessarily selfish or uncaring for the general welfare of the state or that when the public authority interferes its objective is to undermine or destroy the interest of the business class. Hegel is not naive; he is a realistic student of human nature. He knows very well that economic power has a tendency to corrupt. This is why he recommended (1) that a public authority should be erected to supervise the activities of the business sector to make certain that these activities remain within legal bounds and (2) that society should be composed of corporations which guarantee the material and spiritual well — being of its members, on the one hand, and regiment the power of the masses, on the other: "for some time past organizations have been framed with a view to controlling these particular spheres from above, and effort has chiefly been expended on organizations of that type, while the lower classes, the mass of the population, have been left more or less unorganized. And yet it is of the utmost importance that the masses should be organized, because only so do they become mighty and powerful. Otherwise they are nothing but a heap, an aggregate of atomic units. Only when the particular associations are organized members of the state are they possessed of legitimate power." (Add. to § 290) What merits special attention here is that the corporate system is for Hegel a political strategy for organizing all the segments of society into effective socio — political power, a power that can be influential not only in seeking and realizing its interest by direct influence of the market but also through legislation.

Again, the sort of private enterprise system which Hegel adopts in the *Philosophy of Right* is somewhat different from the one proposed by Adam Smith. The system of the latter rests on the basic claim of atomisn, according to which if the invisible hands of supply and demands are given their reign economic justice or balance will result in the end. But Hegel rejects, as we saw, this claim. This is why he introduced the corporate system; and in introducing this system he sought to provide an ethical basis for the economic law of civil society: "as the family was the first, so the corporation is the second ethical root of the state, the one planted in civil society. The former contains the moments of subjective particularity and objective universality in a substantial unity. But these moments are sundered in civil society to begin with; on the one side there is the particularity of need and satisfaction, reflected into itself, and on the other side the universality of abstract rights. In the corporation these moments are united in an inward fashion, so that in this union particular welfare is present as a right and is actualized." (§ 255) In a society where the universality of abstract law is acknowledged and respected it would be extremely difficult, almost impossible, for the basic institutions to go over bounds, i.e., to ignore and step on the meaning and spirit of the law. On the contrary, in such a society although profit and self — enrichment may be given their due claim the right and satisfaction of all are also given their claim. This is exactly why Hegel writes: "within the corporation the help which poverty receives loses its accidental character and the humiliation wrongfully associated with it. The wealthy perform their duties to their fellow associates and thus riches cease to inspire either pride or envy, pride in their owners, envy in others. In these conditions rectitude obtains its proper recognition and respect." (§ 253) But even if a business falls prey to greed and ignores the interest of the state qua public authority the people have the right to interfere and uphold the universal in the life of its particular members. Although the corporations are, as we saw, autonomous and should run their own particular business, still they cannot violate the law; their interest must be subordinated to the interest of the whole: "these circles of particular interest," Hegel writes, "must be subordinated to the higher interests of the state, and hence the filling of positions or responsibility in corporations, etc., will generally be effected by a mixture of popular election by those interested with appointment and rectification by higher authority." (§ 288) This aspect of the relationship between the state and the business class was rightly articulated by Prof. Charles Taylor: "for Hegel there can be no question of abolishing the bourgeois economy. Rather its inherent drive to dissolution must be contained through its sub — ordination to the demands of the more ultimate community which is the state. This higher allegiance and the rules which flow from it must keep men from giving way to those extremes of the drive for self — enrichment which pull society into the slip — stream of uncontrolled growth."[14]

The state, then, has a right to interfere in the economic sphere of civil society only when the interest of the law and the people is ignored or jeopardized, but this interference is justified *only by legal means*. And if the law happens to be unjust or fails to assert the welfare of the state as a living unity of purpose it can, as I argued earlier, be changed, and it can be changed mainly because there is a politico — economical framework within which every member of society can exist and fulfill himself as a particular individual.

SIX

APPENDIX I

JUSTICE AS THE BASIS OF PUNISHMENT

In his widely read essay, *Hegel's Theory of Punishment*[1], J. Ellis McTaggart argues that Hegel's conception of punishment, as it is expounded in *The Philosophy of Right*, (1) cannot be properly applied in jurisprudence, and (2) does not have room for the conscientious offender who knowingly violates the existing bad law in favor of a higher, better law. These criticisms have been accepted, almost without question, by most writers on punishment, even by Hegelian critics.[2] They stem, however, from an erroneous interpretation of what Hegel means by punishment and of how he thinks it is to be justified. McTaggart for example argues that the object of punishemnt, for Hegel, "is that the criminal should repent for his crime, and by so doing realize the moral character, which has been temporarily obscured by his wrong action, but which is, as Hegel asserts, really his truest and deepest nature."[3] McTaggart further argues that punishment tends to improve, reform, the criminal. Thus punishment becomes an instrument of moral reformation, a means to a higher end.[4] One can certainly argue, as McTaggart does, that a reformatory theory of punishment would not apply in jurisprudence if punishment does not improve but rather hinders the moral well — being of the criminal. Thus the questions which we should stress are: does Hegel espouse a reformatory theory of punishment? If so, in what sense? How does he justify the act of punishment? Under what conditions should punishment be inflicted? In this essay I intend to focus attention on these questions. I shall argue that the end of punishment, for Hegel, is not repentence or reformation, but the negation of wrong and the solidarity of justice in the life of the individual and society. I shall also argue that Hegel's view of punishment does apply in jurisprudence, and that his theory leaves adequate room for the individual to protest against a bad law conscientiously and knowingly.

I.

Legal punishment is an act in which pain is inflicted upon a criminal, that is, upon a person who has knowingly violated the law. The question arises: why should punishment be inflicted? Hegel, to begin with, considers two main theories which provide answers to this question: deterrence and reformation.[5] They basically hold that pain is evil. Thus, since crime itself is evil it would "seem quite unreasonable to will an evil merely because 'another evil is there already'.".[6] Accordingly, punishment should, if we have to use it, be inflicted only for a good, humane end. The theory of deterrence views punishment essentially as a threat, and as such it is preventive in character. The threat may relate either to the individual or to society. When the individual is concerned, punishment tends to deter him from repeating the same crime; and when society is concerned, it produces the same result by being a threat which others are bound to observe and recognize. Thus as a deterrent factor, punishment tends to minimize the occurence of crime. But this theory, Hegel objects, dehumanizes the individual; it treats him as a thing, as an animal who needs to be made harmless, not as a dignified human being. It is indeed morally wrong, for it does not respect man as a free, responsible being; on the contrary, it treats him "as if he were not free, and seeks to compel him by the representation of evil. But right and justice must have their seat in freedom and the will, and not in the absence of freedom which is made use of by the menace. When such a ground is alleged for punishment, man is considered, not in his dignity and freedom, but like a dog over which a stick is raised." (§ 99; 246)

The reformatory theory, on the other hand, holds that the end of punishment is to reform or improve the moral well — being of the criminal. Punishment, however, cannot be inflicted unless we are somehow certain that it will make the criminal better and suitable for social life; it is in a sense an educative factor in the life of the criminal. At first glance, this theory appears to be humanitarian in its orientation, for it aims, almost exclusively, at the spiritual improvement of the wrongdoer. But in fact the objections which Hegel advances against the deterrent theory apply to this one also, primarily because it does not treat the culprit as the master of his life. This theory fails, moreover, in two other respects. First, it severs the intimate and necessary relationship between crime and punishment; that is, it views punishment as something indifferent, unrelated to crime. But Hegel has frequently insisted that the concept of crime *implies* the concept of punishment: "crime as the will which is implicitly null, *eo ipso* contains its negation in itself and this negation is manifested as punishment." (§ 101; 72; see also 247) Moreover, if punishment can improve and enrich the spiritual life of man, why not, then, establish a compulsory system of punishment which applies to all the members of society who are morally weak or deficient? Again, if we do not treat punishment as logically presupposed by crime, "then it may become possible to see in punishment proper only an 'arbitrary' connexion of an evil with an unlawful action." (§ 101; 73) Second, the reformatory theory assumes that at the time of the crime the wrongdoer does not fully possess his rational or moral nature; he does not, in other words, act as a fully responsible being. Yet he has potential for free and rational existence. So punishment becomes a means which actualizes this potentiality. But, Hegel argues, a person who is not rational or fully moral at the time of the crime cannot, *eo ipso*, do wrong (cf. § 132; 88). Accordingly only such a man can be punished. Thus punishment on this view loses its meaning as a legal or moral category.

The main objection, however, which Hegel raises against the theories of deterrence and reformation is that they overlook the very meaning and rationale of punishment. Both of them abhor punishment because it is a form of evil. But the question of punishment is not "merely a question of evil or of this, that, or the other good; the precise point at issue is wrong and the righting of it." If we lose sight of this point two unhappy consequences follow: (1) we "brush aside the objective treatment of the righting of wrong, which is the primary and fundamental attitude in considering crime;" (2) we confuse the moral aspect of punishment with its personal, subjective aspect, i.e., with "trivial psychological ideas of stimuli, impulses too strong for reason, and psychological factors coercing and working on our ideas (as if freedom were not equally capable of thrusting an idea aside and reducing it to something fortuitous!)." Hegel does not deny that deterrence, threat, reformation, etc., are relevant to and important features of the concept of punishment; he only asserts that these features presuppose "as their foundation the fact that punishment is inherently and actually just. In discussing this matter the only important things are, first, that crime is to be annulled, not because it is the producing of an evil, but because it is an infringement of the right as right, and secondly, the question of what that positive existence is which crime possesses and which must be annulled; it is this existence which is the real evil to be removed, and the essential point is the question of where it lies." (§ 99; 70)

II

Now let us ask: how does Hegel justify punishment? Why should the criminal be punished? The criminal should be punished because he has violated the law, i.e., committed a crime. In this act, right, which the law expresses, is denied, ignored. Thus crime is unjust primarily because it is an infringement of right. The criminal in his act sets aside the principle of rightness. But right, as such, cannot be ignored or set aside. Accordingly, punishment is inflicted to restore or assert rightness, i.e., justice. Punishment, then, is just, not because it produces this or that result, but because it is an assertion of absolute right.

The infringement of the law exists in the world in two basic respects. It, first, exists as a fact, as an event; and as an event it has a "positive" existence in the external world like any ordinary event or fact, e.g., tree or rain. But *merely* as an event it is not distinguished from other events by any moral or criminal aspects. It, second, exists as a crime; and as a crime it is understood only from the standpoint of the wrongdoer himself, that is, as a conscious, purposeful action. Thus as a crime it lacks the positive existence of ordinary facets or events. What makes it a crime is the fact that it is deliberately chosen, willed, by the criminal (cf. 331). To society, or those who recognize it, it is a *negative act*, for it is an infringement, a denial of rights, and to that extent it is self — destructive — null, to use Hegel's language: "right as something absolute cannot be set aside, and so committing a crime is in principle a nullity: and this nullity is the essence of what the crime effects" (§ 97; 246). Thus if crime is not removed it would, at least implicitly, be accepted as something valid. It is, however, removed by removing what infringes the right "and therein displays its validity and proves itself to be a necessary, mediated reality". (*Ibid.*)

Hegel stresses that punishment cannot be just and, consequently, cannot be justly inflicted upon the criminal, unless two conditions are fulfilled; (A) the criminal act must be willed by the wrongdoer; (B) the wrongdoer must consent to the punishment. (A) Hegel, first, assumes that the criminal is a rational being; he is free and can determine his life. He is therefore a responsible individual. But responsibility is a necessary condition for punishment; that is, one cannot be punished for an act he has performed unless he can be responsible for it. And he cannot be responsible for it unless the act can be imputed to his will, i.e., unless he has freely chosen the act.[7] Thus crime is a purposeful, conscious act; it expresses the will of the criminal[8], and in choosing to commit it he in a sense accepts the punishment entailed by the act. For, as I indicated earlier, the concept of crime implies the concept of punishment; thus if one chooses the former he *ipso facto* chooses the latter. Viewed from this standpoint, punishment is just, for the crime is *committed* freely, willfully. It is also a right, for the action of the criminal is the action of a rational being. In committing a crime he ignores a law which he knows he should recognize and observe. This law is an expression of his will as a universal moral nature. Thus in violating it he denies himself the specific right which the law embodies; punishment is a restoration of this right (cf. § 100; 70). Accordingly the criminal does not receive punishment as something imposed on him by an external, hostile agency; on the contrary, he pronounces his own judgment and declares himself guilty, thereby acknowledging the validity of punishment as right. This is exactly why Hegel held that since crime is a volitional act, "punishment is regarded as containing the criminal's right and hence by being punished he is honored as a rational being" (§ 100; 71). In punishment, then, justice triumphs over crime and the criminal establishes himself once more as a free, self — determined being.

The negation of wrong by punishment is retribution, and this in two basic respects: (1) punishment is in principle a negation of negation, an "injury of the injury"; (2) the concept of crime contains, as we have seen, its negation and presupposes it; hence punishment should be equal to the crime — (but in what sense should it be equal to the crime?). These two aspects of punishment have led some thinkers to interpret the concept either as revenge or as a restatement of the dictum, "an eye for an eye, and a tooth for a tooth", or, "as the criminal has done, so should it be done to him" (Cf. § 100). But Hegel rejects both of these interpretations. He, *first*, denies, as Flechtheim tends to believe, that retribution is revenge. The distinctive character of revenge is that it is a private and not public, legal act. It is arbitrary and determined by the emotions of personal interest of the revengeful person. Accordingly revenge is unjust, for it is an infringement of the law. It creates a demand for justice, i.e., for punishment, which is free from any subjective or arbitrary interest. "Fundamentally, this implies the demand for a will which, though particular and subjective, yet wills the universal as such." (§ 103; 73). Thus retribution is not an act in which pain is inflicted for its own sake; it is rather the realization of the concept of right as such, i.e., justice.

Hegel, *second*, denies that retribution is, at least indirectly, a restatement of the dictum, "an eye for an eye, and a tooth for a tooth." For the dictum assumes that requital can be made equal to the crime. This however, cannot be done; for this equality is not one of quantity or quality, but of value. It is not, in other words, "an equality between the specific character of the crime and that of its negation; on the contrary, the two injuries are equal only in respect of their implicit character, i.e., in respect of their value" (§ 101; 71). The qualitative and quantitative aspects of punishment are external to the concept of crime. That is, the nature or content of punishment is an empirical, practical question. We cannot fomulate a set of rules according to which punishments are determined, for crimes are concrete, unique events. Consequently they should be evaluated by the judge in their special contexts. Even here it is almost impossible to determine absolutely what a certain punishment is or should be; for "in the field of the finite, absolute determinacy remains only a demand, a demand which the Understanding has to meet by continually increasing delimitation — a fact of the greatest importance — but which continues *ad infinitum* and which allows only of perennially approximate satisfaction "(§ 101; 72). This factor makes it extremely difficult to apply the "eye for eye, tooth for tooth" maxim in a court of justice. Yet despite the inability to determine precisely what the punishment should be in a given case it is absolutely necessary that a decision, no matter how arbitrary it may be, should be made with the best possible intention to realize justice. In the third part of *The Philosophy of Right* Hegel writes: "reason cannot determine, nor can the concept provide any principle whose application could decide whether justice requires for an offence (i) a corporal punishment of fourty lashes or thirty — nine, or (ii) a fine of five dollars or four dollars ninety — three, four, etc., cents, or (iii) imprisonment of a year or three hundred and sixty — four, three, etc., days, or a year and one, two or three days. And yet injustice is done at once if there is one lash too many, or one dollar or one cent, one week in prison or one day, too many or too few." (§ 214; 137) This only shows that law, or any abstract rule, cannot *by itself* dictate what punishment a criminal deserves in a concrete situation, otherwise the retributive aspects of punishment would be exhibited as an absurdity: e.g. "theft for theft, robbery for robbery, an eye for an eye, a tooth for a tooth — and then you can go on to suppose that the criminal has only one eye or no teeth." (§ 101; 72)

(B) Before punishment can be inflicted the criminal must, second, freely consent to the punishment; he must confess his guilt. This confession justifies his accepting the punishment which the judge prescribes. In laying this condition Hegel is especially concerned with the dignity and humanity of the criminal; for he does not treat him as an object of pity or revenge, but as a self — determined person, and this for two reasons: (1) the punishment is imposed justly; (2) the criminal freely accepts the punishment, and to that extent he punishes himself — how? There is no good reason, Hegel maintains, to suppose that only the judge or legal expert knows how to assess the facts of the criminal case; "for ability to do so depends on general, not on purely legel education. Determination of the facts of the case depends on empirical details, on deposition about what happened, and on similar perceptual data, or again on facts from which inferences can be drawn about the deed in question and which make it probable or improbable." (§ 227; 275) In a criminal situation we need to be certain of two main factors: (1)whether the facts are considered comprehensively and objectively; (2) whether the criminal agrees that this consideration is both accurate and just. This is the main reason why Hegel insists that the criminal should confess his guilt, and that when this is done the right of self — consciousness "attains a measure of satisfaction; consciousness must chime in with the judge's sentence, and it is only when the criminal has confessed that the judgment loses its alien character so far as he is concerned." (*Ibid.*) Hegel is aware that the culprit may lie or make a mistake. If this happens the cause of justice would be undermined. And yet if the accused is treated according to the subjective will of the judge alone he is no longer a free man. Thus to escape these two extreme possibilities Hegel suggests trial by jury, "which meets the demand that the declaration of guilt or innocence shall spring from the soul of the accused" (*Ibid.*). It meets this demand because the jury is a body of rational men, and since they share this rationality with the accused and identify themselves with him their verdict is the verdict of the criminal's own soul.

Thus punishment for Hegel is not intended, as McTaggart has argued, to reform or improve the moral well — being of the criminal, nor to make him repent of his moral sin. The main difficulty with this interpretation is that it places the "end", "purpose" of punishment in the future, i.e., outside the criminal situation; but, as I have argued, the concept of crime implies the concept of punishment; thus it does not have an end beyond the criminal act. It is inflicted primarily because a certain wrong, which is an irrational act, needs to be righted. Punishment, then, expresses an inner demand for justice, not for revenge or the attainment of a social or psychological end.

III.

We should next ask: does Hegel's concept of punishment apply in jurisprudence? McTaggart thinks that it does not. He argues that the main object of punishment from the standpoint of the state is to prevent crime and not to reform the criminal. He advances four reasons in support of this claim. (1) By inflicting "severe and judicious punishment we can diminish" crime enormously. (2) The deterrent effect of punishment acts not only on the criminal who suffers it, but on all who realize that they will suffer it if they commit a similar offense. The purifying influence can act only on those who suffer the punishment." (3) "There seems grave reason to doubt whether, in a modern state, the crimes dealt with and the attitude of the criminal to the state are such that the punishment can be expected to lead to repentence.[9] (4) Punishment can reform the criminal only by appealing to the moral nature of the criminal, but this nature cannot be easily aroused or realized. Thus, since the innocent in a society are more than the criminals, and since the deterrent impact of punishment is more effective in decreasing crime, the deterrent theory can properly be applied in jurisprudence. This line of reasoning fails in two fundamental respects: (1) If Hegel advocates a reformatory theory of punishment, as McTaggart holds, and *if* we can prove that the over — riding object of punishment is deterrence, and that deterrence does indeed minimize crime, then Hegel's theory of punishment would hardly apply in jurisprudence. But these assumptions are ill founded. The object of punishment for Hegel is not, as I argued earlier, to reform or purify the criminal, i.e., to make him repent of his sin, but to remove a wrong, that is, to realize justice. (2) I do not think that from the standpoint of the state the end of punishment is to prevent or diminish crime, though this is one of the most important *duties of the state*; its end is, as Hegel insisted, to right a certain wrong, or, put differently, to assert the principle of rightness and see to it that justice is promoted in the life of the community. This is a legalistic interpretation of punishment, according to which the sole justification of punishment is infringement of law. In other words, the state has no right whatever to punish a man unless he has violated the law. And I think the world we live in today is, inasmuch as criminal law is concerned, Hegelian in character. When a criminal is presented to a court of justice to account for a crime he has committed the judge makes it clear to the public that the culprit is punished because he has violated the law. And if the criminal discovers in some secret way that he is used as a means to a public or some other type of interest he would certainly feel insulted, degraded, and treated unjustly. This goes to show that in ordinary life punishment is inflicted because the criminal deserves it, because it is just.[10] Accordingly it would be a mistake to say, with McTaggart, that Hegel's concept of punishment is deterrence.

McTaggart, moreover, complains that Hegel's notion of the relationship between the law and the citizen does not leave room for critical, individual conscience. The identification of the moral law with the established authority robs the individual of his moral independence and consequently of his moral self — determination. The individual becomes a slave, so to say, to the state; for in becoming the ground of the law the state assumes the role of a father or a god who cannot be questioned or ignored.[11] Flechtheim advances a similar criticism: "because of the identification of the real with the ideal, of law with justice, Hegel's system leaves no room for the conscientious offender who knowingly violates the oppressive law of today in the interest of the 'better law of tomorrow.'"[12]

These criticisms are based on the assumption that law is, contrary to Hegel's belief, man made; it is not the final expression or embodiment of the principle of rightness. Accordingly it may be mistaken. Thus an individual has the express right to violate an existing law and appeal instead to the moral law when he feels certain that the existing law is wrong or limited. But this type of argument fails to do justice to Hegel's concept of right and its relation to positive law and the individual. The established law of the state in Hegel is as I argued in the preceding essays, neither final nor complete; hence it is possible for the individual to rebel against it and seek its change. "The principle of rightness," Hegel writes, "becomes the law (Gesetz) when, in its objective existence, it is posited (gesetzt), i.e., when thinking makes it determinate for consciousness and makes it known as what is right and valid; and in acquiring this determinate character, the right becomes positive law in general." (§ 211; 134—135) Thus in becoming law, right acquires a determinate, universal character. This means that law does not merely express a rule of conduct; it is also a precept which expresses determinate universality. The determinate identity between the implicit and posited character of law is what gives positive law its binding or obligatory force. This identity, however, is never complete or final; consequently, positive law for Hegel has obligatory force *inasmuch as* it is right. That is, positive laws are not perfectly or completely right. In his analysis of law as a determinate existent Hegel stresses that no legal code is or can be complete: "It is misunderstanding which has given rise alike to the demand — a morbid craving of German scholars chiefly — that a legal code should be something absolutely complete, incapable of any fresh determination in detail, and also to the argument that because a code is incapable of such completion, therefore we ought not to produce something 'incomplete', i.e., we ought not to produce a code at all. The misunderstanding rests in both cases on misconception of the nature of the finite subject — matter like private law, whose so — called 'completeness' is a perennial approximation to completeness, on a misconception of the difference between the universal of reason and the universal of understanding, and also on the application of the latter to the material of finitude and atomicity which goes on for ever." (§ 216; 139) Hegel also stresses that a legal code is "the child of its age and the state of civil society at the time". (§ 218; 140); it is, in short, a human creation. Accordingly any existing penal system is susceptible to further improvement. This shows that law in its positive, determinate existence is not final; it does not, in other words, express the principle of rightness absolutely and ultimately.[13] Again, the knowledge of right as such and the deduction of positive law is not the privilege of the state or an elite of legal experts: "the legal profession, possessed of a special knowledge of the law, often claims this knowledge as its monopoly and refuses to allow any layman to discuss the subject .... We do not need to be shoemakers to know if our shoes fit, and just as little have we any need to be professionals to acquire knowledge of matters of universal interest. Law is concerned with freedom, the worthiest and holiest thing in man, the thing man must know if it is to have obligatory force for him." (§ 215; 273) Hence it would be a mistake to say that the state in Hegel assumes the role of a father or a god who cannot be questioned on moral grounds. On the contrary, Hegel himself admired men like Socrates and Luther who defied the established authority for the sake of a more rational social existence.

One may advance, as I already did, other detailed and elaborate arguments to show that the individual is not, for Hegel, an instrument of the state or of some higher authority. Here I am only concerned to show that within Hegel's theory of right and punishment there is, at least from a logical point of view, room for a critical attitude towards the established authority, and that punishment is not inflicted by the state because the state is an ultimate power but because its infliction is just. The justice of the punishment is established by the fact that positive law expresses the principle of rightness (justice); thus a violation, or negation, of such law would constitute an unjust act.

SEVEN

APPENDIX II

THE BASIS OF OBLIGATION IN INTERNATIONAL LAW

A number of Hegelian scholars and critics hold that Hegel's theory of law and the state does not provide a basis for obligation in international law. They argue that on the international level states, for Hegel, exist in a 'state of nature', a condition in which a state behaves in relation to another state on the basis of superiority and national interest. Thus it is permissible for a state to adopt any course of action inasmuch as that course is conducive to its alleged interest. John Findlay, for example, writes: "states are, and should be (for Hegel), in a state of nature over against one another. The welfare of the State is essentially a *particular* welfare, and the government that concerns itself with it must essentially be a particular wisdom, not a universal providence."[1] In a similar tone Benedetto Croce writes: "Hegel refutes and almost mocks the Kantian idea of perpetual peace, and sees war as the only solution to arguments between States."[2] John Plamenatz, moreover, argues that, for Hegel, "it is right for a State to break a treaty if it finds it to its advantage to do so."[3] This prevalent interpretation certainly raises the question: does Hegel's theory of right (*Recht*) provide a basis for international law? Is international law in Hegel obligatory? If so, what is the basis of this obligation? For, if we argue, as Hegel's critics have done, that states are not bound to honor international law, treaties, or stipulations among themselves it would follow that international law is a useless, ineffective, rule of conduct, and that war, violence, intrigue, is the ultimate arbiter between the nation states of the world.

In this essay I intend to argue that for Hegel international law is not a useless, ineffective, rule of conduct between the states. On the contrary, it is the best means for establishing and promoting international order. The foundation of this order is contract, i.e., the agreement among the states to respect and honor certain rules of international conduct. These rules are obligatory, binding, not only because the states have agreed to observe them but also because they express the general interests of the international community. It is notoriously misleading to say, with Plamenatz, that according to Hegel's theory of law "it is right for a state to break a treaty if it finds it to its advantage to do so." Before we propose an interpretation of Hegel's view of war, or of international relations, we should first understand what he means by international law. For example, in what sense is international law obligatory. Under what conditions, moral or expedient, can a law be obligatory? Much of the misunderstanding and confusion which vitiates Hegelian scholarship on the concepts of war and international law stem from a reluctance to analyze carefully the meaning, ground, and purpose of international law, on the one hand, and of the state, on the other hand. I shall assume the foregoing discussion of the essential nature of the state, mainly because Hegel's conception of the state and international law are logically inter — related: Hegel's view of the basis of the state and of sovereignty are essential presuppositions of his concept of international law. It is, however, important, before I proceed in my discussion, to spotlight once more Hegel's notion of sovereignty, simply because an understanding of this notion is crucial to our understanding of the basis of obligation in international law.

The essential aspect of the state as a political reality is, as we have seen, its unity. This unity exhibits two fundamental features: (1) when we say the state is a unity we mean it is a unified, *organic* whole; its elements, viz., laws, activities, agencies, powers, or institutions are inter — dependent. The one cannot exist or function except in virtue of its inherent relationship to the state as a whole. They are, in other words, determined by the Idea of the whole; "from its might they originate, and they are its flexible limbs while it is their single self." (§ 276) (2) The officials of the state are not appointed on the basis of birth, economic power, or social influence, but on qualification, on "the strength of their universal and objective qualities." (§ 277) These two features "constitute the sovereignty of the state." (§ 278) This only shows that "sovereignty depends on the fact that the particular functions and powers of the state are not self — subsistent or firmly grounded either on their own account or in the particular will of the individual functionaries, but have their roots ultimately in the unity of the state as their single self." (*Ibid.*) Thus sovereignty is not an abstract, superior power divorced from the state as an organically functioning reality; on the contrary, it is "the ideality of all particular authorities" within the state. (*Ibid.*) Accordingly, the basis of this ideality is *not might* but law. "It is precisely in legal, constitutional government," Hegel writes, "that sovereignty is to be found as the moment of ideality — the ideality of the particular spheres and functions. That is to say, sovereignty brings it about that each of these spheres is not something independent, self — subsistent in its aims and modes of working, something immersed solely in itself, but that instead, even in these aims and modes of working, each is determined by and dependent on the aim of the whole," viz., the welfare of the state. (*Ibid.*) Thus the ground of political obligation in Hegel is not power but law. That is, a citizen is under obligation to obey the state because the latter is the concrete reality of the law which embodies the will of the people as a whole, not because the state is powerful or superior. Power is never, for Hegel, the basis of political obligation.

As an ideality of the various institutions of the state, sovereignty expresses itself actually as one individual will, or authority, e.g., the monarch; "this is the strictly individual aspect of the state, and in virtue of it alone is the state *one*." (§ 279) Thus essential to sovereignty is the character of individuality. That is, a sovereign state is an individual, and this individuality becomes concrete in the person the ruler, viz., the sovereign: "the state has individuality, and individuality is in essence an individual, and in the sovereign an actual, immediate individual." (§ 321) Without this aspect we cannot explain, or justify, the action of the state as an activity in which the society as a whole attains its moment of self — realization. In matters of practical conduct problems are faced and decisions have to be made; the state as self and representative of the general will should act: "the weighing of pros and cons between which it lets itself oscillate perpetually now this way and that, and by saying 'I will' does the state *qua* individual determine itself. But to endow the sovereign with this supreme authority does not mean, as we saw, that his power is unlimited, arbitrary, or capricious. "As a matter of fact, he is bound by the concrete decisions of his consellors, and if the constitution is stable, he has often no more to do than sign his name." (*Ibid.*) So the sovereign represents the will of the people, and he embodies the individual character of the state, only in so far as he acts according to the dictates of the constitutional law.

I

When we characterize the state as an individual we mean, moreover, that it is an independent, autonomous entity. It does not derive its privilege to rule and determine its life from an external source or power but from the will of the people who constitute its very being. Consciousness of this individuality is attained when a state encounters and distinguishes itself from other autonomous states; this consciousness manifests itself "as a relation to other states, each of which is autonomous *vis - a - vis* the other." (§ 322) Indeed a state cannot exist as an individual reality except through its relatedness to other states. (Cf. § 331) Thus states co — exist; this co — existence is the basis of international relations. For in its pursuit to realize its aim a state is bound to enter into *definite* relations with other states. In these relations conflict arises. Accordingly, how is this conflict to be settled — by means of law, or war?

Bertrand Russell holds that, for Hegel, "conflicts of states can only be decided by war; states being towards each other in a state of nature, their relations are not legal or moral. Their rights have their reality in their particular wills, and the interest of each particular state is its own highest law. There is no contrast of morals and politics, because states are not subject to ordinary moral laws."[4] *Prima facie* it does not follow that if the interests and rights of states are expressed in their individual constitutional laws then a basis for international law between them is not possible, i.e., the concept of sovereignty, at least à la Hegel, is not mutually exclusive of the concept of international law. Russell, like other Hegelian critics, tends to think that an international law is identical, from the standpoint of its status and purpose, with a moral law, with a law which applies to human beings in a given state. This identity, however, is based on the mistaken assumption that states and human individuals are alike or they exist and behave similarly, but they are not alike and they do not exist and behave similarly. Treating an international law as if it is an ordinary moral law has led to much of the confusion which permeates the analysis of the obligatory basis of international law in general and Hegel's treatment of the concept in particular. In what follows, I shall analyze Hegel's view of the basis of international law and then seek to show that most of the charges levelled against it are either erroneous or one — sided.

II

"International law," Hegel writes, "springs from the relations between autonomous states." (§ 330) These states are, as we have seen, independent and sovereign; they are not governed by a higher or external authority. Yet they are bound to interact with each other; in this interaction "one state would not meddle with the domestic affairs of another." (§ 331) This is based on the assumption that the concept of sovereignty implies the recognition, or respect, of the sovereignty of other states. But in fact it is extremely difficult, if not impossible, for states "to be indifferent to each other's domestic affairs — " hence the need for international law." (*Ibid.*) This law is dictated and made legitimate by the autonomous states; its basis is *contract* "pure and simple." (§ 332)

Hegel admits that an international law should be obligatory, binding: "the fundamental proposition of international law (i.e., the universal law which ought to be absolutely valid between states, as distinguished from the particular content of positive treaties) is that treaties, as the ground of obligations between states, ought to be kept." (§ 333) But if we reflect actually, and historically, on the international scene we discover that neither a universal legislative body nor a universally recognized world constitutional law exists. On the contrary, a state of nature seems to prevail among the sovereign states of the world. In this condition every state gives pre — eminent priority to the value of self — preservation. How? "Since states are related to one another as autonomous entities and so as particular wills on which the very validity of treaties depends, and since the particular will of the whole is in content a will for its own welfare pure and simple, it follows that welfare is the highest law governing the relation of one state to another." (§ 336) We should here ask: how does a state conceive and determine its welfare? Are we to view this conception and determination ideally or factually? Factually, Hegel maintains: "the substantial welfare of the state is its welfare as a particular state in its specific interest and situation and its no less special foreign affairs, including its treaty relations. (§ 337) Thus what a state may take to be its legitimate interest may be in stark opposition to the interest or will of another state. Consequently conflict may arise. If this happens how are we to settle the conflict? Hegel insists that a "relation between states ought (also) to be right in principle, but in mundane affairs a principle ought to have power." (§ 330) This is in my opinion a clear, yet important, recognition by Hegel that international relations are not and should not be capricious, and that international law has in principle obligatory character. But since there is not in fact a power which can determine and *actualize* what is right "it follows that in so far as international relations are concerned we can never get beyond an 'ought' ". (*Ibid.*) Thus if a state finds it to its interest to violate the dictate of a treaty or to sever an established relation with another state it would be justified in doing so. But why? Is it, as Plamentz has argued, because it is superior to its stipulations? Plamenatz holds that a state for Hegel is superior in the sense that "it is right for a state to break a treaty if it finds it to its advantage to do so."[5] If this is what Hegel means by 'superior' then he certainly contradicts himself, for, as Plamenatz remarks, he already acknowledged that there are rules between the states which should be observed. But under what conditions can a state break a treaty if it finds it to its advantage to do so? Does 'superior' mean that a state can under *any* conditions not only break a treaty but also conquer another state if it finds it to its advantage to do so? I am inclined to think that, for Hegel, 'superior' in this context means superiority over treaties made, and this only under certain conditions. Let me support this claim by the following line of reasoning.

First, Hegel repeatedly emphasized that what makes an international law ineffective is not its failure to express a relation of right between two or more states but fundamentally lack of a judicial power which can determine what is right in a concrete situation and enforce the relevant law. This is indeed the crux of his criticism of Kant's idea of securing perpetual peace by a league of nations. This organization would be "a power recognized by each individual state, and was to arbitrate in all cases of dissension in order to make it impossible for disputants to resort to war in order to settle them." (§ 333) But the idea of such an organization presupposes a general agreement on the laws which should be approved by all the states. This idea, Hegel argues, rests on the supposition that a concrete sovereign will be responsible for these laws does in fact exist. But it did not, until Hegel's time, exist. This is why if such an organization exists — and it does exist in the twentieth century — it may arbitrate but it cannot enforce the law. Thus when the welfare of a state is undermined it has the right, i.e., it is justified, to ignore its past agreement and seek to restore its right by force. It is strange that Plamanatz misconceives Hegel's meaning of 'superior' in the context referred to especially when Hegel asserts in the preceding two sentences that "a relation between states ought (also) to be right in principle." Thus in this context when Hegel says that a state is superior to its stipulations he means that the state in question can break a treaty without expecting *justifiable* punishment, for no authority which can execute this punishment exists.[6]

Second, when Hegel refers to the state as 'superior' he means 'sovereign.' As we have already seen, the sovereignty of the state consists in the fact that it is independent, autonomous, and self — determined political entity. Accrodingly what makes the state sovereign is not the political or economic power of certain groups or classes. It is not, in other words, physical power, but law. The sovereign has the power to make decisions concerning the welfare of the state because in his person he is the concrete realization of "the ideality of all the particular authorities" of the state. (§ 278)[7] In his decision the general will of the people, which is expressed in the constitution, becomes actual, concrete. Thus as sovereign the ruler exhibits the rational and ethical nature of the state. His action is not, consequently, capricious or arbitrary. In international affairs he is guided by the supreme principle of the welfare of the state. This means he cannot ignore a treaty, or an international law, *unless* the interests of state is in danger; for the recognition of the treaty, or international law, is, to begin with, justified simply on the ground that it promotes the welfare of the state. Now, suppose a misunderstanding between two states arises — suppose, in other words, a sovereign stipulates that the conditions under which the international law is recognized are changed, and that this change would incur either danger or immediate harm to the state, does then the sovereign have a right to ignore the international law. Of course yes. The sovereign does not have a right to break a treaty (or an international law) if the conditions under which the treaty is to hold remain honored and if, consequently, the interest of the state is not in danger. If, on the other hand, the interest of the state is indeed in danger then the state as a sovereign, i.e., as superior, has a right to break the treaty. The point which we should stress here is that the superiority of the state over its stipulations in Hegel is not absolute but *conditional*; it depends on the extent to which the conditions of the international law are honored. But these conditions are not always honored. States fail to respect their agreements either consciously or unconsciously, because of ignorance or malice. Hegel is quite aware of this fact when he states: "the state is no ideal work of art; it stands on earth and so in the sphere of caprice, chance, and error, and bad behavior may disfigure it in many respects." (§ 258)

Thus if disagreement between states cannot be solved dipolmatially, or politically, war is appealed to. But appealing to war is a last resort: "if states disagree and their particulr wills cannot be harmonized, the matter can only be settled by war." (§ 334) We should stress 'if' in this sentence; for a state cannot go to war unless one of two conditions are fulfilled: (1) if the interest of a state is undermined by another state, and (2) if a state is certain that a danger from another state is forthcoming, "together with calculations of degrees of probability on this side and that, guessing at intentions etc., etc." The strict conditions which Hegel lay for going to war only shows, once more, that a state is not at liberty to ignore its agreements with other states. It is *superior* to its stipulations *only if* the conditions under which these stipulations are not honored. We should here emphasize: from the fact that some states break a treaty, or an international law, it does not follow that the validity of the law, or the treaty, is undermined or ceases to be obligatory. Accordingly, it is not enough, as Hegel frequently pointed out, to construct a valid body of international laws: we should also have a power to enforce these laws. More light will be shed on this point in the remainder of my discussion.

When Plamenatz argues that the state, for Hegel, is unconditionally superior to its stipulations he in effect implies that Hegel's theory of the state does not provide a basis for international law. Hence, as Findley wrote, states "are, and should be, in a state of nature over against one another." This seems to be the standing interpretation of the Hegelian critics to whom I already alluded. But these critics hardly ask: does Hegel have a theory of international law? In what sense should an international law be obligatory? If, for example, we argue that a law is not obligatory because it lacks a power to enforce it, i.e., sanctions, we commit the notorious mistake of equating *obligation* with *force*. But even in ordinary civil or moral laws we make a distinction between the *normative*, obligatory, aspect of the law and its *punitive* aspect; that is, the obligatory aspect of the law is logically different from the implicit promise that if a given law is not obeyed punishment will be imposed.[8] Hegel certainly recognizes this obligatory aspect of the law, for he clearly states that international law ought to be valid between states, and that treaties, "as the ground of obligations between states, ought to be kept." (§ 333) But, as we have already seen, the international community lacks a power to enforce this law. From the fact, however, that such power is lacking it does not follow that the law is not inherently obligatory, or that there is no good reason to obey it. But what is the basis of this law?

The basis, ground, of international law is contract. That is, as a rule of behavior international law is upheld by the various states on the basis of agreement between themselves. This law expresses the particular interests of the states in general. The supreme principle which guides its enactment is the welfare of all the states which will be affected by it. In agreeing to, or in recognizing the validity of, an international law a state acts as a sovereign, i.e., as an individual and independent state; in other words, it acts freely: "since states are related to one another as autonomous entities and so as particular wills on which the very validity of treaties depends, and since the particular will of the whole is in content a will for its own welfare pure and simple, it follows that welfare is the highest law governing the relation of one state to another." (§ 336) An international law, then, expresses the *immediate* interest of a state; it expresses the interest of that state as it exists in a certain place, certain time, and certain cultural setting. Accordingly, it is not something deduced from an abstract law, nor is it a gesture of philanthropy: "the substantial welfare of the state is its welfare as a particular state in its specific interest and situation and its no less special foreign affairs, including its particular treaty relations." (§ 337)

Thus what justifies respect for international law, or treaty, is the promotion of the well — being of the state. So, states behave in relation to one another, not on the basis of an already established law or moral principle but on the basis of national interest. Hegel thinks that it is a mistake to demand that states should act in international affairs according to moral principles, and this for two main reasons: (1) the welfare of a state has claims to recognition totally different from those of the welfare of the individual." (*Ibid.*) (2) A state is quite different from a private person. While the former is sovereign, autonomous, and not subject to a universal jurisdiction, the latter, viz., the private person, is "under the jurisdiction of a court which gives effect to what is right in principle." (§ 330)[9] Again, by it very nature the state is a concrete existent: it is an accomplished fact. Its rights and needs are determinate; this is a main reason why its behavior with other states cannot be determined according to moral laws but according to practical, or pragmatic, rules.

Now, we should ask: is international law, for Hegel, obligatory? What creates international obligation? International law, for Hegel, is obligatory, and the source of obligation is the agreement, i.e., promise, to recognize and respect the international law. Let me elucidate this point in some detail. When a state agrees to the terms of a contract it places itself under obligation to respect its terms. The event of promise creates obligation. This is possible only because in making an agreement a state acts as a sovereign. It does this with a consciousness of its own interest and of the general and practical impact of the contract. This is exactly why Hegel repeatedly stated that an international law has the form of an 'ought'. This 'ought', however, is not moral in character; it is prudential, or pragmatic, for it is based on and serves the interests of the contracting parties. The rules which express these interests cannot be deduced from a universal thought or Providence, simply because the interests are conditioned by historical necessity; they are variable. Consequently the only general principle which should guide their enactment is the promotion of the well — being of the contracting states. We cannot here help but ask: what does it mean for an international law in this context to be obligatory? It means that the law *ought*, as Hegel asserts, to be obeyed; it means, in other words, that there are good reasons to obey it. And the reasons which justify obeying them are: (1) the contracting states have voluntarily agreed to respect the alw; (2) the law expresses the mutual interests of the contracting states. It is a mistake to argue that because a supreme judicial power capable of enforcing the law is absent the law is not obligatory; for, as I said before, we would then equate obligation with physical force. It is, however, generally agreed that this is not a reasonable position to espouse. The absence of a legitimate superior power that can enforce international laws has led Hegel to say that when a conflict cannot be settled between states they resort to war. I should here stress that war, for Hegel, does not determine what is right, nor is it the only means to settle international conflict. It only decides which of two or more conflicting right claims is to give way: "Thus war, or the like, has now decided, not which of the rights alleged by the two parties is the genuine right — since both parties have a genuine right — but which of the two rights has to give way."[10]

At this point of our discussion one may object: how can a sovereign state be bound by an international law? For it would seem that the very notion of sovereignty excludes the idea of obligation to an external law. This objection is based on the assumption that the sovereign is an absolute power, and that this power is somehow above the law; thus it cannot be bound by any authority external to it. I aver that we cannot intelligibly explain the obligatory aspect of international law if we maintain that the sovereign state is an absolute power in the sense just indicated. But we need to stress that Hegel's conception of sovereignty does not in any way involve, or even imply, the notion of absolute power.

We have already seen in some detail in the first part of this paper that a state is sovereign in the sense that (1) it is an individual, independent, autonomous entity; (2) it derives its legitimate power from the constitutional law which expresses the rational will of the people who constitute its pulsing heart. This power becomes concrete in the governmental structure. Accordingly the legitimate power of the state is grounded in the constitutional law, and if the law expresses the well — being of the state as an organic unity, and if this well — being cannot be attained except through an orderly international conduct, then the state can, by means of a contract, place itself under obligation to behave in a certain way to guarantee the continued realization of the general aim of the state. In this contract the state may restrict, or give up, some of its rights: this restriction, however, is relative and practically negligible, for only in this sort of exsitence can the state maintain the peace it needs for its growth and prosperity: "the principles of the national minds are wholly restricted on account of their particularity, for it is in this particularity, as existent individuals, that they have their objective actuality and their self — consciousness." (§ 340; see also § 336) Thus in placing itself under obligation to obey an international law a state may restrict some of its rights, but in this act it realizes its most fundamental right, viz., the right to exist and to actualize itself in the life of the spirit.

One final comment should complete our discussion. When we say that a state places itself under obligation to observe an international law by means of contract, or promise, we should stress that what creates the obligation is not the mere pronouncement of the words 'we agree', whether these words are uttered or formally written, but the fact that the agreement, law, or treaty, expresses a definite complex of mutual interest, i.e., the welfare of the states concerned. The obligation springs, in other words, from the inherent relations (or historical conditions) which exist between the sovereign states of the world. This is why when a new state emerges, and is recognized as a sovereign state by the other states, it ought to observe the already established body of international laws, not only because this body guarantees the general welfare of the international community but also because the very fact of its recognition as a state implies *implicit* acceptance of the laws which are essential for their existence and life. The fundamental principle of international law which regulates the conduct of the international community at the present time is still Hegelian in character. The procedure by which the United Nations was established a few decades ago, the way this organization has been functioning, and the way international treaties and agreements are made, only reveal Hegel's profound understanding of human nature and the history of the world, on the one hand, and the basis and end of international law, on the other. We should thus agree with Brierly when he said that "of all writers on the state his influence (Hegel's) on the theory of international law has probably been the most far — reaching, and certainly it is still the most devastating."[11]

NOTES
ESSAY ONE

1. J. Plamenatz, *Man and Society*, Vol. II (New York: McGraw — Hill Book Co., 1963), pp. 264. Plamenatz, for example, writes: "though Hegel is not as illiberal as he is sometimes presented as being, he is illiberal; he does play down the individual. He does sometimes come very close to suggesting that, because society makes us rational and moral, we ought not to challenge established laws and conventions. He also sometimes speaks as if the state stood to the citizen as God the creator stands to His creature man. He insists so much that man owes everything to the communities he belongs to, and above all to the State, that he seems to be suggesting, whithout wishing to put it into crude words, that he also owes absolute obedience." *Ibid.*, p. 243. See also L. W. Lancaster, *Masters of Political Thought* (Boston: Houghton Mifflin Co. 1959) pp. 66—70; Simone de Beauvoir, *The Ethics of Ambiguity* (New York: Philosophical Library, 1948), pp. 8ff; F. Gregoire, *Etudes Hegelienne: les Points Capitaux du Systeme* (Louvain and Paris 1958); J. Findley, *Hegel: Re-examintion* (New York: Collier Books, 1958). Moreover, in an interesting article included in Z. A. Pelczynski's *Hegel's Political Philosophy: Problems and Perspectives* K.H. Ilting writes: "Hegel's deification of the state is justifiably notorious. It was bound to provoke both the abhorrence of those who object to any profanation of God's name, and the hostility of all militant atheists. This conception of the state is not objectionable solely because Hegel attempted to interpret the political community in terms of the fundamental concepts of ancient metaphysics and theology. What is really objectionable is that he tried to extend this interpretation explicitly to the modern state." Again, "why, then, did Hegel persistently refuse in the *Philosophy of Right* to join Rousseau in his method of overcoming the liberal conception of the state and in his democratic ideals? This is all the more remarkable since he had been sympathetic to Rousseau's ideas from his earliest years and especially shared Rousseau's dislike of 'the particular' (private existence) and his admiration for 'the general life' (public affair). The explanation might be that this was due to political opportunism, which Hegel by no means ignored in writing his major political work." (Cambridge: At the University press, 1971), pp. 102 — 103.

2. J. Maritain, *Moral Philosophy* (New York: Charles Scribner's Sons, 1964), p. 163. I should here remark that Maritain commits, like Karl Popper, what W. Kaufmann has labelled in a recent study the error of 'quilt quotations'. This error is committed when a scholar advances a criticism against a view or theory not on the basis of understanding the inner logic and spirit of the view or theory but on the basis of certain quotations selected 'out of context'. See W. Kaufmann, "The Young Hegel and Religion, in *Hegel*, ed. by A. McIntyre (Notre Dame University Press, 1976) pp. 25 ff.

3. Henceforth the number of the paragraphs and the Additions refer to *Hegel's Philosophy of Right*, tr. by T.M. Knox, (Oxford University Press, 1962).

4. Hegel discusses in detail his objections to the doctrine of the separation of Powers in the state. Cf. par. 277.

5. See Charles Taylor, *Hegel*, Cambridge University Press, 1975), pp. 374 ff.

6. *Man and Society*, p. 268.

ESSAY TWO

1. D. Pickles, for example, writes; "no political system at any time, democratic or not, has ever provided for all the people even to choose the government, much less exercise governmental powers." *Democrary* (Basic Books, Inc., N.Y., 1970), p. 9. And Jean — Jacques Rousseau writes: "if there were a people of gods, it would govern itself democratically. Such a perfect government is not suited to men." *On The Social Contract*, Book III, Chapter 4. See also, J. Plamenatz, *Democracy and Illusion* (Longman Group Limited, 1973); Sir H. S. Maine, *Popular Government* (Indianapolis: Liberty Classics, 1976).

2. We should here point out that Hegel is also critical of Fichte's conception of the general will. This criticism extends, moreover, to the philosophers and intellectuals of the French Revolution. See, for example, *Hegel's Natural Law*, tr. by T.M. Knox, with an Introduction by N. B. Acton (University of Pennsylvania Press, 1975), pp. 85 ff.; *The Philosophy of Right*, § 258, 273.

3. Jean—Jacques Rousseau, tr. by D. Masters and Masters, *On The Social Contract* (New York: St. Martin's Press, 1978), Book I, chapter 6.

4. This premise is central to most versions of democracy in the twentieth century. See, for example, Carl L. Becker, *Modern Democracy* (New Haven: Yale University Press, 1959); H. B. Mayo, *Introduction to Democratic Theory* (New York: St. Martin's Press, 1975); D. Pickles, *Democracy*.

5. *On The Social Contract*, Book I, chapter 7.

6. *Ibid.*, Book II, chapter 1.

7. *Ibid.*

8. *Ibid.*

9. *Ibid.*, Book III, chapter 1.

10. *Ibid.*

11. *Ibid.*, Book IV, chapter 3.

12. *Ibid.*

13. *Ibid.*, Book II, chapter 7.

14. Ibid.

15. S. Avineri, *Hegel's Theory of the Modern State* (Cambridge University Press, 1972), p. 184.

16. For a detailed discussion of how Rousseau abandons his concept of the general will and replaces it with the concept of the will of all see B. Basanquet, *The Philosophical Theory of the State* (London: McMillan and Co., 1958), chapter 5.

17. See also, G. W. F. Hegel, *Phenomenology of Mind*, tr. by J. B. Baillie (London: George Allen and Unwin, 1961), pp. 599 – 610.

18. *On The Social Contract*, Book III, chapter 3.

19. See Charles Taylor, *Hegel*, pp. 408 ff.

20. From the principle "if freedom implies the consent of each individual, then of course only the subjective aspect is meant. From this principle follows as a matter of course that no law is valid except by agreement of all. This implies that the majority decides; hence the majority must yield to the majority." Hegel, *Reason in History*, tr. by R. Hartman (Library of Liberal Arts, 1953), pp. 56—57.

21. *Ibid.*, p. 57.

22. In his early political writings Hegel discusses this difficulty with specific reference to France, England, and Germany during the latter part of the eighteenth century and early part of the nineteenth century. See A. Z. Pelczynski's excellent treatment of this point in *Hegel's Political writings* (Oxford University Press, 1964), chapter 4.

23. *Reason in History*, p. 57
24. Rousseau, like Hegel, views the state as an abstract entity. See *On The Social Contract*, Book I, chapter 6
25. *Rerson in History*, p. 57.
26. *Ibid.*, pp. 61 — 62.
28. *Ibid.*, p. 61.
29. I am of the opinion that Hegel's claim that society is composed of associations, that these associations reflect definite socio — economic or professional interests, is valid in principle even in our contemporary society. In the United States, for example, the president and representatives of the people are not elected directly by the people but indirectly through the electoral college, the existing parties, and other types of caucuses. In addition, a large portion of the legislative business is conditioned by all sorts of lobbying groups which represent the concrete interests of minorities, labor unions, businesses, etc.
30. In the proceedings to the Wurtemberg Diet, Hegel writes with reference to the 'Will of the people': "this is a great Word, and the representatives of the people should take the greatest care not to profane it or use it light — heartedly ... To say 'he knows what his will is' is one of the most difficult, and hence most noble, things one can say of a man. People's representatives must not be picked at random, but rather one should choose the wisest from among the people, since not everyone knows, as it is his duty to know, what one's true and real will is, i.e., what is good for one." Quoted and commented on by Pelczynski in *Hegel's Political Writings*, p. 93

ESSAY THREE

1. J. Maritain,*Moral Philosophy*, p. 165. A similar interpretation is advanced by A. P. d'Entreve in *Natural Law: A Historical Survey* (Harper Torchbooks, 1965). Here he writes: "the doctrine of the ethical state (in Hegel) is a complete substitute for the doctrine of natural law which had accompanied Western thought throughout its long history. It entirely reverses the relationship between the ideal and the real, which was the necessary presupposition of natural law thinking." Again, "there can be no doubt that Hegel's conception of history marks the end of natural law thinking altogether. It eliminates for all purposes that notion of an ideal law which...is another constant feature of the theory of the law of nature. Ideals cease to be immutable and eternal. They are the outcome of history. It is before the bench of history that ideals must be tried." pp. 73—74.
2. *Moral Philosophy*, p. 165.
3. *Ibid.*, p. 166.
4. D'Entreve, for example, asks: "is law an act of will or the intellect?" *Natural Law*, p. 64.
5. When Hegel holds that knowing what one does is a necessary condition for responsible action he only reveals a fundamental aspect of human nature, viz., finitude. Although we may project in our imagination the possibility of an act, and although we may foresee its possible consequences, it does not follow from this that our projection or foreseeing is complete or accurate. Our foresight is never complete — hence always a margin of ignorance relating to future action. This is why being responsible is always a matter of degree: I am responsible for an act *in so far as* I know what I am doing. (Cf. Add. to § 117)
6. Marcus G. Singer, *Generalization in Ethics* (New York: Alfred A. Knopf, 1961), pp. 251 — 252.

7. In *The Fundamental Principles of the Metaphysics of Morals*, Kant writes: "the Categorical Imperative concerns not the matter of the action, or its intended result, but its form and the principle of which it is itself a result; and what is essentially good in it consists in the mental disposition, let the consequences be what they may. This imperative may be called that of morality." (Library of Liberal Arts, 1949), p. 33.

8. This line of reasoning is developed in greater detail in *Natural Law* "what goes beyond the pure concept of duty and beyond the abstraction of the concept in its absolute purity, recognizes full well that practical reason totally renounces the content of law and can do nothing beyond making the *form* of *fitness* of the will's (*Willkhr*) maxim into supreme law. The maxim of the arbitrary will (*willkhr*) in choosing has a content and includes a specific action, but the pure (*wille*) is free from specification." p. 75.

9. I. Kant, *Critique of Pure Reason*, tr. by L. W. Beck (New York: The Bobbs — Merril Co., 1956), pp. 22 — 27.

10. It should here be mentioned that this is also how Dewey, Mill, and Bradley, to mention a few outstanding ethicists, interpreted Kant.

11. *Natural Law*, p. 77 Cf. M. . Gram, "Kant and Universalizability Once More," *Kant - Studien*, No. 58, 1967.

12. We may interpret Kant as saying that I should not withhold the deposit because acting on the universalized maxim would lead to the annihilation of the institution of deposit. But this institution is *important*, i.e., valuable, and because it is important it should be kept. Therefore if my act sanctions its annihilation it will be immoral. If this is what Kant means by the preceding quotation, and this meaning is suggested by Singer (pp. 252 — 253) he certainly presupposes what he consciously sought to avoid; he, in other words, smuggled in the notion that what makes the act immoral is the fact that it violates a presupposed principle which is accepted somehow as valid. See Hegel, *Natural Law*, pp. 78 — 81; A. Schopenhauer, *On The Basis of Morality*, tr. by E. F. J. Payne, with an introduction by R. Taylor (The Library of Liberal Arts, 1965), part II.

13. *Critique of Practical Reason*, p. 27.

14. See Jonathan Robinson, *Duty and Hypocrisy In Hegel's Phenomenology of Mind*, (University of Toronto Press, 1977), pp. 107 ff; Hegel, *Phenomenology of Mind*, pp. 642 ff.

15. Cf. *Hegel's Philosophy of Right*, pp. vi, 319, 346; Taylor, *Hegel*, p. 376.

16. T. M. Knox, *Hegel's Philosophy of Right*, p. 319.

17. *Nicomachaean Ethics*, Book II, 1103a, 15 — 25.

18. *Ibid.*, 1103a, 30 — 1103b, 2.

19. C. d'Entreve, *Natural Law*, pp. 72ff.

20. Cf. K.H. Ilting, "The Structure of Hegel's Philosophy of Right", and J. N. Shklar's "Hegel's Phenomenology: An Elegy for Hellas", in Pelczynski's *Hegel's Political Philosophy*

21. Hegel, *Natural Law*, p. 128.

22. *Ibid.*, p. 126. The same idea is stressed in *Reason and History*: "a state is then well-constituted and internally vigorous when the private interest of its citizens is one with the common interest of the state, and the one finds gratification and realization in the other — a most important proposition." p. 30.

23. *Ibid.*, P. 128.

24. *Ibid.*, p. 112

25. *Reason in History*, P. 37

26. Cf. Hegel, *Natural Laws*, P. 115.

27. *Ibid.*, P. 12.

28. *Ibid.*, p.113.

29. Hegel, *The Philosophy of History*, p. 269.
30. Hegel discusses in detail the process of moral decision — making in the *Phenomenology of Mind*, pp. 611 ff.
31. Cf. *Reason in History*, pp. 37 ff.
32. Hegel, *History of Philosophy*, p. 250.
33. Quoted by H. B. Acton in his Introduction to Hegel's *Natural Law*, PP. 38 — 39.
34. *Reason in History*, PP. 27 — 28.
35. *Ibid.*, p. 46.
36. Hegel, *Natural Law*, p. 116.
37. Cf. K. H. Ilting, "The Structure of Hegel's Philosophy of Right"; N. Riedel, "Nature and Freedom in Hegel's *Philosophy of Right*, in Pelczynski's *Hegel's Political Philosophy*.

ESSAY FOUR

1. J. Maritain, *Moral Philosophy*, pp. 259 — 177.
2. In the second paragraph of the section which is devoted to Property, Hegel writes: "what is immediately different from free mind is that which, both for mind and in itself, is the external pure and simple, a thing, something not free, not personal, without right." (§ 42) See also *System of Ethical Life and First Philosophy of Spirit*, tr. by H.S. Harris and T. M. Knox, (State University of New York, 1979), pp. 127 — 128, 232 ff.
3. Cf. *Ibid.*, pp. 231 ff., 127 ff.; see also, Hegel, *Early Theological Writings*, pp. 302 ff. Again, Hegel, "Two Fragments of 1797 on Love", *Clio*, Vol. 8, 1979. For an interesting discussion of love and its place in marriage and the family, see R. Siebert, "Hegel's Concept of Marriage and the Family: The Origin of Subjective Freedom," in *Hegel's Social and Political Thought*, ed. by D. P. Verene (The Humanities Press, 1980).
4. Hegel, *Ecyclopedia of Philosophy*, tr. by G. E. Mueller (Philosophical Library, 1959), p. 246.
5. For an enlightening historical study of Hegel's conception of education, see, George A. Kelly, *Idealism, Politics, and History: Sources of Hegelian Thought* (Cambridge: At the University Press, 1969), pp. 269 ff.
"6. It is, I think, important to consider what a twentieth century philosopher, Alfred N. Whitegead, says on this point: "we have to remember that the valuable intellectual development is self — development, and that it mostly takes place between the ages of sixteen and thirty. As to training,the most important part is given by mothers before the age of twelve." *The Aims of Education* (The Free Press, 1957), p. 1.
7. Even in the domain of law — making the capacity to intuit the universal content of right and the good into law requires education. In § 209 Hegel writes: "the relatedness arising from the reciprocal bearing on one another of needs and work to satisfy these is first of all reflected into itself as infinite personality, as abstract right. But it is the very sphere of relatedness — a sphere of education — which gives abstract right the determinate existence of being something universally recognized, known, and willed, and having a validity and an objective actuality mediated by this known and willed character."
8. *System of Ethical Life and First Philosophy of Spirit*, pp. 232 ff.
9. I should here remark that Hegel repeatedly pleaded for the dignity and humanity of the child as a possible human being. In the paragraph to which I already alluded, he writes: "one of the blackest marks against Roman legislation is the law whereby

children were treated by their fathers as slaves. This gangrene of ethical order at the tenderest point of its innermost life is one of the most important clues for understanding the place of Romans in the history of the world and their tendency towards legal formalism." Cf. § 180, and also *Philosophy of History*, pp. 285 ff.

10. It would, I think, help if I make the following remark. Education is an activity of loving. The parents show, reveal, their love for the child by educating him: their love for the child is an objectification of their love for each other. In this activity the parents give of themselves; they give ideas, ways of acting, desires, habits, life, discipline, in short, character. It seems at first look that the character is a product, something fashioned by the parents, but this is not necessarily the case for at least three reasons:

A. What the parents impart, viz., love, is itself a unique reality, for it is the unity of both parents who are themselves in love, and *individuals*.

B. What the parents impart is not merely theirs, i.e., an exclusive, subjective possession, but has a social and hence universal character.

C. As lovers and conscious of their individualities, the parents would be reluctant, adamantly opposed, to any constriction upon the potential sense of individuality of the child. On the contrary, their supreme goal is to see to it that what they say, do, or plan for the child, they teach the child to grow as a self — determined being. Like the real artist: although the work of art comes from the soul of the artist the work is unquely different from the artist as a psycho — physical fact in the world.

ESSAY FIVE

1. Maritain, *Moral Philosophy*, pp. 169 — 170.
2. *Ibid.*, p. 167.
3. G. W. F. Hegel, *Logic*, tr. by W. Wallace (Oxford University Press, 1965), pp. 144 — 145.
4. *Ibid.*, p. 254.
5. *Ibid.*, p. 145.
6. In the *Philosophy of History* Hegel writes: "real liberty requires... freedom in regard to the trades and professions — the premission of everyone to use his abilities without restriction." p. 448.
7. In § 189 Hegel writes: "political economy is the science which starts from this view of needs and labour but then has the task of explaining mass — relationships and mass — movements in their complexity and their qualitative and quantitative character. This is one of the sciences which have arisen out of the conditions of the modern world. Its development affords the interesting spectacle (as in Smith, Say, and Ricardo) of thought working upon and endless mass of details which confront it at the outset and extracting there from the simple principles of the thing, the Understanding effective in the thing and directing it." Hegel grants, as we see, the fundamental principle of capitalism, according to which economic reality is governed by inherent universal principles, of which the laws of supply and demand would be an example.
8. Taylor, *Hegel*, p. 433. Cf. *Philosophy of Right*, § 201.
9. Here the following objection may be raised: does one not limit himself by restricting himself to a vocation and by occupying a specific place in the totality of the social scheme? For when a person restricts himself in this way he automatically deprives himself of many other valuable possibilities or opportunities. Hegel is aware of this sort of objection. In § 207 he remarks: "at first (i.e., especially in youth) a man chafes at the idea of resolving on a particular social position, and looks upon this as a

restriction on his universal character and as a necessity imposed on him purely *ab extra*." But this sort of objection, Hegel argues, is mistaken because it exposes an abstract way of thinking. A person who is reluctant to pursue a definite vocation refuses to step into actuality; he refuses, in other words, *to be somebody*, for, as we saw, in order for a man to be somebody, "he should belong to some specific social class, since to be somebody means to have substantative being. A man with no class is a mere private person and his universality is not actualized. (Add. to § 207)

10. Cf. Taylor, *Hegel*, pp. 432 — 433.

11. For Hegel's view on poverty and his inability to find a solution, or perhaps a radical solution, to the problem of poverty within his political scheme, see S. Avineri, *Hegel's Theory of the Modern State*, pp. 89 — 98, 146 — 151; R. Plant, "Economic and Social Integration in Hegel's Political Philosophy," in *Hegel's Social and Political Philosophy*, ed. by D. P. Verene, pp. 59 — 87.

12. In § 245 Hegel writes: "in Britain, particularly in Scotland, the most direct measure against poverty and especially against the loss of shame and self — respect — the subjective bases of society — as well as against laziness and extravagance, &c., the begetters of the rabble, has turned out to be to leave the poor to their fate and instruct them to beg in the streets."

13. For a thoughtful discussion of the legal — political status of the corporation and its role in the whole political structure, see Heiman's essay, "The Sources and Significance of Hegel's Corporate Doctrine," in Pelczynski's *Hegel's Political and Social Philosophy*.

14. Taylor, *Hegel*, p. 433.

ESSAY SIX

1. J. Ellis McTaggart, "Hegel's Theory of Punishment," in J. Feinberg, *Reason and Responsibility* (Belmont: Dickerson Publishing Co., 1968), 320—330.

2. Cf., e.g., Ossip K. Flechtheim, "Hegel and the Problem of Punishment," in *Journal of the History of Ideas*, Vol. 8, 1947; J. O. Mabbott, "Punishment," *Mind.*, vol. 48.

3. "Hegel's Theory of Punishment," p. 321.

4. A similar interpretation is adopted by Flechtheim in "Hegel and the Problem of Punishment." A fairer interpretation is found in H. Reyburn, *The Ethical Theory of Hegel* (Oxford: At the Claendon Press, 1921). McTaggart distinguishes Hegel's version of reformation from the standard, utilitarian version of it. He observes that "the reformatory theory says that we ought to reform our criminals *while* we are punishing them. Hegel says that punishment itself tends to reform them. The reformatory theory wishes to pain criminals as little as possible, and improve them as much as possible. Hegel's theory says it is the pain which will improve them", p. 321. Despite these qualifications McTaggart fundamentally attributes a refomatory theory of punishment to Hegel, for he thinks that punishment for Hegel is inflicted to reform, purify (p. 327) the criminal. This is certainly a utilitarian interpretation of the concept."

5. An important anthology which contains key discussions of the theories of reformation and deterrence, and related positions on punishment, especially in recent years, is *Philosophical Perspectives on Punishment*, ed. by G. Ezorsky (Albany, 1972). See also, J. Feinberg, *Reason and Responsibility*; A. C. Ewing, *The Morality of Punishment* (London, 19229); H. L. A Hart, *Punishment and Responsibility* (Oxford University Press, 1968).

6. *Hegel's Philosophy of Right*, § 99.

7. See paragraphs 115 ff.; 79 — 81. In this connection Hegel writes: "the subject's right to know action in its specffic character as good or evil, legal or illegal, has the result of diminishing or cancelling in this respect too the responsibility of children, imbeciles, and lunatics, although it is impossible to delimit precisely either childhood, imbecility, etc., or their degree of irresponsibility." § 132, 88.

8. In *Natural Law* Hegel seeks to show that punishment "originates in liberty and remains in liberty, even though it brings constraint." op. cit.

9. McTaggart, "Hegel's Theory of Punishment," p. 327.

10. See F. H. Bradley, *Ethical Studies*, (Oxford University Press, 1959), chapter I; See also R. A. Wasserstrom, "Strict Liability in Criminal Law," *Stanford Law Review*, Vol. 12, 1960.

11. McTaggart, "Hegel's Theory of Punishment," pp. 328 — 329.

12. Flechtheim, "Hegel and The Problem of Punishment", p. 308

13. *Hegel's Philosophy of Right*, paragraphs 134 — 135.

ESSAY SEVEN

1. J. N. Findley, *Hegel: A Re - examination* (Collier Books, 1962), p. 330.

2. Benedetto Croce, *Politics and Morals* (Philosophical Library, 1945) p. 75.

3. J. Plamenatz, *Man and Society*, vol. II, pp. 26 — 261. Moreover, D. A. Zoll writes: "states (for Hegel) are independent, bound by none of the moral restraints or obligations appropriate to private individuals. The trial of the state is *war*, which is not only inevitable among states, but is a laudable means of restoring the vitality and temper of a state." *Reason and Rebellion* (Prentice — Hall, Inc., 1963), pp. 234 — 235. Again, E. Cassirer writes: "the negative role of political life (for Hegel) is contained in the fact of war. To abolish or terminate war would be the death blow of political life. It is a mere utopianism to think that the conflicts between nations could ever be settled by legal means — by international courts of arbitration." *The Myth of the State* (Yale University Press, 1946), p. 266. See also Z. A. Pelczynski *Hegel's Political Philosophy*; L. Strauss and Cropsey, *History of Political Phylosophy* (Chicago: Rand NcNally and Company., 1963), pp. 648 ff.; K. Popper, *The Open Society and Its Enemies* (Princeton University Press, 1950).

4. B. Russell, *A History of Western Philosophy* (New York: Simon & Schuster, 1963), pp. 741 — 742.

5. *Man and Society*, p. 260.

6. The current events in Southeast Asia, whether between China and Vietnam or Vietnam and Cambodia, certainly validate Hegel's claim that an international law sponsored by an organization called the United Nations can only arbitrate. When we consider the political facts between these nations we discover that the powerful nation determines what right should be cancelled and what right should be upheld. See, moreover, Hegel's *The German Constitution* in Pelczynski's *Hegel's Policital Writings*, pp. 209 — 211.

7. Hegel is quite emphatic on this point. In § 279 he writes: "in the organization of the state — which here means in constitutional monarchy — we must have nothing before our minds except the inherent necessity of the Idea. All other points of view must vanish. The state must be treated as a great architectonic structure, as a hieroglyph of the reason which reveals itself in actuality. Everything to do with mere utility, externlity, and so forth, must be eliminated from the philosophical treatment of the subject."

8. From the premise that the obligatory aspect is generically different from the

sanctions which accompany the law it does not follow that any rule, since it is a rule, may have an obligatory aspect. Specific conditions must obtain a rule is to be obligatory.

9. In *Natural Law* Hegel, moreover, writes: "it is inherently self — contradiction if, in international law, the relation of absolutely independent and free nations (which are ethical totalities) is to be regulated after the model of a civil contract which relates directly to the individuality and independence of the citizes." p. 124. One could here ask: can a state be responsible the way a person can? Or, how could a state, the way Hegel conceives it, assume responsibility for an act it has committed? If we say that an International Court can be established to determine the nature and extent of the wrong done, we still can ask: when does this court derive its power? Does it proclaim universal authority? If so, how is it determined? How can we be sure that it does not express, or serve, the interest of a given group.

10. Hegel, *The German Constitution*, p. 210. We should here emphasize that Hegel makes a distinction between the concept of individuality and particularity: although a state is individual it is nevertheless particular: "individuality is to be distinguished from particularity. The former is a moment in the very idea of the state, while the latter belongs to history." (§ 259) Thus when we say, with Hegel, that the state is sovereign we do not mean that its power is absolute or that this power is not subject to check, revision, or modification. A state is entitled to be sovereign and to demand that other states recognize its sovereignty, but at the same time "this title is purely formal, and the demand for this recognition of the state, merely on the ground that it is a state, is abstract". § 331. The absoluteness of a state cannot be determined *a priori*, nor can it be deduced from an already established principle; it depends on its particular condition, on its actual content viz., its constitution, activities, relation to other states, achievements, etc. Thus, for Hegel, sovereignty as a concept does not *logically entail* absoluteness of power.

12. James L. Brierly, *The Basis of Obligation in Internation Law* (Oxford: At the Clarendon Press, 1958), p. 36. Current literature on international law shows that most international scholars agree with Hegel that the ultimate basis of international law is contract. They also agree that, factually, force, whether it is in the form of political pressure, economic boycott, alliances, regional or U.N. military force, etc., is needed to enforce the law.

INDEX

Aristotle, 96, 97, 104, 105, 123, 147
Austin, J. 61
Avineri, S. 9, 10, 11, 42, 193

Basedow, J.H. 129
Bentham, J. 61
Bradley, F.H. 190
Brierly, J. 185

Cassirer, E. 194
Categorical Imperative 58, 83 ff.
Civil Society 18 ff.
Conscience 32, 88 ff.
Corporation 158 ff.
Constitution 23 ff., 40, 177
Croce, B. 176

Dewey, J. 190
Diogenes 144
Education 126 ff.
d'Entreves, A.P. 99, 189
Duty 80 ff.

Fichte, J.G. 39, 107, 188
Findley, J. 176, 182
Flechtheim, O.K. 170, 173, 193
Freedom 12 ff., 39 ff.
Fuller, L. 65, 112

General Will 20, 39 ff., 189
Goethe, J. 69, 145, 146
Goodness 79 ff.

Haller, Herr von 63

Harris, H.S. 9
Hart, H.L.A. 61
Heiman, 193
Hobbes, T. 61
Holmes, H. 65

Ilting, K.-H. 12
Kant, I. 17, 81, 83, 95, 97, 107, 117, 121, 180, 190
Kelly, G.A. 191
Kelsen, H. 61
Knox, T.M. 92

Law 41 ff., 49, 60 ff., 110 ff.
Love 115 ff.
Luther, M. 108

McTaggart, J.E. 176 ff.
Marcuse, H. 45
Maritain, J.-J. 15, 16 ff., 26
Marriage 115 ff.
Mill, J.S. 190
Montesqieu 63, 100
Morality 73 ff.

Napoleon 24
Niebhur, R. 9

Pelczynski, Z.A. 9, 11, 12, 189
Personality 31 ff.
Pickles, D. 188
Plant, R. 9, 193
Plamenatz, J. 9, 10, 11, 15, 26, 176, 180, 182

Plato 39, 104, 117, 123
Poverty 154 ff.
Property 123 ff.
Public Opinion 35 ff.

Rationality, of State 28 ff.
Representation 39 ff.
Responsibility 75 ff.
Ricardo 192
Rousseau, J.-J. 26, 39 ff., 129, 143, 187, 188
Russell, B. 179

Say 192
Schlegel 122
Singer, M. 84 ff.
Sittlichkeit 91 ff.
Smith, A. 133, 164, 192
Social Contract 39 ff.
Socrates 24, 90, 108
Sophocles 122
Sovereignty 26 ff., 39 ff., 48, 51 ff., 177 ff.
Steinkraus, W.E. 9

Taylor, C. 9, 10, 11, 92, 149, 165
Totalitarianism 16 ff., 25

Virtue 96 ff.

Welfare State 152 ff.
Whitehead, A.N. 191
Will 64 ff.

ELEMENTA. SCHRIFTEN ZUR PHILOSOPHIE UND IHRER PROBLEMGESCHICHTE. Hrsg. von Rudolph Berlinger und Wiebke Schrader.

Band 1. Amsterdam 1975. 60 S. Hfl. 20,–
SCHRADER, WIEBKE: Die Auflösung der Warumfrage. 2. unverändert Auflage.

Band 2. Amsterdam 1975. 240 S. Hfl. 50,–
BERLINGER, RUDOLPH: Philosophie als Weltwissenschaft. Vermische Schriften.

Band 3. Amsterdam 1975. 295 pp. Hfl. 56,–
SCHELER, MAX: Logik I. Mit einem Nachwort von Jörg Willer.

Band 4. Amsterdam 1976. 319 S. Hfl. 70,–
FARANDOS, GEORGIOS D.: Kosmos und Logos nach Philon von Alexandria.

Band 5. Amsterdam 1977. 217 S. Hfl. 40,–
SAUER, FRIEDRICH OTTO: Physikalische Begriffsbildung und Mathematisches Denken. Das Philosophische Problem.

Band 6. Amsterdam 1977. 207 S. Hfl. 40,–
KÖNIGSHAUSEN, JOHANN-HEINRICH: Kants Theorie des Denkens.

Band 7. Amsterdam 1977. 196 S. Hfl. 40,–
SCHRADER, WIEBKE: Das Experiment der Autonomie. Studien zu einer Comte- und Marx-kritik.

Band 8. Amsterdam 1978. 177 pp. Hfl. 40,–
SCHRADER, WIEBKE: Die Selbstkritik der Theorie. Philosophische Untersuchungen zur ersten innermarxistischen Grundlagendiskussion.

Band 9. Amsterdam 1978. VII,175 pp. Hfl. 40,–
NEUMANN, THOMAS: Gewißheit und Skepsis. Untersuchungen zur Philosophie Johannes Volkelts.

Band 10. Amsterdam 1979. 175 pp. Hfl. 40,–
BAILEY, GEORGE W.S.: Privacy and the Mental.

Band 11. Amsterdam 1980. II,219 pp. Hfl. 45,–
DJURIC, MIHAILO: Mythos, Wissenschaft, Ideologie. Ein Problemaufriß.

Band 12. amsterdam 1980. II,171 pp. Hfl. 40,–
ETTELT, WILHELM: Die Erkenntniskritik des Positivismus und die Möglichkeit der Metaphysik.

Band 13. Amsterdam 1980. 135 pp. Hfl. 30,–
LOWRY, JAMES M.P.: The Logical Principles of Proclus' ΣΤΟΙΧΕΙΩΣΙΣ ΘΕΟΛΟΓΙΚΗ as systematic ground of the cosmos.

Band 14. Amsterdam 1980. X,240 pp. Hfl. 50,–
BERLINGER, RUDOLPH: Philosophie als Weltwissenschaft. Vermischte Schriften. Band II.

Band 15. Amsterdam 1980. 485 pp. Hfl. 90,–
HELLEMAN-ELGERSMA, W.: Soul-Sisters. A Commentary on Enneads IV 3 (27), 1-8 of Plotinus.

Band 16. Amsterdam 1981. 153 pp. Hfl. 30,–
POLAKOW, AVRON: Tense and Performance. An Essay on the Uses of Tensed and Tenseless Language.

Band 17. Amsterdam 1981. 113 pp. Hfl. 25,–
LANG, DIETER: Wertung und Erkenntnis. Untersuchungen zu Axel Hägerströms Moraltheorie.

Band 18. Amsterdam 1981. 149 pp. Hfl. 30,–
KANG, YUNG-KYE: Prinzip und Methode in der Philosophie Wonhyos.

Band 19. Amsterdam 1981. 203 pp. Hfl. 40,–
OESCH, MARTIN: Das Handlungsproblem ein systemgeschichtlicher Beitrag zur ersten Wissenschaftslehre Fichtes.

Band 20. Amsterdam 1981. 284 pp. Hfl. 60,–
ECHEVERRIA, EDWARD J.: Criticism and Commitment. Major Themes in contemporary 'post-critical' philosophy.

Band 21. Amsterdam 1982. 156 pp. Hfl. 30,–
THOMAS HOBBES: His View of Man. Edited by J.G. van der Bend.

Band 22. Amsterdam 1982. X,139 pp. Hfl. 30,–
TRÄGER, FRANZ: Herbarts Realistisches Denken. Ein Aufriss.

Band 23. Amsterdam 1982. 190 pp. Hfl. 40,–
TAKEDA, SUEO: Die subjektive Wahrheit und die Ausnahme-Existenz. Ein Problem zwischen Philosophie und Theologie.

Band 24. Amsterdam 1982. 181 pp. Hfl. 35,–
MAGER, KURT: Philosophie als Funktion. Studien zu Diltheys Schrift "Das Wesen der Philosophie".

Band 25. Amsterdam 1982. 233 pp. Hfl. 50,–
HEINZ, MARION: Zeitlichkeit und Temporalität im Frühwerk Martin Heideggers.

Band 26. Amsterdam 1982. 268 pp. Hfl. 50,–
PUNTER, DAVID: Blake, Hegel and Dialectic.

Band 27. Amsterdam 1982. 178 pp. Hfl. 35,–
MCALISTER, LINDA: The Development of Franz Brentano's Ethics.

Band 28. Amsterdam 1983. 275 pp. Hfl. 60,–
PLEINES, JÜRGEN-ECKARDT: Praxis und Vernunft. Zum Begriff praktischer Urteilskraft.

Band 29. Amsterdam 1984. 239 pp. Hfl. 50,–
SHUSTERMAN, RICHARD: The object of literary criticism.

Band 30. Amsterdam 1984. 206 pp. Hfl. 40,–
VOLKMANN-SCHLUCK: Von der Wahrheit der Dichtung. Interpretationen: Plato – Aristoteles – Shakespeare – Schiller – Novalis – Wagner – Nietzsche – Kafka. Hrsg. v. Wolfgang Janke und Raymund Weyers.

Band 31. Amsterdam 1984. 195 pp. Hfl. 40,–
DECHER, FRIEDHELM: Wille zum Leben – Wille zur Macht. Eine Untersuchung zu Schopenhauer und Nietzsche.

Band 32. Amsterdam 1984. 146 pp. Hfl. 30,–
WEPPEN, WOLFGANG VON DER: Die existentielle Situation und die Rede. Untersuchungen zu Logik und Sprache in der existentiellen Hermeneutik von Hans Lipps.

Band 33. Amsterdam 1984. 182 pp. Hfl. 40,–
WOLZOGEN, CHRISTOPH VON: Die autonome Relation. Zum Problem der Beziehung im Spätwerk Paul Natorps. Ein Beitrag zur Geschichte der Theorien der Relation.

Band 34. Amsterdam 1984. 197 pp. Hfl. 50,–
MITIAS, MICHAEL H.: Moral Foundation of the State in Hegel's. 'Philosophy of Right': Anatomy of an Argument.